FOOD LOVERS'
GUIDE TO
TUCSON

The Best Restaurants, Markets & Local Culinary Offerings

1st Edition

Mary Paganelli Votto

Guilford, Connecticut

Editor: Amy Lyons
Project Editor: David Legere
Layout Artist: Mary Ballachino
Text Design: Sheryl Kober
Illustrations © Jill Butler with additional art by Carleen Moira Powell and MaryAnn Dubé
Maps: Alena Pearce © Morris Book Publishing, LLC

ISBN 978-0-7627-8121-8

Printed in the United States of America

10 9 8 7 6 5 4 3 2 1

All the information in this guidebook is subject to change. We recommend that you call ahead to obtain current information before traveling.

Contents

Introduction, 1

How to Use This Book, 4

Neighborhoods & Transportation, 8

Keeping Up with Food News, 10

Tucson's Restaurants, 15

Central, 17

Foodie Faves, 17

Landmark, 61

Foothills, 63

Foodie Faves, 63

Landmarks, 74

Northwest, 78

    Foodie Faves, 78

    Landmark, 94

West, 97

    Foodie Faves, 97

    Landmark, 109

East, 111

    Foodie Faves, 111

    Landmark, 121

South & South Tucson, 123

    South: Foodie Faves, 124

    South Tucson: Foodie Faves, 130

Downtown, 137

Foodie Faves, 137

Landmarks, 150

U of A & Fourth Avenue, 156

Foodie Faves, 157

Landmark, 173

Regional Gastronomic Info, 175

Specialty Stores, Gourmet Shops & Purveyors, 176

Specialty Food Markets, 177

Butchers, 191

Bakeries, 193

Coffee, Tea & Dessert, 202

> Tearooms, 202
>
> Coffeehouses, 206
>
> Dessert, 215

Farm Fresh, 225

> Farmers' Markets, 225
>
> Vendor Spotlights, 232
>
> Community Supported Agriculture (CSA), 235
>
> Pick Your Own, 237

Food Trucks, 239

Native Foods, 248

> Edible Plants, 250
>
> Where to Find These Foods, 254

Foodie Festivals & Events, 256

Recipes, 269

Clear, Ageless Skin Smoothie (Courtesy of Miraval Arizona Resort & Spa), 271

Fresh Organic Apple-Cumin Vinaigrette (Sigret Thompson of The Tasteful Kitchen), 272

Ceviche with Minted Ginger Syrup & Candied Jalapeños (Junos Wilder of Downtown Kitchen + Cocktails), 274

Traditional Green-Corn Tamales (Todd Martin of Tucson Tamale Company), 277

Tepary Bean Soup (Scott Uehlein of Canyon Ranch Resorts), 279

Black Rice Horchata (Ryan Clark of Lodge on the Desert), 281

Appendix: Eateries by Cuisine, 283

Index, 288

About the Author

Mary Paganelli Votto is a graduate of Vassar College and holds Master Certificates in Cooking and Baking from the New School for Social Research Culinary Arts Program. She is a chef, writer, recipe tester, and editor. She loves to cook and eat!

A foreign service "brat," Mary traveled the world throughout her childhood, eating her way through the Middle East, Italy, France, and England. While living in New York City after college, she was an extern with the Food Network and worked as a private chef.

In Tucson since 1999, Mary has spent the majority of her time here working with Tohono O'odham Community Action (TOCA), a nonprofit organization dedicated to the reinvigoration of culture and health on the Tohono O'odham Nation. As the chef/writer for TOCA, Mary has been responsible for documenting traditional foodways. Her work with elders and community members resulted in the publication of the book *From I'itoi's Garden: Tohono O'odham Food Traditions,* a collaboration with TOCA and Elder Frances Manuel that celebrates the culinary traditions of the Tohono O'odham and the bounty of the Sonoran Desert. She is also the author of the travel guide *Insiders' Guide to Tucson* and a contributor of food and restaurant articles to *Tucson Lifestyle* magazine.

In addition, Mary works as a recipe tester for Canyon Ranch Resorts, was the food stylist and production assistant for the Tohono O'odham episode of the PBS program *Seasoned with Spirit: A Native Chef's Journey,* and the food stylist for *Primal Grill,* season 3. She is also an adjunct professor of culinary arts at Tohono O'odham Community College and the consulting chef for the Desert Rain Cafe.

Acknowledgments

Thank you to the many, many people who helped me put this book together—friends, family, food lovers, acquaintances, colleagues, coworkers, people on the street . . . no one was immune to my constant question, "What's your favorite restaurant in Tucson?"

I'd like to especially thank my terrific husband Ernest, and my son Eric who fortunately also love to eat and dined at many a restaurant with me.

Many thanks to the busy chefs and restaurant owners who contributed their delicious recipes: Janos Wilder, Keanne and Sigret Thompson, Scott Uehlein, Todd Martin, Ryan Clark, and Miraval.

Friends and fellow food lovers were terrific resources, especially Terrol Dew Johnson, Tristan Reader, Karen Wyndham, Stephanie Lip, Nina Altschul, Debbie Graves, Ellen Rauch, David Berryman, Lisa Falk, the Community Garden group at Teddy's, Edie Jarolim, Rita Connelly, Kate Reynolds, Jennifer Duffy, Carol Tepper, Karyn Zoldan, Susan Lobo, Mike Lee and the Tucson Chinese Cultural Center, Chrissy and George Sokol, and Alejandra Cardena. Melissa Colosimo deserves a special thanks for arranging numerous tastings and interviews.

Introduction

For a relatively small city, Tucson offers hundreds of restaurant choices—from the tiny mom-and-pop to the exclusive spa, you will find it all here. Founded in 1776, Tucson didn't become part of the United States until 1854. During that time, the flags of several nations flew over the "Old Pueblo," so Tucson is the home of many culinary influences, from Native American to Spanish to Mexican, all reflected in the variety of restaurants available here. You'll find Sonoran Mexican, Oaxacan Mexican, New Mexican, Cantonese, Korean, Bosnian, Jordanian, Japanese, gluten-free, vegan, raw, Southwest, barbecue, and much, much more here.

Home to over half a million residents, the 500-square-mile city of Tucson is in the center of eastern Pima County, which stretches over 9,000 square miles and includes the communities of Marana, Oro Valley, South Tucson, the Tohono O'odham Nation, and Green Valley. Thought to be one of the oldest continually inhabited areas in the United States, Tucson is surrounded by five gorgeous mountain ranges and is home to the stately saguaro cactus. The some-what intimidating landscape is surprisingly bountiful, providing fascinating indigenous foods like saguaro cactus fruit and tepary beans, used for centuries by Native people, along with citrus, pomegranates, and olives.

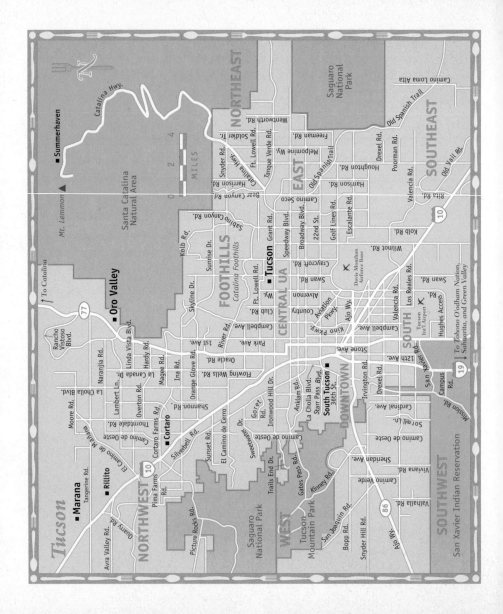

Still a somewhat sleepy town, Tucson attracts people from all over the globe who come here to enjoy the 350 days of sunshine and lovely desert landscape. Longtime residents, students, families, snowbirds, and tourists love to eat here and locals are justifiably proud of the many dining options in town.

Many of the Mexican restaurants here feature the cuisine from the state of Sonora to our south in Mexico. This is home-style cooking using a variety of meats, often grilled (*carne asada*) or dried (*machaca* and *carne seca*); herbs like oregano and *epazote;* chiles of all kinds, both fresh and dried; local fruits and vegetables (Mexican gray squash, key limes, nopales, purslane); a wide variety of Mexican cheeses (*cotija, panela, queso blanco*); and seafood from the Sea of Cortez, including deep-fried whole fish, oysters, and shrimp. You'll find these ingredients and more transformed into burros, burritos, soft tacos, chimichangas, stews, and soups, often accompanied by refried pinto beans and rice.

"Chili," "chile," "chiles"—you'll see all sorts of spellings of this word in stores, on labels, restaurant menus, and signs. There are literally hundreds of varieties, heat levels, and names for the many chiles that grow and are used in cooking here and all over the world. Generally speaking, the word **chile** is used here to describe the fresh, cooked, or dried pod, **chili** is used to describe the cooked stew, and traditional chili here does not usually include beans. Chile powder here is simply that—a dried chile that has been ground into powder—not the mixture of spices that are usually sold as "chile powder" in the spice section of the grocery store. This is by no means the final word, but it can be confusing so I hope this helps.

Many of the Asian restaurants here offer dishes from many different regions and sometimes even different countries under one roof—you will find Japanese sushi, Korean barbecue, and Chinese buffet offered together and interesting Mexican-influenced sushi combinations.

"Southwest" (or "South West") and "Southwestern" are terms you will see as a classification for restaurants and also referenced on many menus in Tucson. Not just a geographic area, this has also become a culinary term, usually indicating, in its purest sense, the use of local and indigenous products used in combination with a wide variety of other ingredients and culinary styles.

You will find every kind of eatery imaginable here, from the roadside cart to the exclusive multimillion-dollar spa and resort hotel. There is truly something for everyone, from old-fashioned cowboy grub to four-star resort cuisine and multiethnic choices from Malaysian to Jamaican. You name it, chances are you will find it here.

How to Use This Book

This guide is organized into multiple sections with sidebars that highlight interesting food facts and insider information. Here's what you get:

RESTAURANTS

The restaurant part of this book is separated into geographic areas within the city of Tucson and Pima County that in general correspond to how locals describe these different parts of town. You'll find restaurants big and small, from sandwich shops to upscale resorts, but you won't find national chain restaurants in these listings. Landmark restaurants, defined as those in a unique historic location, are listed separately at the end of each geographic section. Unless otherwise noted, places are open daily.

The restaurants in each geographic area are organized alphabetically. Specific streets and landmarks delineate each geographic area as follows:

Central

Wetmore and River Roads on the north, I-10 on the west, Wilmot Road on the east, and 22nd Street to the south.

Foothills

Catalina Mountains to the north, Oracle Road to the west, Sabino Canyon to the east, and River and Tanque Verde Roads to the south.

Northwest (includes Oro Valley, Marana, and Catalina)

I-10 on the west, the Pinal County border on the north, Oracle Road on the east, and Wetmore on the south

West

Avra Valley Road to the north, the city of Ajo and the Tohono O'odham Nation to the west, I-10 to the east, and Ajo Way to the south.

East

Catalina Mountains to the north, Saguaro Park to the east, Wilmot Road to the west, and I-10 to the south.

South & South Tucson

Starr Pass Boulevard/22nd Street to the north, I-19 to the west, the towns of Green Valley and Sahuarita to the south, and Wilmot Road to the east.

The city of South Tucson is an independent mile-square community surrounded by the city of Tucson. The boundaries are 25th Street to the north, South 12th Avenue to the east, West 40th Street and I-10 to the south, and South Second Avenue to the west.

Downtown

Railroad tracks to the north, I-10 to the east, South 22nd Street to the south, and 4th Avenue to the west.

University Area & Fourth Avenue

Stone Avenue to the west, Speedway Boulevard to the north, Alvernon Way to the east, and Broadway Boulevard to the south.

Restaurant Price Key

Dollar signs are included with each restaurant listing and represent the following price ranges:

$	inexpensive, entrees in the $10 or less range
$$	moderately priced, entrees in the $10 to $20 range
$$$	expensive, most entrees over $20

REGIONAL GASTRONOMIC INFO

Festivals & Foodie Events

A month-by-month listing of culinary events around town, both free and paid.

Specialty Stores, Gourmet Shops & Purveyors

An alphabetical listing of the terrific specialty markets in town. If you're looking for rattlesnake (yes, we have it), pig's blood, banana flowers, or just some great pastrami, it's all here.

Coffee, Tea & Dessert

Craving a java, a cuppa, or something sweet? This chapter covers coffee shops, tea houses, ice cream, and dessert places that do not necessarily serve full meals but put out a good cup of joe or a super sundae.

Farm Fresh

A listing of area farmers' markets along with profiles of some of our local vendors and sidebars about where to pick your own and join a CSA for farm-fresh products.

Native Foods

This chapter explores the amazing bounty of the Sonoran Desert, and the traditional foods of the Tohono O'odham (the Native American people whose nation is a part of Pima County). Organizations, resources, and cookbooks are included.

Recipes

Mouthwatering signature recipes contributed by some of the area's top chefs and restaurant owners are included in this chapter.

Neighborhoods & Transportation

Tucson, like many cities, is divided into a variety of neighborhoods. Some are identified geographically (the Catalina Foothills) or historically (Barrio Historico), or have unique place names (Pie Allen, Sam Hughes). For the purposes of this book, Tucson also includes Pima County, which surrounds the actual city of Tucson and includes areas not strictly within the city of Tucson geographic boundaries.

CULINARY TOURS

Tucson Food Tours (foodtourstucson.com; 520-477-7986), founded by locals Brad and Maria Lawrence, offers 3-hour culinary tours (don't worry, Gilligan, it's not on a boat). The walking tours focus on the fast-growing downtown area, which has become a magnet for restaurants. Brad and Maria have extensive front-of-the-house experience and have worked for numerous top restaurants in town, so you will get a real insiders' tour. You'll visit a minimum of six restaurants and get lots of food with a "side of history" as they point out interesting architectural and historical details about the neighborhood. The tastings are generous, so don't eat a lot before you go!

If you're interested in tasting local Sonoran cuisine, Gray Line Arizona (graylinearizona.com; 520-622-8811) offers a "Best of the Barrio" tour that takes you to select restaurants in South Tucson. The tour takes 4 hours and requires a minimum of six people. You'll spend more time eating than driving, visiting four different family-owned restaurants that offer tastings and samples including a frosty margarita. Book ahead of time and come hungry!

The city is fairly spread out and navigable most easily by car. The bus system, Sun Tran (suntran.com) does not reach all outlying areas and street taxi service is limited primarily to the airport area and some downtown and University areas (a full listing of all local

cab companies is at the city of Tucson website, thecityoftucson
.com). There are some private car and limousine services available
but they can be expensive. A light rail system is in the works but
will primarily service the University and Downtown areas. So, buckle
up, 'cause driving is the best way to get to most parts of town.

Keeping Up with Food News

There are lots of ways to keep up with what's happening on the
restaurant and dining scene in town.

Publications

Arizona Daily Star, azstarnet.com. The insert in the Thursday
edition of the paper, called "Caliente," is a good source for up-
to-the-minute food news in the "Morsels" section. There is usually
fairly extensive coverage of area restaurants in the "Good Eats" section. A rotating list of restaurants is included in the "Grab a Bite"
section, organized by type of cuisine. The Wednesday edition of the
paper technically features the food section, but it consists mainly
of national articles culled from other news sources.

Arizona Gourmet Living, arizonagourmetliving.tripod.com.
Scattered about town, this freebie, low-budget magazine comes
out four times a year and offers in-depth profiles of local chefs and
restaurants and provides recipes for signature dishes. It's more a

business-to-business than a consumer food magazine and the website has no content.

DesertLeaf, desertleaf.com. This tabloid-size monthly is delivered free to Foothills residents and complimentary copies are available at local libraries. It usually features a restaurant profile of a select advertiser, a column with cookbook reviews and recipes, and an alphabetical listing of local restaurants by cuisine.

Tucson Guide Magazine, tucsonguidemagazine.com. Local food writer Edie Jarolim pens a column in each issue of this local lifestyle magazine that focuses on area restaurants. The "Chef Says" Q&A feature offers interesting interviews with local chefs along with a signature recipe. The "Things to Do" section features occasional fun food facts and great ideas for things to do around town—food-related and otherwise. A dining section, the "Desert Dining Guide," lists area restaurants alphabetically, while seasonal events are listed in the "Festivals & Fiestas" section. Each full issue is available online at their website.

Tucson Lifestyle, tucsonlifestyle.com. Each issue of this monthly glossy features an article that highlights several local restaurants (full disclosure: I write for this publication) and a dining guide organized by cuisine. A month-by-month calendar also includes local events. The website has full magazine content and a searchable restaurant database by cuisine and neighborhood.

Tucson Weekly, tucsonweekly.com. Published every Thursday, this alternative paper has lots to say about food around town. Each issue has a restaurant review written by locals (in the "Chow" section), a rotating list of restaurants by cuisine, and a column called "Noshing Around" that provides updates on new restaurants, events, and food-related activities. They don't pull any punches with their reviews, so you'll hear it like it is! Their website provides a daily dispatch of foodie news called "The Range," current articles and reviews, and an archive of restaurant reviews dating back to 1999.

Zocalo Magazine, thezmag.com. This free publication primarily covers downtown area businesses and events with a focus on news and the arts. The "Food & Drink" section features an article or two on an area restaurant and occasionally a recipe. Their website offers a full digital edition of the magazine.

Online

Metromix Tucson, tucson.metromix.com. Although part of a national online network, this is a great resource for finding area restaurants, bars, and clubs. It's all here and easily searchable by type of cuisine and neighborhood, with a great map feature.

Metropolitan Tucson Convention and Visitors Bureau, visit tucson.org. The Convention and Visitors Bureau does a great job of keeping up with area restaurants and events. Online, you'll find a comprehensive, searchable (by cuisine and key word) restaurant database with capsule descriptions and a helpful map feature. If you want something more personal, the folks who man their Visitors Center in Plaza Palomino downtown always have suggestions and a slew of sample menus on hand.

Tucson's Restaurants

Tucson has always been proud of its culinary diversity and its large number of restaurants. Here in one of the oldest continuously inhabited regions in the United States, we have an amazing variety of restaurants, culinary styles, and cultures represented in our small city. We also have some of the oldest continuously operating and historic restaurants in the country—several have been in business since the early 1900s. Despite our seemingly intimidating landscape, the desert yields many fascinating indigenous ingredients that find their way into many items on our menus. Home to Native American, Mexican, Spanish, Asian, and many other ethnic groups, Tucson is truly a culinary "melting pot," with restaurants here offering the cuisines of many nations, our own "cowboy" cuisine influenced by our long history of ranching, and what has come to be referred to as Southwest cuisine—a melding of many of these styles and indigenous foods into a unique blend. This diversity is also reflected in the many different types of restaurants you'll find here, from the upscale resort with talented chefs preparing sophisticated fare to tiny mom-and-pops cooking home-style food, it's all done casual style. You'll rarely find anyone in a suit and tie, but more often in shorts or khakis and a comfortable shirt. The restaurants included here represent the varied cultures, flavors, and cuisines that make Tucson a special and exciting place for food lovers.

Central

The majority of restaurants in Tucson are located here, in this central corridor that encompasses a large swath of town and several main thoroughfares. You'll find an amazing variety including just about every ethnic cuisine from Jamaican to Korean, Middle Eastern, and Indian, and every style of restaurant from fast food, coffee shops, cafes, takeout, upscale, downscale, offering breakfast, lunch, and dinner. You could spend months eating just along Speedway, there are so many places on this major road alone.

Foodie Faves

AI Bistro, 5099 E. Grant Rd., Tucson, AZ 85712; (520) 318-2726; artinstitutes.edu/tucson; International; $. Not too many people know about this tiny little bistro housed inside the Art Institute of Tucson. Culinary students in the Associate and Bachelor degree programs work the front and back of the house under the strict guidance of experienced culinary instructors. You can watch it all through the big windows that show the entire working kitchen. The menu changes weekly, showcasing the regions, cuisines, and styles that the students are studying (what a great way to study!). You will be treated to a wide variety of culinary treats, served up in style. The students rotate through the program, experiencing the realities of the competitive restaurant world. The 3-course prix-fixe menu is ridiculously reasonable, but the hours of operation are limited to when school and these master classes are in session. Be sure to share any comments or thoughts with the students and instructors; they are anxious to learn and improve their skills. The small space has only 12 tables and gets booked fast. Advance reservations are a must. Open for lunch only, Tues through Thurs only during the academic year with seatings at 11:30 a.m., noon, and 12:30 p.m.

Blue Willow, 216 N. Campbell Ave., Tucson, AZ 85719; (520) 327-7577; bluewillowtucson.com; American; $. Homey and friendly, the Blue Willow is a favorite breakfast destination, serving Tucsonans since 1978. The croissants are famous and the hearty full breakfasts are served all day. After you browse through the small gift shop that greets you at the entrance, there are several seating options. The main dining room is a restored 1940s adobe house with lots of little rooms and hallways. The patio is highly popular and people wait patiently for a table here, among the plants *en plein air*. Breakfast, breakfast,

breakfast, it's the most important meal of the day and this is the place to have it. All breakfast entrees come with crispy potatoes, brown rice or beans, and whole-wheat raisin toast (choose this) or a tortilla. The Blue Willow Special is a top pick—eggs are scrambled with chicken, green chiles, tomatoes, chopped corn tortillas, cheddar, salsa, and sour cream. It's a huge and incredibly satisfying combination. The fresh fruit crepes are filled with a fantastic mix of fresh strawberries, bananas, pineapple, blueberries, and yogurt, topped with real whipped cream and a dusting of cinnamon. Omelets are so big you could probably use them as a raft to cross the ocean. There are many choices of fillings from the classic three cheese to the Southwestern avocado, jack, and green chiles. French toast is made with the amazing whole-wheat cinnamon-raisin bread (choose this!) or egg bread and is dense and perfectly sautéed. There's lots, lots more on the menu for lunch and dinner, including soups, sandwiches, and Southwest-inspired entrees but the breakfast is tops. Open weekdays from 7 a.m. and weekends from 8 a.m. for breakfast, lunch, and dinner.

Bobo's, 2938 E. Grant Rd., Tucson, AZ 85716; (520) 326-6163; bobostucson.com; American; $. It's not pretty and some may even call it a "greasy spoon." In fact you might even wonder why Bobo's is here, but you won't wonder once you try one of their amazing, humongous pancakes, made from scratch and as big as your head. That's right. Bobo's is famous for their pancakes, light, fluffy, slathered in butter and drenched in syrup (bring your own if you like the real stuff), it'll be amazing if you can eat the whole plateful. Once you go home, you will dream of Bobo's pancakes and crave more and more. And you can get them all day, which is very dangerous. There are other things on the menu here, excellent hash browns, fried eggs, and they even serve lunch and dinner, but I don't know what they offer because, for me, the only thing to get here is the pancakes. Warning: This place is packed, especially on the weekends, so plan accordingly. Open at 5:30 a.m. daily, closes at 2 p.m. on Sat and Sun.

BrushFire BBQ Company #1, 2745 N. Campbell Ave., Tucson, AZ 85719; (520) 624-3223; brushfirebbq.com; Barbecue; $$. The guys at BrushFire may seem laid back but they are very serious about their barbecue. Jared Wren and Ben Rine opened this little place in 2007 after stints cooking in India. Somehow barbecue took over for Indian food and BrushFire was born. This super-casual hot spot, with limited tables and counter service only, puts out some terrific barbecue. Two big wood smokers that hold over a thousand pounds of meat sit out back, belching out some mighty nice-smelling smoke. All meats are dry rubbed, smoked over pecan and mesquite wood, and sauced to order. The sweet, spicy, peppery, thick, tomatoey BBQ sauce is a secret recipe that only Jared and Ben are privy to—the rest of us just have to guess and keep eating it to figure out the ingredients. It's served on just about everything—fries, beans, meats, even salads! What to order? Messy fries—a glob of fries tossed with meat, sauce, and cheese (cheddar, swiss, jalapeño jack, or provolone); delicious baked beans—cooked in the smoker with chunks of barbecue pork, molasses, chile powder, and onions, so they have a deep smoky flavor; pulled-pork sandwich—soft, shredded meat piled onto a soft bun that's been brushed with garlic butter and grilled; you can get

it with tons of optional toppings including pickles (my choice); hot, sweet, or red onions; sweet or hot peppers; and jalapeños—a delicious mouthful. Ribs, brisket, chicken, sausages, and turkey all come pink and moist out of the smoker and are available in family packs or by the pound. Even prime rib is smoked here, available only on Tues after 5 p.m. with two sides and garlic bread; it's tender and full of flavor. On holidays, they even smoke Tur-Duck-Hens (the infamous turkey stuffed with a duck stuffed with a chicken). Available by special order only, they come whole and cut in half . . . half a Tur-Duck-Hen, who knew? Open daily starting at 11 a.m.

CeeDee Jamaican Restaurant, 1070 N. Swan Rd., Tucson, AZ 85711; (520) 795-3400; jamaicanrestauranttucson.com; Jamaican; $$. Be prepared to squeeze into the booths and single aisle or take out at this extremely small outpost of homemade Jamaican food, decorated floor to ceiling with Jamaican flags and posters. Family members work hard as they dish out stews, curries, and fricassees from the bubbling vats behind the counter, or grab a patty (chicken, beef, or veg) out from under the hot lights. The menu is small but tasty. Just get in line and point to whatever looks good. It all smells good. The servers are usually too busy to answer lots of questions and there aren't many signs but you will enjoy tender jerk chicken (made here with lots of pungent herbs and spices), thick, rich curried goat (there are bones so be careful), and the meaty "frigazee" (stew) of the day (usually chicken and oxtails). All come with rice and peas (peas here are kidney beans) and two sides—festival (similar to a hush puppy), plantains, or vegetables. Unusual drinks, homemade and canned, are also available. You may see sorrel punch, Irish Moss, or peanut punch in the refrigerated case—just try one! Limited but tasty desserts include rum cake by the slice and dense potato pudding. Open Tues through Sun for lunch and dinner from 11 a.m.

Dakota Cafe & Catering, 6541 E. Tanque Verde Rd., Tucson, AZ 85715; (520) 298-7188; dakotacafetucson.com; American; $$$. This upscale cafe is located at the edge of the pseudo-Western attraction Trail Dust Town. When (if?) you tire of cowboy gunfights, train rides, and panning for gold, Dakota offers a comfortable, cool respite for drinks, lunch, and dinner. The outdoor porch is the place to sit. With live music offered nightly, it's a private, cozy place far from the hustle and bustle of the town. You will find classic, seasonal cafe food prepared well and professionally served here. Lunch is the most popular time to dine here, with excellent sandwiches, soups made from scratch, and generous salads. As for sandwiches, perennial favorites include the grilled portobello (a meaty mushroom cap layered with eggplant, roasted red peppers, tomatoes, spinach leaves, and Havarti cheese with dill on a nice crusty roll) and the Parmesan grilled cheese (thick sourdough with three cheeses, ham, and a spicy horseradish Dijon mustard). Top salads are the orange beef with cashews and dressed with orange vinaigrette, and the classic-with-a-twist salmon niçoise with baby tomatoes, green beans, and roasted potatoes with an orange-dill dressing. Soup choices change daily. Open Mon through Sat at 11 a.m., Sun at 10 a.m.

The Dish, 3131 E. First St., Tucson, AZ 85716; (520) 326-1714; rumrunnertucson.com; Continental; $$$. You'll find this little bistro tucked away inside the Rum Runner retail wine shop. Intimate is the only word to describe the small space that includes a separate dining area with a bar and a few tables hidden among the wine racks and in little alcoves around the store. Dinner only is served here, prepared *à la minute* by Chef Michael Muthart as "small" (appetizer), "green" (salads), "deep" (soup) and "big" (entree) dishes. The small-scale menu changes frequently, showcasing seasonal ingredients. Among the appetizers, you might find a creamy goat cheese brûlée with tomato confit, sprinkled with fresh oregano and served with toasted baguette slices; salads include baby greens with spiced pumpkinseeds and a tomato vinaigrette; and wild mushroom amaranth cakes with raisin chutney, or slow-cooked lamb loin with caramel sauce are entree choices. The best deal of all is to be had on Tues,

Wed, and Thurs nights when a bowl of saffron mussels and a glass of fine wine at the bar will set you back only $12. Open for dinner Tues through Sat at 5 p.m.

El Mezon del Cobre, 2960 N. First Ave., Tucson, AZ 85719; (520) 792-0977; (520) 791-0977; Mexican Seafood; $$. Isolated on a rather barren stretch of First Avenue, this family-run Mexican restaurant specializes in seafood. The bright, clean restaurant interior is decorated with colorful tile work, brightly painted walls, and wood carvings. Owner Consuelo Medina and sons Manny and Octavio are friendly, welcoming, and committed to cooking with the very freshest seafood, which comes in fresh directly from Guayamas. And seafood is what you must order here. Start with the whole yellow jalapeños stuffed with shrimp and wrapped in bacon (*El Mezon chiles toritos* on the *antojito*/appetizer section of the menu). I don't know how they do it, but the bacon strips hugging tightly to the jalapeños are super crispy but not greasy and the shrimp inside are soft and tender. Scallop ceviche is available in season as are plump and briny oysters on the half shell. Snapper is cooked in several ways, all good. The signature snapper dish is a whole fish deep fried (*pargo frito*), but the snapper fillets can be had grilled, breaded, foil-wrapped, sautéed with green chiles, and *a la Veracruz* in a rich but light tomato sauce with capers and olives. There are so many super shrimp entrees (at least 10), and they range from the basic (deep-fried) to the unusual (sautéed with ketchup and Huichol hot sauce). You'll just have to come in and try them all. If you have even a bit of room left, try Consuelo's *pastel de tres leches,* a super-spongy, dairy-infused cake frosted with whipped cream. Open daily for lunch and dinner from 11 a.m.

El Molcajete, 633 S. Plumer Ave., Tucson, AZ 85719; (520) 623-8886; Mexican; $. It's all homemade here at this off-the-beaten-track family-run restaurant. Don't expect anything fancy, this is a real homey place frequented by cops and neighborhood residents who enjoy the simple, delicious, Sonoran Mexican food. The interior is cool and dim with bright plastic-coated tablecloths on the tables, and the vibe is friendly and low key. Mom Olivia Salazar is in the kitchen daily making her famous soups: *albondigas* (meatball), *caldo de queso* (cheese), *gallina pinta* (hominy, beef, and bean), *fideo* (noodle), and lentil. You'll also find some of the best green-corn tamales here. It's truly a family restaurant, with daughter Mirza working the front of the house with a smile and dad Reyes is behind the scenes washing dishes and doing everything else! Open Mon through Sat 7 a.m. to 3 p.m. for breakfast and lunch.

Feast, 3719 E. Speedway Blvd., Tucson, AZ 85712; (520) 326-6500; eatatfeast.com; American; $$. Doug Levy has no culinary degree—in fact his degrees are in sculpture and linguistics, but he can cook! This Tucson original has been in the kitchen since he was 16, tasting, testing, and creating. His constantly changing menu (he changes eight to twelve menu items on the first Tuesday of every month!) reflects his continuing interest in seasonal, local ingredients and just about every culinary genre you can think of. Although the menu changes frequently, you will find signature items on it regularly. These include an ethereal lobster, corn, and scallion bread pudding that arrives tableside in little ramekins. Soufflé-like, it is light, rich, and airy. Another regular is the crispy duck salad (shredded duck confit with field greens, grapes and goat cheese, dressed in a maple vinaigrette). And you'll always find the Feast grilled cheese—seared haloumi cheese layered with honey-roasted eggplant, sliced tomatoes, and red onion and served on a crusty French roll. The small vegetable garden out back, newly planted pear trees, and herb and edible flower patch on the side of the restaurant provide daily inspiration, finding their way into unique sauces (like oregano cream), appetizers (like English pea gratin with tarragon and leeks), and salads (like nasturtium citrus caprese salad). Doug also likes to use indigenous ingredients—he makes his own popular variation on the classic cassoulet using local tepary beans. If you fall in love with a dish and fear that you might not see it again on the rapidly changing menu, take heart. During the summer months Doug will make it for you, just put in a special request. To discover his other inspirations, you'll just have to make a reservation. Seating is available in a modern, chic front dining area, a back dining room, and a small side patio right on the parking lot, and it all books up fast. Open Tues through Sat at 11 a.m., Sun at 10 a.m.

Frankie's, 2574 N. Campbell Rd., Tucson, AZ 85719; (520) 795-2665; frankiescheesesteaks.com; Cheesesteak; $. You don't have to go to Philly to get a cheesesteak, Frankie's makes a great one right here in town. In business since 2003, owner Frankie Santos really is from South Philly so he knows his cheesesteak. It's plain and simple in here: counter, tables, and lots of happy people eating Frankie's delicious sandwiches. You must get the cheesesteak, thin sliced, grilled certified Angus beef, bright orange Whiz cheese, and sautéed onions nested in a soft Amoroso roll imported all the 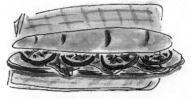 way from Philly. It's a mouthful of goodness. If you're not a purist about your cheesesteak, add some extra toppings. The broccoli rabe is amazingly good and garlicky. There are also roasted sweet and hot peppers, sautéed mushrooms, extra-sharp provolone and homemade marinara sauce to put on top if you wish. Frankie's is not just about cheesesteak, even though that's what I come here for. You'll also find hoagies, roast pork, chicken, salads, fish, and Wise potato chips from back East on the menu; they're all good too. Open daily at 11 a.m.

Frank's/Francisco's, 3843 E. Pima St., Tucson, AZ 85716; (520) 881-2710; franksrestaurant.com; $. Let me tell you right up front, this place is truly a dive. Not only is it a dive but is has a dual personality and the best sign in all of Tucson—Frank's, Fine Dining Elsewhere. They know whereof they speak. Completely unassuming and a bit grimy, this place has been cooking up bountiful breakfasts and Michoacan-style Mexican dinners for a long, long time (actually since 1972). Open kitchen is perhaps too fancy a word to describe the interior. The small diner-like space is almost completely taken up by the grill top that puts out real home fries, all kinds of eggs, sunny-side up and otherwise along with chicken-fried steak, corned beef hash, and pancakes. Portions are huge and people line up for seats. At 5 p.m., the place becomes Francisco's, offering some unusual items like pig's feet enchiladas, *sopes con desembrada* (thick corn tortillas with seasoned, stewed beef), and pork chops with red chile garlic sauce along with tacos, tostadas, flautas, burritos, and quesadillas, also in generous portions. Open for breakfast and lunch Mon through Fri 6 a.m. to 2 p.m., Sat 7 a.m. to 2 p.m., Sun 8 a.m. to 2 p.m. Dinner daily at 5 p.m.

Ghini's French Caffe, 1803 E. Prince Rd., Tucson, AZ 85719; (520) 326-9095; ghiniscafe.com; French; $. Pronounced variously as "genie" and "ghee-nee" (the correct version is "ghee-nee"), this restaurant's name comes from Chef-Owner Coralie Satta (nicknamed Ghini and originally from Marseilles). Since 1992 she has brought a taste of southern France to this strip mall with a huge menu of delicious breakfast and lunch items, many featuring breads made at the neighboring bakery. You'll find many French-inspired signature dishes here. An all-time favorite is the eggs Provençal: butter-basted fried eggs served atop soft, caramelized tomatoes sautéed in garlic and thyme. Another choice is the *omelette de soleil* featuring three eggs whisked with herbes de Provence. The simple *baguette au jambon* (warm baguette with butter and paper-thin slices of ham) transports you to Paris. Ghini's version hits the mark, made with a freshly baked baguette from the bakery and unsalted, creamy butter. *Croque monsieur* and *croque madame,* dipped in egg and sautéed until crispy and melty, are other lunchtime favorites. Crepes folded over fresh strawberries, bacon pea salad in a creamy Dijon dressing, chicken cordon bleu, escargots, triple-crème brie, there are just too many good things to eat here. Drinks include steamy café au lait served in big cups and freshly squeezed lemon, lime, and orange juice. The outdoor front patio (dog-friendly) with cooling misters is a prime spot; small tables fill the intimate dining area inside. Closed Mon, open Tues through Sat from 8:30 a.m. to 3 p.m., Sun from 8 a.m. to 2 p.m.

Govinda's, 711 E. Blacklidge Dr., Tucson, AZ 85719; (520) 792-0630; govindasoftucson.com; Vegetarian; $. A meal at Govinda's, housed in the Chaitanya Cultural Center, is an experience that should not be missed. Be prepared to join the long line of people waiting for some excellent, simple vegetarian food. The quiet, hushed, garden environment complete with lily pond, fountains, caged birds, strolling peacocks, and rustling palms is a real oasis. All profits from the restaurant go to feed the homeless locally and to support the ashram. You never know exactly what you'll find on the buffet line, and many people bring containers so they can take home food for the week, it's so tasty. Whole-wheat bread is made here, as is all the food, and it can go fast. It is very casual: The buffet items are set out on a counter, with plates and silverware stacked at the start of the line and servers ready to fill your plates. A weekly menu is posted on the restaurant's website if you want to get a feel for what might be on the buffet. Thursday nights are always vegan and Tuesdays usually feature more Indian-style cuisine (curries, dhal, poori, raita, and chutneys.) Everything is subtly spiced and carefully prepared with some very interesting combinations and textures. It's truly amazing what can be made with vegetables and how creative the cooks here are with dishes that are not made with dairy. There is seating inside the small dining area and outside on the lovely patio where you can hear the caged birds sing. Don't miss the nice little store on property that sells hand-printed cotton bedspreads, spiritual books, clothing, and lots of interesting knickknacks. Open for dinner Tues through Sat at 5 p.m., for lunch Wed through Sat from 11:30 a.m. to 2 p.m., and brunch Sun from 11 a.m. to 2 p.m.

Greek Taverna, 3225 S. Swan Rd., Tucson, AZ 85712; (520) 784-7335; greektaverna.biz; Greek; $$. Greek wine! Greek cheese! Greek coffee! Greek owner! Gregarious owner George Markou has put his heart and soul into Taverna (also known as Fat Greek 2). He is not only a cook but also a farmer. His 3-acre farm is home to 22 goats, 2 cows, 18 sheep, 30 chickens, and loads of tomatoes, eggplants, zucchini, and garlic. All of these farm-fresh ingredients go into the food here. Goat and sheep's milk is processed into feta and haloumi cheese, cow's milk into homemade yogurt, and the veggies into

Greek specialties like eggplant dip, *tzatziki,* Greek salad, moussaka, and pastitsio. George grew up in Piraeus and prides himself on offering some of the specialties of the region, made from family recipes, on his extensive menu. These include calamari *saganaki* (whole, lightly fried calamari); zucchini patties with feta and herbs; slow-cooked green beans with tomatoes and parsley; and beef *kokinitso,* a rich stew seasoned with cinnamon and allspice. Ask George for his specialty dessert, *galaktobouriko,* a delicious pastry of layered phyllo, goat's-milk custard, and honey. Open Mon through Thurs 11 a.m. to 8:30 p.m., Fri and Sat 11 a.m. to 9 p.m., closed Sun.

Gus Balon's, 6027 E. 22nd St., Tucson, AZ 85711; (520) 747-7788; American; $. Breakfast at Balon's and you'll never eat anywhere else. Especially after you taste the homemade breads, cinnamon rolls, and pies. The food here is really, really good and tastes like Mom made it. Breakfast is served all day, eggs perfectly cooked with big hunks of grilled, smoked ham, American fried potatoes, and a thick slice of buttered toast (wheat, seeded rye, and white—the rye is to die for) with a cup of good old American coffee, what could be better than that? Chicken-fried steak, liver and onions, meat loaf, tuna melt, egg salad, grilled cheese, maybe. Whole loaves of bread and pies can be purchased to go, I'm happy to report. Closed Sun, open 7 a.m. to 3 p.m. Tues through Sat.

Ha Long Bay, 6304 E. Broadway Blvd., Tucson, AZ 85710; (520) 571-1338; halongbaymenu.com; Vietnamese; $. Located on the corner of the El Mercado shopping plaza, this simple, cozy spot is clean and welcoming, with bamboo curtains, light wood tables and chairs, and a plant-filled fountain. You'll find well-seasoned, authentic Vietnamese food here, served by pleasant, soft-spoken staff. Start with the fragrant lemongrass beef or chicken on a stick; garlicky roast pork slices; and delicate summer rolls filled with herbs and thin bean-thread noodles. Vietnamese hot and sour fish soup is spicy and tangy with nice chunks of white fish and unusual vegetables. There are several *pho* selections, served in giant bowls with fresh cilantro and basil leaves, limes, and sliced green chiles. The broth is nicely flavored and not greasy, and the meats and seafood you can choose to add are fresh. The baby rice platters

are a favorite here. Tiny grained rice cooked with fried shallots is sticky but not gluey and is a great base for grilled shrimp, lemongrass pork, or sliced pork; the dish comes with cucumber slices and the house special *nuoc mam* sauce, a slightly spicy, sweet, vinegary dipping sauce. There are other options on the extensive menu including vegetarian dishes, fried rice, vermicelli noodles, and low-carb items (really!) that omit starch in favor of lettuce leaves. Bubble teas filled with black tapioca balls are the beverage of choice. Open Mon through Sat at 11 a.m. and Sun at noon for lunch and dinner.

Impress Hot Pot, 2610 N. First Ave., Tucson, AZ 85719; (520) 882-3059; Chinese; $. You won't find another hot pot place in town. What is a hot pot? A big, huge bowl of soup base that you will bring to a boil at your table and dip a wide variety of meat and vegetables into. The Impress is a clean, neat, spare space with calligraphy and delicate drawings on the walls and a scattering of granite-topped tables. Owner Li Pei, who looks about 12 and is extremely polite and solicitous, will bring you a paper menu with color pictures and spaces for you to check what you want. He will patiently and clearly explain all your options. First you must select the type of broth. Original, spicy, or half and half. Listen very carefully to Li when he tells you that spicy is VERY SPICY. Don't be like some of us (me) who think they know better and insist on ordering the spicy broth, a red, angry brew with tons of tiny, red chile peppers, black peppercorns, whole garlic cloves, and assorted other incendiary spices. Take my word for it, it is SPICY. The regular broth is a thin concoction of chicken and beef broth and is a much safer choice unless you are a certified chile head. If you order the half and half, a huge bisected metal bowl arrives at your table and is placed on the center heating unit. You can select a variety of combinations of meats, greens, mushrooms, and tofu, to dip into your broth. Once you've checked your choices on the menu, Li heads back into the kitchen and emerges with a platter of whatever you chose. BUT, before you can dip, Li escorts you to a side table covered with little bowls filled with condiments—minced garlic, chopped cilantro, sesame paste, chile oil, and more are here for you to mix and match into your very own special dipping sauce. Now you are ready to dip, and double and triple dip. Using your chopsticks, place the food into the broth and swish it around until it's cooked just right. The amount of food is staggering and incredibly filling. Unusual canned Asian sodas can be had to douse the flames, if you did choose the SPICY broth. Open Mon through Sat 11:30 a.m. to 2:30 p.m. for lunch, and from 5:30 p.m. for dinner, Sun from 1:30 p.m. for lunch and dinner.

Kingfisher, 2564 E. Grant Rd., Tucson, AZ 85716; (520) 323-7739; kingfishertucson.com; Seafood; $$$. Culinary Institute of America grad and fish lover Jim Murphy is the owner-chef here. The richly decorated, dark, cool interior is home to perfectly prepared seafood dishes. The bar is a major gathering place at happy hour (Mon through Fri 4:30 to 6:30 p.m. and 10 p.m. to midnight). People squish together on the banquettes for great cocktails and signature menu items in smaller portions and at smaller prices. The Lemon Aide, a heady mix of vodka and lemon juice with a sugared rim is a signature drink, but the drinks menu is full of delicious choices as is the award-winning wine list. Happy hour mussels are the top pick. Gleaming black shells housing the soft, saffron mollusks are bathed in a delicious broth (the mix depends on the day and might be white wine, shallots, and herbs, or a spicy sriracha-spiked fish broth). Kingfisher is known for its oysters, flying in over 15 varieties on a daily basis—you'll find them on the Oyster Bar section of the menu. The rest of the frequently changing menu offers the familiar (creamy New England clam chowder, baked oysters, steamed littleneck clams) and not so familiar (unusual soups with Asian accents, ceviches with unusual spices, macadamia-crusted

Hawaiian fish fillets, chicken-fried trout). The Kingfisher lobster roll is not to be missed: a grilled, buttered roll filled with lobster chunks mixed with bell peppers, celery, and scallions in a creamy mayo base—you won't find anything like it in town. Whole lobsters are flown in seasonally and served up with a bib, silver lobster crackers, and drawn butter, nothing else and that's all you need. While many of the main seafood proteins on the menu (oysters, shrimp, salmon, trout, sea bass) stay the same, Chef Murphy likes to experiment with sauces and sides, using different spices (coriander, fennel, lemongrass) and sauces (scallion tartar, horseradish aioli, garlic sherry cream, lime *crema*) to create unusual combinations on the plate. Chef Murphy has a real appreciation and respect for his ingredients, never over-seasoning or over-saucing but letting the fish shine on its own. Open Mon through Fri 11 a.m. to 3 p.m. for lunch, 5 to 10 p.m. for dinner.

Le Rendez-vous, 3844 E. Ft. Lowell Rd., Tucson, AZ 85716; (520) 323-7373; lerendez-vous.com; French; $$$. Blink and you might miss this little place right on the edge of the road just west of the corner of E. Fort Lowell and E. River Roads. Watch for the little square tower and pull into the small parking lot in the back. Inside you'll find some of the best classic French food in town. As soon as you step in the door, you'll be greeted by heavenly smells and debonair owner Gordon Berger. There are two seating areas, but choose the lovely enclosed patio covered with a burgundy domed roof; it's a super spot for a romantic evening. There's even a teensy-weensy table for two in the far corner. Tables are set with linens, candles, fine china, and crystal wineglasses and waiters dressed in black with starched aprons are ready for service. Order the classics here, they are lovingly and beautifully prepared using original recipes from Gordon's dad, French native and restaurant founder Claude Berger. I love that everything on the menu is in French, it just gives it all an extra European flair and sense of authenticity. Things to order: *soupe a l'oignon gratinée, salade de betteraves,* chateaubriand with béarnaise sauce, *escargots au Chablis, coquilles Saint-Jacques, ris de veau, canard Montmorency,* and Grand Marnier soufflé. Translation? Baked French onion soup, a deeply rich beef broth topped with melted gruyère; roasted beet salad with creamy goat cheese; soft beef tenderloin with *herbes de Provence* and a buttery tarragon herb

sauce; snails in garlic butter and wine; pillowy scallops baked under a bed of cheese; tender sweetbreads; roasted duck with cherries; the Grand Marnier soufflé is a light, orange-flavored cloud. Open for lunch Tues through Fri 11:30 a.m. to 2 p.m., dinner at 5 p.m.

Lerua's, 2005 E. Broadway Blvd., Tucson, AZ 85719; (520) 624-0332; Mexican; $. Lerua's (leh-roo's) is famous for their green-corn tamales, and that's what you should order here because they are some of the best in town. Owner Mike Hultquist, who has worked here in one capacity or another since he was eight, is a green-tamale aficionado. He sources his corn from special farmers who grow it just for him and it's delivered weekly to his back door. Ladies who have worked here for at least 60 years collectively remove the husks and slice off the fresh corn kernels to make the delicious masa that's inside these delectable steamed husks. It takes 11 hours to make just 60 tamales here, they are so careful about quality and taste. Watch for the little handwritten sign that says "green corn tamales" on the roadside at the northwest corner of busy Broadway Boulevard and Campbell Road—the restaurant has been at this location since 1938! Inside you'll find a small, brightly tiled space with booths, tables, and chairs and lots of other Sonoran Mexican dishes on the menu, including red chile beef tamales and chicken tamales. At holiday time, they also make sweet bean tamales filled with masa, beans, and raisins and spiced with cinnamon and cloves. Closed Sun, open Mon through Sat from 8:30 a.m. to 10 p.m.

Lodge on the Desert, 306 N. Alvernon Way, Tucson, AZ 85711; (520) 320-2000; Southwestern; $$$. Chef Ryan Clark, a graduate of the Culinary Institute of America, was named a top young chef by the American Culinary Federation and has won many culinary competitions in town. On top of his success, he's a cheerful, unassuming, friendly chef. Chef Clark is both the executive chef and the mixologist here, creating delicious Southwest-inspired drinks and food. The restaurant is housed in the back of the Lodge on the Desert resort hotel, a collection of hacienda-style buildings surrounding lovely, grassy grounds. You can sit inside in one of two intimate dining areas, on the outdoor patio complete with fireplace, or at the separate bar. The bar offers a super happy hour where you can sample some of Chef Ryan's culinary creations and his signature drinks. The **Black Rice Horchata** cocktail is the one I order every time, a delicious, creamy combination of cinnamon-infused bourbon, rice milk, and sugar (see the recipe on p. 281) and the Mussels Nopales, a bowl of shell-on mussels, strips of fresh grilled prickly-pear cactus pads, and house-made chorizo in a smoked tomato broth. The layering of flavors and textures is superb. The dinner menu features many of Chef Clark's signature dishes. The "twice-cooked" New York strip is dry rubbed with a house-made spice blend, slow roasted then grilled, which gives it a tender interior and crusty exterior—a perfect combination. A filet of moist, grilled Loch Duarte organic salmon sits on a mound of amazingly delicious Dungeness crab and leek mashed potatoes napped in a smoked paprika *nage*. Complimentary truffles, hand-rolled and dusted with cinnamon, are served after the meal so you needn't stress over picking out one of the many desserts. The truffle flavors change daily and you might find curry toasted coconut, jalapeño, or just plain dark choco-late—all dense and creamy, the perfect little bite of dessert. Open for breakfast from 7:30 to 10:30 a.m., lunch 11 a.m. to 2 p.m., and dinner from 5 p.m. daily.

Lovin' Spoonfuls, 2990 N. Campbell Ave., Tucson, AZ 85719; (520) 325-7766; lovinspoonfuls.com; Vegetarian; $. **Vegans, vegetarians, and those of us who like inventive nonmeat-based food all head to Lovin' Spoonfuls. Owner Peg Raisglid became a vegan in 1989 and has made it her personal mission to promote veganism and healthful eating. She has definitely succeeded here, with an extensive menu of vegetarian options in a comfortable, bistro-like setting with high ceilings, wood furnishings, soft lighting, and flowers on every table. Service is at the counter so get hold of a menu first and take your time reading about the interesting choices here before you get all the way up to the register and have to order. Home-style waffles, thick and crunchy, can be had for breakfast. Traditional, buckwheat, or gluten-free, they come with real maple syrup and nondairy topping; you can add fruit, nuts, and chocolate chips if you want something extra. Burritos and scrambles are made with tofu, and you can build your own, adding veggie ham, vegan cheese, soy chorizo, and lots of fresh veggies. The lunch and dinner entrees really showcase how creative Peg is with her foods. You'll find curries, lasagna, pasta, cashew nut loaf, soy chicken, and mock shrimp (they look exactly like the real thing and are sculpted from potatoes!). Save room for dessert because Peg makes one of the best carrot cakes in town—rich moist layers of cake, crushed pineapple, and mock cream-cheese frosting coated in chopped walnuts—it's delicious. Breakfast is served Mon through Sat 9:30 to 11 a.m., lunch 11 a.m. to 3 p.m., and dinner begins at 5 p.m. Open Sun 10 a.m. to 3 p.m.**

Mays Counter Chicken and Waffles, 2945 E. Speedway Blvd., Tucson, AZ 85716; (520) 327-2421; mayscounter.com; $$. Chicken and waffles. Who came up with this concept and why did it take so long? You can't beat the crispy, crunchy chicken and thin, crispy waffles here at May's. This former fast-food pizza place has been transformed into a retro-style diner and haven for fried chicken and down-home Southern-style cooking. Grab a booth, tuck your napkin into your collar, and get ready to eat. And eat. And eat. You may wish to wear stretch pants when you come here because there's a lot of tempting stuff on the menu and breakfast is served all day. Now, back to those waffles. You don't *have to* get them with fried chicken on top, but . . . the slightly malt-flavored waffles soak up all that nice chicken juice and the little crunchy pieces of skin that miss your mouth on the way in. Topped with a nice pour of maple syrup, they are wonderful. Should you not want waffles with chicken (what?!) you can choose battered, fried pickle chips, giant corn dogs, steak and eggs, fried catfish, shrimp and grits, and tater tots drowning in melted cheese and jalapeños. There are drinks here too, cocktails and beer on tap and by the bottle. The bacon Bloody Mary is hard to beat, a perfect mix of tomato juice, horseradish, and bacon-infused vodka with a strip of bacon as a swizzle stick. Open Mon through Fri at 11 a.m., Sat and Sun at 8 a.m.

McMahon's Prime Steakhouse, 2959 N. Swan Rd., Tucson, AZ 85712; (520) 327-7463; metrorestaurants.com; Steak; $$$. As you pull up to the circular driveway you may think this is a private club, complete with rich leather banquettes, humidors, porters, and valets. You're not too far off the mark! McMahon's is truly the epitome of fine dining. This upscale, extremely elegant and understated steak house is renowned for its personalized service, excellent steaks, and award-winning wine list. The jewel in the crown of the Metro Restaurant Group, McMahon's offers classic steak house fare. Famous for their USDA prime meats, beef is the protein of choice here. Start with paper-thin filet mignon carpaccio with Parmesan curls, minced red onion, diced hard-boiled egg, and salty capers, or mini beef Wellingtons, three puff pastry–wrapped tender-loins on a slick of rich Madeira demi-glace. McMahon's prime cuts, all expertly cooked, include hanger steak, rib eye Delmonico, filet mignon, and bistro tender steak. Creamed spinach and McMahon's own creamy scalloped potatoes (layered with green chiles and cheese) are the sides of choice. The Ivory Lounge offers a cigar-friendly outdoor porch and piano music seven nights a week if you care to retire there after dinner for a postprandial drink and a Cuban. The building is also home to Smoke, a small, cozy side bar off the main entrance. Extremely popular during happy hour, you'll find perfectly prepared drinks and an accessible and reasonably priced happy hour menu available here. You can also order the full menu at the bar if you wish. Lunch Mon through Fri from 11:30 a.m., dinner 5 p.m. Mon through Fri and from 4 p.m. on Sun; happy hour at Smoke Mon through Thurs from 3 to 7 p.m.

Millie's Pancake Haus, 6530 E. Tanque Verde Rd., Tucson, AZ 85715; (520) 298-4250; millies pancakehaus.com; Breakfast; $. Stuck in the back corner of a strip mall, the black awnings and faded sign signal you've found Millie's. The plain brick exterior belies the cozy kitchen feel inside. Robin's-egg blue walls, blue and white Delft plates, and lace curtains make

for a homey breakfast spot. There's even a nice bench to sit on while you wait for your table. And you will wait because Millie's is always crowded, especially on the weekends when it's family time and you'll find multi-generations sitting together tucking in to some great breakfast food—mostly pancakes—which is what Millie's is known for. There are all sorts of pancakes here: fluffy buttermilk with apple butter, thin Swedish with lingonberry sauce, crepe-like French with orange liqueur, Russian blintzes with sour cream, German with cinnamon-spiced apples, potato with apple sauce, Belgian a la mode, and whole-kernel corn cakes with bacon. And that's just one-third of the menu! Breakfast is served all day but you can also get a great comfort-food lunch (after 10:30 a.m.). House-made Swedish meatballs on top of egg noodles is a great choice, served with *smierkase* (cottage cheese) and apple butter on homemade bread. Grilled cheese, chicken salad, and BLTs are all on the menu too. Open Tues through Sun, 10:30 a.m. to 2 p.m.

Neo of Melaka, 6133 E. Broadway Blvd., Tucson, AZ 85711; (520) 747-7811; neomelaka.com; Malaysian; $$. Sophisticated, serene, authentic, Neo of Melaka is one of the few places in town to taste Malaysian food, a multiethnic mix of Malay, Chinese, Indian, Nyonya, and Indian flavors. The menu is a real mix of some familiar Chinese, Thai, Vietnamese, and Indian dishes and several unusual Malay specialties. On the appetizer menu, start with satay beef. These meaty skewers are served with a chunky, thin, slightly sweet peanut sauce for dipping, so good you will want to order several—there are four to an order. Curry puffs are a favorite, little flaky puffs filled with a mild curried potato mixture and so very easy to pop into your mouth. Tempura shrimp are delicate and light and come with a vinegary ginger chili dipping sauce. There are a number of house specialties you'll find only here including *lemak, sambal,* and *masak merah*—different styles of broth and sauces that you can order with seafood, chicken, beef, vegetables, or tofu. A favorite is the *lemak,* a sweet coconut broth flavored with garlic and lemongrass (you can order this with a nice fillet of salmon on top). The *sambal* here is a tamarind juice–based broth seasoned with shrimp paste, onions, and kefir lime leaves, great with tofu. The *masak merah* is a tangy sweet-and-spicy blend of potatoes, tomatoes, and Japanese eggplant in a garlicky, ginger-infused sauce, nice with beef or chicken. More familiar items include curries, wonton soup, sesame beef, *kung pao,* and pot stickers. Everything here is nicely prepared and plated fine dining style. Open Mon through Fri from 11 a.m. for lunch and dinner, Sat and Sun from 11:30.

Pastiche Modern Eatery, 3025 N. Campbell Ave., Tucson, AZ 85719; (520) 325-3333; pasticheme.com; American; $$. Plan your Friday nights around Pastiche. Start with the amazing wine tasting held from 5 to 6:30 p.m. at the wine shop just to the right of the restaurant entrance. Amanda Wahl (aka Amazing Amanda) hand-selects the evening's tastings from her vast wine cellar, and you can taste up to five fine wines, with gourmet cheese and crackers, for only $5.05 per person. You will learn a lot about wine and if you find one that you like, take it along to sip with your dinner next door for only a small corkage fee. Pastiche is a longtime Tucson favorite, known for its eclectic American/world cuisine. The interior is restful and lovely with soft lighting, Monet-like paintings by local artists, and pastel-colored walls. Service is on point and attentive. Pastiche thoughtfully offers smaller "bistro portions" of many of its menu items, so you can choose lots of things to taste without breaking the bank or getting too full. Owner Pat Connors is known for his commitment to local causes and the "Chicken Soup for Tucson's Soul" on the appetizer menu reflects this—for each order a donation is made to the local food bank, so what better way to feel good about what you eat? A signature appetizer to try

 here is the unusual panko-crusted, deep-fried avocado with spicy chipotle aioli. Other menu items offer a fusion of flavors: Porcini and pistachio-crusted ahi, bourbon salmon, and Jamaican-spiced rotisserie chicken are just some of the unusual choices. Get cookies for dessert. Pastry Chef Kristie Guest, a Johnson & Wales grad, bakes

up an amazing assortment daily with a fab chocolate dipping sauce. Open Tues through Fri for lunch and dinner from 11:30 a.m., Sat and Sun dinner only from 4:30 p.m.

Pinnacle Peak Steakhouse, 6541 E. Tanque Verde Rd., Tucson, AZ 85715; traildusttown.com; Steak; $$. Put on your cowboy boots and an old tie before you head here for a meal. A tourist and family favorite, they grill up some of the best steaks in town. Part of Trail Dust Town, a re-created old Western town with shops, rides, and entertainment, this is a kid favorite. Tucson residents have spent many hours here riding the mini train, buying candy at the Chocolate Depot, scouring the five-and-dime store for old-fashioned treats and kitschy knickknacks, attending the cowboy shootouts, and spinning around on the old-fashioned carousel. And that's all before eating a giant meal at Pinnacle Peak, the featured attraction! This place is packed all the time but the lines move fast and they will give you a pager so you can head back out into the fun at Trail Dust Town (did I mention the shooting gallery and the old-time photo studio?) until your table is ready. The interior is a combination Victorian parlor and saloon, with antique couches in the waiting area and rustic furnishings in the dining areas. Order steak: the big bone-in Cowboy, Cowgirl, and even bigger Big Cowboy are the ones to get. Mesquite grilled over open flames (you can watch them cooking in the back), they are juicy and delicious. Everything comes with a bowl of pinto beans, a basket of Texas toast bread (untoasted), and a side salad. Yee ha! Watch for the strolling balloon maker and listen for the bell that announces what happens to those of you who dare to wear a tie! Open Mon through Fri at 5 p.m., Sat and Sun at 4:30 p.m.

Pho # 1, 2226 N. Stone Ave., Tucson, AZ 85750; (520) 670-1705; Vietnamese; $. There are those who hesitate to enter here because it's definitely off the beaten track and this part of town is rather deserted during nighttime hours. But those who do walk past the golden lions that guard the entryway will be rewarded with excellent *pho*. It's basic and bare inside, but you'll find over 50 Vietnamese soups and rice dishes on the menu. The *pho* is the way to go. The broth is rich and greaseless, the condiments fresh and clean, and the meats nicely marbled and icy cold. I like to start with #0, the sampler plate with egg and spring rolls, sugarcane, charbroiled meatballs, and shrimp paste in tofu wraps. Then on to the *pho* (numbers 9 through 22), steak, shank, brisket, tendon, meatballs, shrimp, tofu, chicken, all these are available to mix into your broth along with several sauces, cilantro, and Thai basil leaves, mung bean sprouts, sliced jalapeños, and a side of sweet pickled carrots and jicama. Other soups feature a variety of noodles: egg, thick rice, potato, and vermicelli simmered in broth with seafood, pork, tofu, and chicken. Dry rice bowls (*bun*) feature giant bowls of vermicelli noodles topped with meats and vegetables. Choose a funky drink from the refrigerated case, front and center of the restaurant as you come in.

Decor is not a strongpoint here! Open Mon through Sat from 11 a.m. for lunch and dinner.

Polish Cottage, 4520 E. Broadway Blvd., Tucson, AZ 85711; (520) 891-1244; polishcottageaz.com; Polish; $. The aptly named Polish Cottage is a simple, one-room place lovingly decorated by owners Robert and Agnieszka Stawicki with delicate handmade paper cut-outs (*wycinanki*) framed on the walls, hanging at the windows, and under the glass on each table. They cook homemade Polish food here and you'll find lots of families digging into delicious family-style meals. Start with the pierogi. A sampler plate gets you a taste of each one, the sweet farmer cheese and sauerkraut fillings are especially good. Order a side of sweet caramelized onions and sour cream to go with them. The unusual white borscht is a house specialty. Made with a base of sour rye, the thin, rich broth is full of kielbasa chunks and pieces of hard-boiled egg. Stuffed cabbage rolls are wrapped around a light pork and rice filling, and served with a homemade tomato sauce. Other choices include breaded cutlets, kielbasa, beet soup, and hunter's stew. The waitstaff here is superb—not only do they speak Polish but they are experts on Polish cuisine and will answer any questions (even the most mundane about the decor), with enthusiasm and lengthy explanations. Open Tues through Sat 11 a.m. to 8 p.m., Sun noon to 7 p.m.

Sausage Deli, 745 E. Grant Rd., Tucson, AZ 85719; (520) 623-8182; sausagedeli.com; Deli; $. They have great grinders here. Top-of-the-line deli meats, thick, bready rolls, homemade vinaigrette, finely shredded lettuce, thin-sliced tomatoes. It's all just right. Lots of people go out of their way just to get a sandwich here. It's all counter service with booths, tables, and chairs inside and an outdoor patio. Most customers get their sandwiches to go, swinging into the parking lot, ordering at the counter, and grabbing their grinder wrapped up in butcher paper, with a side of potato salad or chips, to eat elsewhere. I think the grinders improve as they travel, the bread absorbing the vinaigrette and the meats and cheeses compressing into the soft bread, but that's probably just me. The Italian is a top pick, with Genoa salami, pastrami, provolone, lettuce, tomato, bell and peperoncini peppers, dried oregano, and Italian dressing. Open wide, it's a big, messy, delicious mouthful. Others like the Susie Sorority (turkey and Havarti with sprouts) and the hot meatball sub (homemade meatballs, marinara, and Parmesan cheese). There are 17 other hot and cold sandwich choices and you can build your own too. Open Mon through Sat from 10 a.m. to 5 p.m.

Scordato Pizzeria, 4280 N. Campbell Ave., Tucson, AZ 85718; (520) 529-2700; pizzeriavivace.com; Pizza; $$. This is not a fast food, take-out pizza joint. In fact, they advise you not to take out because it will compromise the texture of the crust. That's how much they care about their pizza here and your ability to enjoy it at its most delicious. Artisan pizza is what you will find at this upscale, elegant pizzeria. Sit in the airy front room or on the secluded back patio with a nice view of the Rillito River wash and get ready for perfect pizza. Cooked at extremely high temperatures, the crust is slightly blackened, crispy, and chewy and comes with a variety of decidedly upscale toppings. If you want plain, choose the Margherita, a light tomato sauce topped with mozzarella and fresh basil leaves, it's simple and delicious. The all-cheese with melted robiola, fontina, and mozzarella cheeses strewn with kalamata olives, roasted mushrooms, and fresh arugula, is a wonderful combination of flavors. Other choices include three mushroom with creamy fontina, Parmigiano-Reggiano, and Romano cheeses; chicken meatball and ricotta; and fennel-scented sausage with tiny cipollini onions. This is truly artisan pizza at its best and if you have some favorite toppings, you can mix and match to your heart's content to design your own special pizza. Appetizers and salads are available on the menu as well—the Gorgonzola cheese and grape salad sprinkled with pine nuts is wonderful, as are the chicken- and spinach-filled cannelloni. Open Mon through Fri from 11 a.m. to 2 p.m. for lunch, and dinner Mon through Sat from 5 p.m.

Sher-e-Punjab, 853 E. Grant Rd., Tucson, AZ 85719; (520) 624-9393; sher-e-punjabtucson.com; Indian; $. Ask local expats from India and Indian specialty market shopkeepers where to go in town for authentic Indian food and the name Sher-e-Punjab comes up time and time again. You'll find it in a strip mall, with a modest front entrance and small sign above the door. Once you step inside, you'll be pleasantly surprised to find an attractive, well-decorated space devoted to home-style Punjabi cuisine. A big lunch buffet offered daily will give you a great idea of all the tastes and flavors of India offered here, but if you come for dinner, start with the appetizers, featuring a wide variety of samosas and *pakoras* with all kinds of fillings (veggie, potato, lamb, spinach, fish, onion, and cauliflower). They specialize in tandoori here and you can order a half or whole chicken from the clay oven in the back. Bright pinky-orange, it arrives tableside cut up on a sizzling platter with sliced bell peppers and onions. Curries are another specialty item, with beef, chicken, vegetable, seafood, and an unusual pumpkin version available. There are over 100 items on the menu to choose from so it can be a bit overwhelming the first time you visit. They are very busy and pleasant here, and are happy to answer any questions about the foods on the menu. I particularly enjoy the lamb tikka masala (#37), a creamy rich sauce filled with big pieces of tender lamb; the vegetarian *karahi paneer* (#72), a stew of cubes of soft homemade cheese, onion, ginger, and garlic with spicy chiles; and the *chana* masala (#78), stewed garbanzo beans. A full drinks menu includes specialty beers from India (try the "Karma Ale") and a variety of cocktails. Open daily from 11:30 a.m. to 2 p.m. for lunch buffet, 5 p.m. for dinner.

Shish Kebab House, 5855 E. Broadway Blvd., Tucson, AZ 85711; (520) 745-5308; shishkebabhousetucson.com; Middle Eastern; $$. Opened in 1993 by Jeff Wer (originally from Salt, Jordan), the restaurant is family-run and he brings his authentic Jordanian Arabic specialties to the menu here. The best way to start your meal is with the appetizer combination platter. You can only select five things from the list of terrific appetizers, and although you may want to choose many, many more, save them for your next visit, because you will be back. For starters, I recommend the hummus with meat. The creamy chickpea dip is topped with ground lamb sautéed with onions and pine nuts. Next, choose *motabal,* the Jordanian version of baba ghanoush. The creamy eggplant dip has a slightly bitter, smoky flavor. Both come with warm whole Arabic pita bread, just rip a piece off and dig in. Zatar "pizza," is another favorite, warm pita sprinkled with a pungent herb mix that contains oregano, thyme, and sesame seeds. Meat pies here are excellent: Homemade dough surrounds sautéed ground beef, onions, and pine nuts. *Kousa* is a special Middle Eastern gray squash, here stewed in yogurt and garlic. I could go on and on . . . but I won't. I will leave it to you to discover the many other delicious things to eat here. (hint: *bamia, lahim mashwi, kabsas*). Open Mon through Sat at 11 a.m. and Sun at noon for lunch and dinner.

Son's Bakery Cafe, 5683 E. Speedway Blvd., Tucson, AZ 85712; (520) 885-0806; American; $. Son Bui is the friendly, outgoing chef-owner of Son's Bakery Cafe, a cozy diner where the walls are covered in a mural depicting the deep jungle of his native Vietnam. The tempting smells of freshly baked bread, frying eggs, and bacon greet you as you come in for breakfast. Son's french toast is extremely popular, and he takes great pride in it. Once you order, he looks you in the eye and says with a smile, "You are going to love this!" and you do! Made with his thick Texas-style homemade bread, it's crispy on the outside and eggy and soft in the middle without being soggy or overdone. Sprinkle it with powdered sugar and you have perfection! If you're on a budget and you're hungry, this is the place to come to eat. The full breakfasts offered here are bountiful and amazingly reasonable. Son's traditional breakfast #1 brings you two eggs, two sausages, home fries, and a toasted piece of his homemade bread, while Son's 18-wheeler #4 is a huge platter of eggs, ham, biscuits, and gravy, both for under $5—amazing! Lunch is super and budget-friendly too. Sandwiches (half or full portions) are served on Son's homemade bread (nine types at last count), or you can go more exotic with a bowl of Son's homemade Vietnamese beef soup—a steaming bowl of thin-sliced steak, rice noodles, cilantro, bean sprouts, and basil for a mere $3.99. Son even makes all the desserts—where does he get the energy? Perhaps from the caffeine in his wonderful brownies or his famous chocolate mountain cake. Open Mon and Tues 11 a.m. to 2 p.m., Wed through Sat 7 a.m. to 2 p.m., and Sun 8 a.m. to 2 p.m.

Takamatsu, 5532 E. Speedway Blvd., Tucson, AZ 85712; (520) 512-0800; takatucson.net; Korean; $$. Come here with a large group of close friends. Pile into the big booths with the barbecue in the middle of the table and order lots of stuff to put on the grill. It's fun, it's tasty, and you'll have a good time cooking and sharing your food with everyone (you can only barbecue with two or more). You will see a lots of other things on the menu—sushi, tempura, noodles, teppanyaki, rice bowls, but do not be distracted, skip past these and go directly to the Korean barbecue entrees and specials. Once you tell your waitperson that you will be barbecuing, the gas jets will be turned on so the grill top will get blazing hot. Meanwhile order your proteins—*kalbi* (beef short ribs), *bulgogi* (teriyaki-marinated rib eye), beef tongue, spicy marinated sliced pork, scallops, and jumbo shrimp. Each of these raw options comes with five little side dishes for dipping, saucing, and seasoning, or just eating. They include an incendiary kimchee, sweet pickled vegetables, and a vinegary soy dipping sauce. Each protein arrives on an oval platter with a variety of vegetables (mushrooms, scallions, onions, bok choy). Now it's time to cook. Grab a set of chopsticks and start placing your food directly on the grill. The sizzle and the smell will start your mouth to watering. When the food is cooked, you might have to compete with your friends to grab it and place it on your own plate. Dab on some sauces or dip it and pop it in your mouth. Salty, sweet, slightly charred, the marinated meats are favorites. If you don't feel like cooking your own supper, other Korean specialties include *bibimbap* (stir-fried vegetables and beef over rice with an egg on top), *haemul pa jeon* (seafood and scallion pancake), *denjang chigae* (fermented soybean, beef, and sardine soup), and *yeom soh tang* (spicy goat stew). Who needs regular old sushi with all this to choose from! Open from 11 a.m. daily for lunch and dinner.

Tino's Pizza, 6610 E. Tanque Verde Rd., Tucson, AZ 85715; (520) 296-9565; tinospizza.com; Pizza; $. I only get one thing here—the white pizza—because it's good with a nice, chewy crust that's not too thick and not too thin and they use real ricotta cheese. If you, or someone you love (that's you Eric, my son), do not like tomato sauce, get your pizza here. The white pizza is a blend of mozzarella and Parmesan dolloped with large blobs of real ricotta cheese (yes, I said it again because it's rare to see), sprinkled with dried oregano, a bit of chopped garlic, and drizzled with oil. You can eat in or out, it's casual, and access is easy with a large parking lot (look for the sign with the mustache). Inside is basic with booths, tables, chairs, and a pinball machine. They do offer hot and cold sandwiches, other kinds of pizza (with tomato sauce!), and a variety of toppings and some nice desserts— the tiramisu is made in house. Open Mon through Sat at 10:30 a.m. and Sun at 4 p.m.

Tucson Tamale Company, 2545 E. Broadway Blvd., Tucson, AZ 85716; (520) 305-4760; tucsontamalecompany.com; Mexican; $. If you like tamales, make a beeline to the Tucson Tamale Company because that is all they make, sell, and serve. There are over twenty amazing varieties of tamales at this little market/cafe, the brainchild of tamale lover Todd Martin. Todd and his crew make everything in the back kitchen from scratch. It's busy in here, with lots of people coming in to get tamales to go or ordering at the counter to eat in, while the tamales are being produced at the same time. You will find tamales for breakfast (tamale omelet, anyone?), tamales for lunch, tamales for dessert (pineapple/mango with coconut masa), tamales to go, and packs of frozen tamales, and they are all delicious. The masa is fluffy and tender (Todd uses 100 percent organic masa) and the fillings are incredibly creative. Todd's signature tamale is the the Tucson Tamale, a spicy blend of grilled jalapeño masa and lots of cheese wrapped up in a corn husk. A favorite is the Santa Fe, succulent slow-cooked pork, tangy green chile sauce, and cheddar—it's moist, meaty, and tasty. The seasonal, mildly spicy **Green-Corn Tamale,** a mouthwatering blend of fresh corn, green chiles, and cheddar cheese, is extremely popular (see Todd's recipe on p. 278). Unusual choices include the Dogmale (available frozen only), Todd's take on the Sonoran hot dog, with cooked hot dogs, bacon, onion, pinto beans, chiles, and cheese) and the vegan New Delhi, with carrots, corn, green beans, coconut milk, and curry powder. There is something for everyone here and Todd is constantly experimenting with new combinations, so if you have an idea, let him know and you might see it on the menu next time you come in! Open Mon through Sat from 10 a.m. to 7 p.m. and Sun from 8 a.m. to 3 p.m.

Union Public House, 4340 N. Campbell Ave., Tucson, AZ 85718; (520) 329-8575; uniontucson.com; American, $$. The lovely St. Philip's Plaza is home to this stylish restaurant. The bar that dominates the elegant space is the big draw here, attracting well-dressed

businesspeople, well-toned women in cocktail garb, athletic guys in casual wear, and lots of fetching couples. The bar sports 10 large-screen televisions, angled for a great view from any part of the restaurant. The dining area is slightly crowded with groupings of marble-topped tables. If it seems too claustrophobic inside, you can escape to the comfortable outdoor patio with couches and tables and a great view of the plaza. The menu aims to please with "honest food and clever libations" and, based on the crowds that come in daily, it succeeds with a mix of upscale bar and comfort foods. Arrive here for the "social hour" that takes place daily between 4 and 7 p.m., and 10 p.m. to closing, and features lots of specials and special prices on appetizers and drinks. Even if you're not particularly hungry, your eyes will feast on the attractive crowd bunched around the bar. Ask for the cocktail menu for a view of the specialty drinks made here (go for the signature CuBall, an effervescent mix of cucumber vodka, St-Germain, and 7-Up, served on a green ball—I have no idea why—with a slice of lime), or choose one of the 30 draft beers from around the world. The pretzels on the happy hour and "share it food" section of the menu are a real hit. House-made, they are sprinkled with smoked sea salt and come with a creamy white cheddar sauce and stone-ground mustard. Toffee popcorn with candied pecans are a close second. Unique artisan flatbreads are crispy and laden with unusual toppings like duck confit, spinach, roasted apples, and pickled onions, or prosciutto, cremini mushrooms, arugula, and fresh thyme juice (how do you juice a thyme leaf? It's a house secret!). Main winners are the decadent mac and cheese, as far from the orangey stuff in the box as you can imagine with campanelle pasta, leek *crema,* and white cheddar under a cracked-pepper crust; and the better-than-homemade pot pie, a rich creamy base packed with vegetables, chicken, potatoes, and bacon under a flaky crust. Dessert? Strawberry shortcake—buttery biscuits, sweetened fresh berries, with whipped cream on top! Open daily at 11 a.m.

Vivace Restaurant, 4310 N. Campbell Ave., Tucson, AZ 85718; (520) 795-7221; vivacetucson.com; Italian; $$$. The entrance to Vivace is discreetly located on the edge of St. Philip's Plaza. The interior is warm and sophisticated, with muted colors, fine art, floral arrangements, and recessed lighting. The lovely outdoor patio, with a view of the fountain in the plaza, is a popular spot if you want to dine alfresco. Vivace is a great pick for a business lunch if you want to impress clients and equally good for an intimate dinner tête à tête, with impeccable service and a hushed, cosmopolitan ambience. Well-heeled customers here are dressed for success and expect a fine dining experience. They are never disappointed with Chef Daniel Scordato's high quality, sophisticated Northern Italian cuisine. Ethereal spinach and cheese soufflé, creamy, rich and amazingly light, is a favorite starter followed by a bright pear and walnut salad with "live" soft-leafed butter lettuce, thin-sliced ripe pear, and a crumble of Gorgonzola. Manicotti and lasagna are made with tender handmade pasta, the manicotti filled with ricotta, fontina,

pecorino, and Parmigiano-Reggiano cheeses and floating on a light tomato sage mushroom sauce, while the lasagna noodles are layered with seafood and spinach in a fresh tomato and basil broth. Signature entrees include osso buco, meaty fall-off-the-bone veal shanks in a deeply rich red wine sauce, and pork Sorrentino, Chef Scordato's version of the classic saltimbocca, here made with thin slices of pork tenderloin topped with prosciutto and melted fontina cheese, baked in a light, rich white wine sauce. The wine list here is extensive and your server will be happy to recommend pairings, either by the glass or bottle. Warm molten chocolate cake for two is the dessert of choice (it takes 20 minutes, so alert your server at the start of your meal). Warm chocolate cake, soft truffle center, it's the perfect ending to your fine evening. Open Mon through Sat from 11:30 for lunch and dinner.

Yoshimatsu Healthy Japanese Food, 2660 N. Campbell Ave., Tucson, AZ 85719; (520) 320-1574; yoshimatsuaz.com; Japanese; $. Part noodle house, part sushi bar, part retail store, Yoshimatsu has many identities. There are two distinct parts of the restaurant—

Yoshimatsu in the front and Sushimatso in the back where you can get only sushi. The decor is funky, the clientele is all across the board from business people to tattooed students, and the food is a real mishmash (in a good way). You'll find bento boxes, soup bowls, udon, curry, tempura, yakisoba, *okonomi, tatikomi,* vegan, spicy, vegetarian . . . it could take you all day just to read through the menu. What I like about this place is that there are so many intriguing choices. Go for the lunch specials offered daily from 11:30 a.m. to 2:30 p.m. for amazingly reasonable prices. The sushi and noodle soup combination lunch special is probably the best fusion of the dual personalities of the restaurant, but there's also the lunch plate and "mini and mini set" lunch specials to choose from. There's a great selection of teas here: *sencha,* oolong, *genmai cha,* and *matcha,* served hot or cold. Beer, sake, and wine are available along with unusual Japanese yogurt drinks and sodas. No matter how I try to describe it, Yoshimatsu just has to be experienced. Go there. Eat. Be healthy. Be happy. Open daily for lunch from 11:30 a.m. to 2:30 p.m., dinner starting at 5 p.m. and ending at 9 p.m. Sun through Thurs, Fri and Sat ending at 10 p.m.

Zayna Mediterranean, 4122 E. Speedway Blvd., Tucson, AZ 85712; (520) 881-4348; zaynamediterranean.com; Middle Eastern; $. I love Middle Eastern food, especially Lebanese food, and you will find it here, prepared fresh daily by Lebanese-born Chef-Owner Riad Altoubal. The small, colorful space with a wall of windows overlooking busy Speedway is homey and friendly, with great background music featuring famous Lebanese singer Fairouz. Things are casual here. Step up to the counter, grab a menu, and have a chat with the sociable front of the house staff, who will be happy to walk you through the simple menu. A top pick here is the *mujadara.* It's a wonderful rice dish made with short-grain rice cooked with brown lentils and topped with sweet caramelized onions and toasted pine nuts. Order it with a side of thick, homemade garlicky yogurt, or it's even better with the yogurt on top. There is something incredibly satisfying about the combination. The *fatoosh* salad is a classic Lebanese dish featuring crispy pieces of pita bread, dried mint leaves, and an olive oil and lemon dressing—the bread softens as it soaks up the nice lemony dressing. *Fool mudammas* is a delicious blend of giant fava beans, mixed with tomatoes, parsley, lemon, and lots and lots of garlic. To drink? Lebanese Pilsner beer and a selection of Lebanese wines are available too. *Sahtein!*

Zivaz Mexican Bistro, 4590 E. Broadway Blvd., Tucson, AZ 85711; (520) 325-1234; zivaz.com; Mexican; $$. At first glance this may seem like a standard quick-serve Mexican place, but it isn't. The food here is delicious and unusual, a blend of Latin American cuisines with some unique specialties and interesting marinades and sauces featured on the menu. Stick with the *platillos zivaz,* a selection of 15 signature entrees. Try *pescado ajillo,* a moist, perfectly sautéed filet of ahi served in a spicy *guajillo* chile tomato sauce and sliced mushrooms. The chocolate-based mole poured over grilled chicken breasts (*pechuga en mole*) is rich and satisfying and also available over chicken, veggie, or cheese enchiladas. *Pollo en pibil* (achiote and sour orange–marinated grilled chicken) is one of my favorites, moist and flavorful with a deep rust color. The unique *milanese de berenjena* is the Latin version of eggplant parmigiana—breaded, fried eggplant slices, sprinkled with *queso fresco* cheese and sauced with a tomatillo salsa. If you simply can't choose, let the chefs here choose for you, the "Tour de Zivaz" sampler is available after 5 p.m.

A restaurant with a cookbook in the bathroom is my kind of place, and you'll find a full-color, coffee table–style Mexican cookbook on a special stand next to the tiled sink here. Open Mon through Sat from 11 a.m. for lunch and dinner.

Landmark

Arizona Inn, 2200 E. Elm St., Tucson, AZ 85719; (520) 325-1541; arizonainn.com; Continental; $$$. Built in 1930, this is a timeless Tucson treasure. The original owner Isabella Greenway was the first congresswoman from Arizona and her descendants still own the inn. Anyone who lives in or visits Tucson simply must come to the Arizona Inn at least once. The classic interior is furnished with handmade chairs and tables, antiques, oriental rugs, vintage photos, paintings, pottery, and baskets. The main dining room is home to formal dining tables clothed in starched white linens set with blue crystal glasses. Chandeliers hang from the ceiling and gorgeous floral arrangements grace the side tables. The staff are highly trained, unobtrusive, and instantly at your service. The classic menu harks back to the days when people had formal dinner parties, servants, and private chefs, and gentlemen puffed on cigars and ladies sipped cordials in the drawing room after dinner. Think shrimp cocktail, vichyssoise, French onion soup, Caesar salad, duck breast, crème brûlée—all offered at dinner along with fine wines. If the dining room is too formal for you, there are several other equally lovely dining options. The octagonal Audubon Bar, with historic Audubon prints hung on the walls and a full bar, is a great place for a drink and dinner or lunch. In this cool, intimate, and comfortable setting, you can order soups, sandwiches, and select entrees while you listen to nightly live piano music. A beautiful outdoor patio is a prime location for breakfast and lunch, with a restful view of the manicured lawns, ancient trees, and flowers on the property. The breakfasts here are extremely popular, offering several styles of eggs Benedict (with salmon, pork loin, portobello mushrooms, or chorizo); omelets, pancakes, and the Inn's signature granola. A light continental breakfast can also be had poolside, at the colorfully tiled outdoor patio beside the deep-blue pool hidden away among the guest rooms and suites. Wherever you dine, take your time here, exploring the gorgeous grounds and getting a real taste for Tucson's varied, interesting history. The Main Dining Room serves breakfast daily starting at 6:30 a.m., lunch from 11:30 a.m. to 2 p.m. and brunch Sun at 11:30 a.m. The Audubon and patio serve lunch and dinner daily starting at 11:30 a.m.; poolside dining is seasonal.

Foothills

Most Tucsonan's refer to the area at the base of the Catalina Mountain range as "the foothills." This is a primarily residential part of town, with lots of hiking trails, a national park, an upscale shopping center, art galleries, resorts and spas, and lots of homes nestled into the hills. You'll find restaurants housed in luxurious landmark resorts and restaurants with spectacular city and mountain views here.

Foodie Faves

The Abbey Eat + Drink, 6980 E. Sunrise Dr., Tucson, AZ 85750; (520) 299-3132; theabbeytucson.com; $$. You'd never know that this used to be an ice cream parlor. Owner Brian Metzger has transformed a bland, industrial space on the corner of a parking lot into an upscale, attractive restaurant (with a great view of the Catalina Mountains) that packs in foothills foodies nightly. You'll find diners of all kinds here, from families grabbing a bite to bejeweled matrons having a leisurely supper to hip young folks drinking at the outdoor bar and patio. There is something for them all on this approachable menu. Warning: Do not stuff yourself with the addictive truffle popcorn that adorns each table. You may think you can just have one little handful, but it's delicious and the servers love to refill it over, and over! *Stop* yourself, and leave room for the snacks, salads, soups, and mains on the short but evolving menu. The heirloom tomato salad has a super-tasty, light buttermilk dressing with seasonal leafy greens; a dense pot pie changes seasonally; and the juicy burger is a hit, with homemade shallot marmalade, a fried egg, and bacon served on an English muffin. Ask about the Breakfast for Dinner, a daily creation by Executive Chef Ginny Wooters. Open daily at 4 p.m. for happy hour, 5 p.m. for dinner, and 10:30 a.m. on Sun for brunch.

Acacia Real Food & Cocktails, 3002 E. Skyline Dr., Tucson, AZ 85718; (520) 232-0101; acaciatucson.com; Global/SW; $$$. With one of the most amazing views in Tucson, Acacia's giant picture windows look out over the city and beyond to the mountains. Chef-Owner Albert Hall has created a masterpiece here with a lovely interior of dark woods and a soft, rich color palette of deep reds and browns. A veteran of the Tucson culinary scene, he and wife Lila Yamashiro have developed a sophisticated menu with unusual pairings. Chef Hall makes a point of sourcing the most sustainable and seasonal local ingredients, buying local, all natural, pesticide- and herbicide-free, and certified organic products from micro farmers in Southern Arizona and the University of Arizona Agricultural Cooperative, and meats from the University's Meat Sciences Department. Chef Hall's standards are so exacting, he even flies salmon in all the way from Scotland, which he then cures himself and serves with a blood orange–fennel compote and chive *crema*. The bar-lounge area with comfortable and spacious seating offers up some delightful cocktails and is a great spot to sit and chat with a drink and an appetizer. The spicy chipotle shrimp and warm spinach and artichoke dip with sliced baguettes are great starters to accompany your drink. While the menu here changes seasonally, you'll always find inventive pairings combining Southwest ingredients with global influences. Pillowy gnocchi paired with crisp plantains and creamy house-made ricotta, and sea bass swimming in miso and shiitake broth atop a purple Peruvian potato mash are just two examples of Chef Hall's inventiveness. Cioppino is a real winner—Chef Hall has put his own touch on this satisfying soup filled with generous portions of clams, mussels, shrimp, salmon, scallops, and crabmeat in a spicy tomato pepper broth. Meats are well prepared and juicy; pecan wood–fired pork chops, double lamb chops, veal chops, duckling, and tender steaks are all on the menu with numerous accompaniments. You'll find excellent service here, with an experienced and knowledgeable waitstaff and the ever-present Lila and Albert making sure you are treated just right! And that view—amazing! Closed Mon, lunch and dinner from 11 a.m.

Anthony's in the Catalinas, 6440 N. Campbell Ave., Tucson, AZ 85718; (520) 299–1771; anthonyscatalinas.com; Continental; $$$. Anthony's has been offering upscale continental cuisine in the foothills since before most of the foothills were developed. It predates the several restaurants, housing developments, and malls that now surround it, but it soldiers on, providing great service, food, and an award-winning wine list in a soothing, plush atmosphere with a true continental style reminiscent of fine dining in days gone by. How many places still do Caesar salad tableside? Anthony's does. Escargots? Shrimp cocktail? French onion soup? All here, expertly prepared. Chateaubriand with béarnaise sauce, roast duckling, rack of lamb, filet mignon? Also here, served with vegetables, soup du jour, or a field salad. Dinner specials are available nightly as well, check with your very professional server for details. If you are looking for a classy meal in a classy place, make a point to get to Anthony's; the view and the food will make you happy you dined here. Dinner served nightly from 5:30 p.m.

Blanco Tacos + Tequila, 2905 E. Skyline Dr., Tucson, AZ 85718; (520) 232-1007; foxrc.com; Mexican; $$. Tacos can be pretty basic. A tortilla, filling, wrap it up and you're all set. Not here, this is sophisticated taco land. Located in the upscale shopping mall La Encantada, Blanco Tacos is definitely not your local taco stand. As the Grand Champion winners of the 2012 Tucson Taco Festival competition, this place takes its tacos seriously. Attractive young hosts and

CANYON RANCH
HEALTH RESORT CULINARY SPA DAY

One of the top spas in the nation, Canyon Ranch is a Tucson treasure tucked away in the Catalina Mountain foothills. Owners Mel and Enid Zuckerman, who founded Canyon Ranch in 1979, have been at the forefront of health and fitness in this country, advocating healthy eating for decades. You can access the beauty of this gorgeous spa and its delicious cuisine with a spa day. Renowned for his cutting-edge, healthy cuisine, Corporate Chef Scott Uehlein, who is based in Tucson (see his recipe on p. 279) sources only the very best, organic, sustainable ingredients and works with the Ranch's Food Development and Nutrition departments to create healthy, delicious menus. Dining options include the Main Dining Room restaurant and the Double U Cafe. The restaurant is sit-down while the counter-service poolside cafe offers casual indoor seating and an outdoor patio. The menus at both venues change daily, and it's all delicious. For a full culinary immersion spa day, start with an early meal at the Cafe or Main Dining room, then attend the daily Lunch and Learn cooking demo (usually held at noon), which includes a full meal, and then sign up for the hands-on cooking class held daily from 2 to 4 p.m. You'll emerge from your day with a wealth of culinary knowledge and a great perspective on healthy eating. Spa day details are available only by phone (520-749-9655). General information about Canyon Ranch is at their website, canyonranch.com.

servers will be sure you are greeted, seated, and treated to a great taco experience. There's a great outdoor porch, with nice views of the city and it's a little bit quieter than inside the bustling restaurant. Start off with guacamole, made here with roasted chiles, caramelized onion, and sprinkled with *cotija* cheese. Then move on to the tacos, and there's lots to choose from: fish, shrimp, chicken, braised short rib, ahi, along with mushroom for the non–meat eaters. Try them all with a side of spicy jalapeños and carrots or vegetarian black beans. Mexican chocolate cake, a moist cinnamon chocolate confection, will not disappoint for dessert. Open daily from 11 a.m. for lunch, happy hour, and dinner.

El Corral, 2201 E. River Rd., Tucson, AZ 85718; (520) 299-6092; traildusttown.com; American; $$. Do you like prime rib? That soft, cut-with-a-fork, pink, fat-larded piece of juicy beef? If you do, then El Corral is *the* place to go. Famous for their perfectly cooked, delicious prime rib, this is a favorite destination for meat lovers. Comfortable and cozy with a Southwest/cowboy theme, it's nothing fancy, welcoming one and all for a big plate of beef, every day of the week. Located in a historic territorial ranch house, the restaurant has been in continuous operation for over 60 years! You'll find a family-friendly menu and atmosphere here, with burgers, seafood, steaks, and ribs on the menu but stick with the main contender—

 that famous prime rib, available in petite (ah, who wants a small prime rib?), regular, and large. It comes to your table on its very own platter, surrounded by its own juice and accompanied

by a large knife. Who could ask for anything more? Well, I could, and I do, because the tamale pie is a house favorite, dense and full of corn kernels and green chiles. Open daily for lunch and dinner, starting at 5:30 p.m. Mon through Thurs, 4:30 p.m. other days.

Flying V Bar & Grill, 7000 N. Resort Dr., Tucson, AZ 85750; (520) 529-7936; loewshotels.com; Southwest; $$$. The jewel in the crown on the gorgeous property of Loews Ventana Canyon Resort, Flying V has it all—great views of the rolling green golf course, the Tucson city vista, and a waterfall in the background. What could be a better combination? Fireplace? Excellent bar? Great food? Flying V succeeds on all counts. You can sit inside at the bar, at one of the many well-positioned tables in this soothing, restful interior by a window or near the subtle and warming fireplace on chilly desert nights (yes we do have them!). The outside patio, elevated above the golf course, is tops for outdoor dining. Start off your meal with a terrific signature drink, the prickly-pear margarita. Get it frozen and prepare for an icy, magenta drink that's sure to give you a brain freeze, and it's worth it. Not only is it great to look at in a blue-rimmed, hand-blown margarita glass, but it tastes amazing, just the right blend of sweet, salt, and citrus. *The* appetizer to get here is the guacamole, made tableside by your very own guacamoliere who rolls out a cart filled with perfectly ripe avocados, a black *molcajete,* and lots of optional "mix-ins" (I go for garlic, jalapeños, and a splash of tequila). Watch and learn as the experts slice, dice, and mash up the best guac you may ever have. The entree menu changes seasonally, and features unique local ingredients and supporting local farmers and producers. Starters include a unique soup made with local tepary beans—you might find them in a rich bisque napped with regional Queen Creek olive oil and a spike of sage brittle or a in a creamy-cool vichyssoise topped with ground cholla cactus buds. Side dishes are tasty, served up in adorable mini cast-iron pots. The green chile cornbread is house-made and hard to stop eating, but do hold back because the entree choices are equally tasty. Favorites include fall-off-the-bone, agave-glazed baby back ribs, grilled quail, and perfectly seared ahi. End your meal with the all-chocolate dessert, a trio of chocolate brioche, flourless espresso torte, and Ibarra brownie—the plating alone is a work of art. Closed Mon, open at 5:30 p.m. Tues through Thurs and Sun, Fri and Sat at 5 p.m.

Ginza Sushi, 5425 N. Kolb Rd., Tucson, AZ 85750; (520) 539-8877; ginzatucson.com; Japanese; $$. Master sushi chef Jun Arai, from Nagano, Japan, makes sushi look easy as he uses his well-honed thin-bladed knives to carve delicate slices of hamachi, salmon, and tuna behind the counter at this upscale and welcoming restaurant. The interior is cool and restful with red banquettes, black lacquer dining tables, and pebbly floor. Chef Arai and his wife Diana run this friendly neighborhood spot, keeping people coming back with their very fresh, artfully presented sushi and interesting Japanese *izakaya* specialties. Watch for specials, listed on the whiteboard, Chef Jun is always sourcing the freshest seafood from across the United States and beyond—you might find oysters from Canada or lobster from Maine. Lunch anyone? Super deals are to be had with a variety of bento boxes, served up in sectioned boxes imported from Japan, which can include delightful combinations of sushi, sashimi, salad, rice, and tempura. The sashimi lunch, with rice, miso soup, and a mixed green salad is another winner. Tempura here is light and crispy, the prawns are large and especially tasty. *Natto* (fermented soybeans) and *yamaimo* (mountain potato) are unique specialties not found elsewhere. Do ask Chef Jun-San for his recommendations—he's always to be found working hard at the sushi bar, with a bandana around his forehead, and is friendly and approachable. Dessert options include flan, prepared by Diana who is of Mexican origin. I know it's not Japanese, but it is good and I can't resist it. Dense and eggy and sitting in a pool of luscious caramel sauce, it's a great way to end your meal. Open daily for lunch Tues through Sat at 11:30 a.m., dinner daily at 5 p.m.

Shlomo & Vito's New York Delicatessen, 2870 E. Skyline Dr., Tucson, AZ 85718; (520) 529-3354; shlomoandvitos.com; Deli; $$. There aren't many places in town here to find real New York deli food—Shlomo and Vito's is the closest you can get. Owners Shlomo and Vito (they do exist) grew up in Brooklyn, New York, so they should know their deli. The front of the restaurant serves as deli counter, slicing up corned beef, tongue, and other deli meats and cheeses in case you want some to go. But head on in to the somewhat cavernous restaurant or out to the lovely back patio and

let them do the cooking for you! Corned beef and pastrami come in from Sy Ginsberg's in Detroit. (Why reinvent the wheel? They do it well already.) Soups and desserts are made in house. The huge menu should offer at least one option for ex–New Yorkers missing Katz's or the Carnegie Deli (oh, how I miss that chopped liver!). Sandwiches are huge and packed with meats, served on Jewish rye with brown mustard, and you'll find egg creams, New York cheesecake, brisket, stuffed cabbage, matzo ball, and kreplach soup along with salads, pastas, and fried chicken for those not into deli food. The portions are generous and this place is extremely popular with families and large groups, especially on the weekends. Open daily from 8 a.m. for breakfast, lunch, and dinner.

Tavolino, 2890 E. Skyline Dr., Tucson, AZ 85718; (520) 531-1913; tavolinoristorante.com; Italian; $$. Chef-Owner Massimo Tenino is from the Liguria region in northwestern Italy and has brought his native cuisine to the foothills. Handmade pasta, lasagna, sauce, dessert, it's all homemade from Massimo's family recipes. It's all about family here—the house wine comes all the way from his brother Paolo's vineyards in Alba and family photos line the walls. The open, airy space with a busy, open kitchen is rustic and simple. A lovely outdoor patio looks out onto a courtyard and fountain, occasionally home to a local festival or musicians. A wood-fired grill puts out moist, juicy chicken, savory pork loin, and a variety of pizzas, but pasta is the thing to get here—as authentic as you'll

Local Chain: Zin Burger

A burger seems like such a simple thing to make—after all it's just a patty, bun, and some toppings, right? But I've had my share of awful burgers, dry, greasy, thin, raw, so there's a lot that can go wrong. Happily everything goes right, every time, at these clean, bright burger joints that are part of the Arizona-based Fox Restaurant Concepts Group. Soft grilled buns, juicy meat that's just the right size, and burgers cooked to perfection are what keep people coming into Zin Burger. The young, cheerful staff aims to please and the food is consistently good. Kids of all ages love the shakes, and they also have a nice selection of beers, wines by the glass, and mixed drinks. You'll find all kinds of burgers on the menu. I love the ahi burger here. It's not so easy to cook ahi, it can get dry or overdone, but the cooks do a great job. The generous slab of teriyaki-marinated ahi is seared on the outside and warm and tender on the inside. Sandwiched between buns and topped with avocado, it's just right. Do leave room for dessert, huge portions of chocolate cake, homemade pies—if you can't eat it here, take it home, it'll taste good tomorrow too! The daily happy hour between 4 and 6 p.m. gets you half-price drinks, sides, and two bucks off the "Plain and Simple" burger. 1865 E. River Rd., (520) 299-7799; 6390 E. Grant Rd., (520) 298-2020. Open daily from 11 a.m. for lunch and dinner.

find outside the "boot." You'll see the pasta, in all shapes and colors, dangling from racks as it dries. The lasagna *al forno* is a personal favorite, with thin noodles, a layer of creamy béchamel, and a thick, rich, meaty sauce. Pappardelle and tagliatelle are perfectly made and married beautifully with pesto and Bolognese sauces, respectively. You just can't go wrong with any of the house-made pastas, all noted clearly on the menu, and you can ask to substitute any of them for the non-homemade pastas on the menu. *Branzino* (sea bass flown in from Greece) is a top seller, grilled whole and presented with garlicky broccolini and a white wine–caper sauce. For dessert do not pass up the Bonet, a terrific combination of crunchy Amaretti cookies; rich, bittersweet caramel; and dense chocolate. The recipe has been handed down from Massimo's grandma—I've tried to get a hold of it, but it's a closely guarded secret so I just have to keep coming in to eat it here. I'm not complaining, it's that good! The happy hour is extremely popular, and features some interesting *cichetti* (small appetizers), including the *farinata,* little fritters made with garbanzo-bean flour and only available during happy hour. *Buon appetito!* Closed Sun. Open for lunch at 11 a.m., happy hour at 3 p.m., and dinner at 5 p.m.

Landmarks

Gold at Westward Look Resort, 245 E. Ina Rd., Tucson, AZ 85704; (520) 917-2930; westwardlook.com; Southwest; $$$.

Westward Look is a top Tucson destination, both for its lovely setting and for its food. The historic part of the property was built in 1912, making it one of the oldest resorts in town. Chef James Wallace presides over the restaurants here with the Four Diamond, *Wine Spectator* award-winning Gold as his crown. Schooled in Portland at the Western Culinary Institute, he uses his creative culinary experience (he's cooked in the Caribbean, Hawaii, and Mexico) to present unique breakfast, lunch, and dinner menus. Chef Wallace is a smoker—he smokes his own signature bacon, salmon, and specialty meats. You'll find his one-of-a-kind smoked pork bacon on the perfectly poached eggs Benedict at breakfast and his smoked salmon in the house-made salmon hash, combined with crunchy hash browns. The gorgeous property is home not only to trails, swimming pools, and terrific views, but also to an extensive kitchen garden, lovingly planted, pruned, and fertilized by a full-time gardener. Lucky chef Wallace has his pick of fabulous seasonal fruits, herbs, and vegetables that find their way into his menu. Mission figs, limequats, pineapple guava, purple fava beans, grapes, and bay laurel are all grown and harvested right here. Make a reservation for sunset—the comfortable dining room or outdoor patio are the perfect spot to enjoy the setting sun, awe-inspiring red-orange sky, and a magnificent view of Tucson's twinkling lights when darkness takes over. Dinner is a testament to Chef Wallace's passion for textures, opposing flavors, seasonal ingredients, and technique. The seasonal menu always features a surprise amuse bouche, which showcases simple flavors and textures—you'll find anything from an Asian spoon of soup to an avocado ice cream to start your meal. Dinner signature items include the Short Stack (no, it's not pancakes), layers of petit filet of beef, ahi tuna, and dayboat scallops in a red wine demi-glace with smoked tomato butter and smashed Yukon potatoes. Dessert? The crème brûlée in a fanciful phyllo cup for dessert is a house special. Interested in what happens behind the scenes? Join Chef Wallace for his monthly cooking demo and a tour of the garden followed by a multicourse meal. Open daily at 7 a.m. for breakfast, lunch Mon through Fri only from 11 a.m. to 2 p.m., and dinner Wed through Sat from 5:30 p.m.

The Grill at Hacienda del Sol Guest Ranch Resort, 5601 N. Hacienda del Sol Resort Rd., Tucson, AZ 85718; (520) 299-1501; haciendadelsol.com; Continental; $$$. A historic property, Hacienda del Sol has been a haven for society girls, movie stars, and celebrities since its opening in 1929 as a private girls' school. Converted to a guest ranch in 1948, this lovely, restful and beautiful resort in the hills attracted a number of celebrity guests, including Katharine Hepburn, Spencer Tracy, Clark Gable, and John Wayne. You travel up, up, up a winding road to what looks like a private hacienda surrounded by a low, whitewashed adobe wall leading into a beautiful courtyard. The main restaurant, The Grill, is a restful, relaxing space with dark woods, beamed ceilings, and heavy hewn-wood furnishings. Hand-painted murals and gorgeous Talavera pottery pieces accent the decor. Top-notch service and attention to detail, from the crisp linen tablecloths to the perfectly filled crystal water glasses, make for a five-star dining experience. A small, well-tended garden provides greens, herbs, and a variety of seasonal vegetables for the continental menu with Southwestern touches. Signature dishes include grilled buffalo sirloin with caramelized shallot jus and a cauliflower corn gratin; achiote-marinated New York steak with wild mushrooms; and house-made mushroom ravioli, filled with cremini and seasonal squash in a mushroom Parmesan *brodo*. An extensive wine list features over 1,500 labels and 10,000 bottles, ably paired for you, if you wish, by the sommelier. Chocolate desserts are winners here—really: Pastry Chef Marcos Castro's chocolate bread pudding won him the title of 2011 Tucson Pastry Chef of the Year. Keep an eye out for the occasional chocolate-themed dinner, lauded by *Food Network* magazine. Do take some time before or after dinner to explore the property. The main lounge is home to an amazing beehive fireplace, a central courtyard is lovely, and the walls throughout the resort are filled with fascinating historic photos. Open for breakfast Mon through Sat at 7 a.m., lunch Mon and Sat from 11 a.m. to 4 p.m., dinner nightly starting at 5:30 p.m. Sunday brunch begins at 9:30 a.m.

Northwest

When you hear "Northwest," it usually refers to the rather large and rapidly growing area of town that stretches northwest from downtown Tucson to Oro Valley and on up to Marana and Catalina (all part of Pima County). There are many different types of restaurants here, all found primarily on Oracle Road, which is the main artery running north and south through this section of town. There's an interesting mix of unusual ethnic places, family owned cafes, a tearoom in a botanical garden, a top spa, and resorts to be found here.

Foodie Faves

Alisah's Restaurant, 5931 N. Oracle Rd., Tucson, AZ 85704; (520) 887-5305; alisahrestaurant.com; Bosnian; $$. Welcome to Bosnia! Chef-Owner Ahmet Alisah has brought his home cooking to town and it is hearty and good. The purple hued, simply decorated space is warm and welcoming, just like Chef Alisah! He bounds from the kitchen to greet you as soon as you get settled at your table, bearing a basket of homemade bread and, if you're lucky, a bowl of his special vegetable stew (no charge, of course, you are now family!). His handsome son, lovely wife, or daughter may take your order and can answer any questions about the items on the menu, many of which may be unfamiliar. Chef Alisah makes everything from scratch here, from the specialty sausages to the delicious condiments. The best way to get a taste of it all is with the Chef Alisah's Surprise Plate. This *huge* platter is full of almost everything on the menu. I can't tell you exactly what's on it, because it has to be a surprise and if you don't finish it all, you have to do the dishes (at least that's what they tell you, I have yet to finish it all and I haven't had to do any dishes). The homemade grilled sausages here (*cevapi*), made with ground beef and special spices, are wonderfully meaty; the generous sized sis kebabs arrive still on their metal skewers, accompanied by homemade tomato accented soft rice. *Jajentina sa grahom,* lamb stew with giant butter beans in a thick, meaty sauce, is rich and filling. The thick Bosnian-style *tzatziki* is creamy and garlicky and is great dolloped on just about everything, ditto the tangy/sweet *ajvar,* made with red peppers, onions, eggplant, and tomatoes. If you are a lamb lover, do not miss the whole roasted lamb dinners—advance reservations a must, it fills up way in advance and you will see why (huge portions, great value). Closed Mon. Open for lunch Tues through Sat 10:30 a.m. to 1:30 p.m., dinner Tues through Sun from 5:30 p.m.

Caffè Torino, 10235 N. La Canada Dr., Oro Valley, AZ 85737; (520) 297-3777; caffetorinooorovalley.com; Italian: $$$. This upscale, well-appointed restaurant is as close to Northern Italy as you can get without getting on a plane. Executive Chef-Owner Daniela Borella has created a lovely paean to her native land here, with a terra-cotta and saffron color palette, retro Italian background music, and soft lighting. She uses mom Edy's recipes to create authentic Northern Italian dishes like lasagna with homemade noodles and a rich meat sauce, soft gnocchi in a perfectly balanced pesto sauce, and greaseless, cheesy eggplant Parmesan. The warm sticks of house made focaccia, sprinkled with rosemary leaves and coarse salt, are delicious and come with a dish of extra-virgin olive oil for dipping. Entrees include several veal dishes, well made and generously portioned. The veal *piccata al limone* and veal *alla marsala* are winners, and come with a nice side serving of pasta—you can choose your sauce and style of pasta (gnocchi are extra but worth it). Indulge in the tiramisu for dessert, made in true Italian style with liquor-soaked ladyfingers, mascarpone, and dusted with cinnamon and cocoa powder. *Salute!* Breakfast and lunch daily, dinner Tues through Sun from 5 p.m.

China Phoenix, 7090 N. Oracle Rd., Tucson, AZ 85704; (520) 531-0658; chinaphoenixrestaurant.net; Chinese; $$. This is *the* place to go for dim sum, served only on the weekends from 10 a.m. to 3 p.m. It's also one of the few places in town to get duck and chicken feet, available on the "House Special" section of the

LOCAL CHAIN: BEYOND BREAD

An absolute favorite with locations in Northwest, East, and Central parts of town, these bakery/restaurants are packed day and night with carbaholics enjoying the terrific bread that's made into equally terrific sandwiches, bowls for soups, French toast, and crispy croutons for salads. Founded by Shelby and Randy Collier in 1998, you will need to get here early to miss the long lines but take heart, they move fast. Grab a menu at the door and tuck into the free bread and butter as you check out the many, many sandwich options available at lunch and dinner. There are lots of daily specials too, always noted on signs hung above the cashiers. Curt's Club, my husband's favorite, is huge, with at least 10 layers (I may be exaggerating just a bit) of real turkey slices, toasted white bread, bacon, swiss, mayo, tomato, and lettuce, all pierced with giant toothpicks. I lean toward Brad's Beef—also huge, it's a hot one with roast beef, green chiles, red onion, and Russian dressing on crusty white bread. The soup bowls are huge, hollowed out bread boules that become home to a variety of soups. My favorite is the tomato basil, a rich puree of fresh tomatoes with a scattering of basil leaves. You really can't go wrong with anything on the menu that incorporates bread, it's all made daily and has the perfect texture and crunch. All locations are open Mon through Fri from 6:30 a.m. to 8 p.m., Sat from 7 a.m. to 8 p.m., and Sun from 7 a.m. to 6 p.m.; beyondbread.com.

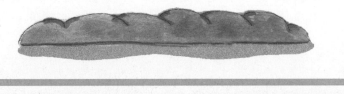

menu. The somewhat cavernous, clean, and neat space is perfect for big parties, with large round tables featuring center lazy Susans that will let you spin your dishes around for easy sharing. Let's talk dim sum. My special Chinese culinary advisor (thank you Mike Lee at the Chinese Cultural Center) suggests that if you want to be "safe," choose the *char siu bao* (barbecue buns). These sculptural delicacies can be had steamed or baked with a honey glaze and are filled with sweet, soft barbecued pork. He also recommends shrimp Ha *Gaau* (steamed shrimp dumplings in translucent rice wrappers), *lo baak gou* (shredded daikon mixed with dried shrimp and rice flour, steamed then sliced and panfried), and *shaomai* (a juicy, soft pork meatball inside a wonton wrapper, steamed and drizzled with sesame oil). He suggests *haam sui gaau* (deep-fried chicken and pork dumplings with minced water chestnuts) and *wu gok* (steamed dumplings filled with mashed taro root, pork, and mushrooms) for the more adventurous, and the aforementioned duck and chicken feet for the super adventurous. His pick for dessert is the *daan taat,* egg custard tarts, gorgeous little pastries with scalloped edges filled with a bright yellow yolk of cooked egg custard. If you can't make it for dim sum, the regular menu is quite extensive. Favorites are the House Specials: snow pea leaves in garlic sauce (seasonal); Chinese greens chow fun with bean cake and black mushrooms; Singapore noodles and, yes, duck feet with oyster sauce. The deep-fried sesame balls filled with sweet red bean paste (*jin deui*) are tops on the dessert list. Open daily for lunch and dinner starting at 11 a.m. Dim sum served 10 a.m. to 3 p.m., Sat and Sun only.

Claire's Cafe, 16140 N. Oracle Rd., Catalina, AZ 85379; (520) 825-2525; American; $. If you're heading up to the cooler climes of Catalina, Claire's should be on your radar, especially for breakfast (which is served all day). In a little strip mall next to a hardware store, this homey place has been making homemade pecan cinnamon rolls from scratch every day since it opened in 1986. Don't expect anything fancy here, it's a real mishmash of tables and booths crammed into tiny spaces with a kitschy decor. Claire (yes, there really is a Claire—Chef-Owner Claire Johnson) and husband Jim work hard and fast to keep customers' coffee cups and stomachs filled. Eggs come every which way: fried, scrambled, with ham steak, sirloin patties, or steak; whipped into three-egg omelets with corned beef, avocado, spinach, cream cheese, chile . . . you name it. Breakfast burritos and quesadillas, Mexican frittatas, huevos rancheros are all made to order behind the grill. Homemade corned beef hash is hard to find these days, and they have it here, grilled up nice and crispy with two eggs any style you want them. Homemade biscuits (are you in the car yet heading up to Catalina?), pancakes, thick-cut french toast, waffles, and homemade buttermilk biscuits covered in sausage gravy . . . need I say more? Open daily for breakfast and lunch until 3 p.m.

Com Tham Thuan Kieu, 1990 W. Orange Grove Rd., Tucson, AZ 85704; (520) 638-7912; Vietnamese; $. I think this Vietnamese restaurant must have the biggest menu in town—there are 240 items to choose from here. Being right next to the amazing Lee Lee market must be the reason, it's easy to find the many traditional ingredients needed to make all these dishes. Put on your glasses and take your time looking at the menu. Happily each dish is described clearly and concisely because the friendly waitstaff are not all native English speakers. This bodes well for the food but makes choosing what to order a little challenging. If I may be of assistance, I recommend starting with #14, the delicate and quite large crepe filled with bean sprouts, shrimp, pork, and lettuce leaves. The crepe is yellow and crispy and has a light coconut flavor, and it's enough for two. Next, #20, broken rice with "10 kinds of food," a large bowl of cooked rice topped with shredded pork skin, steamed egg, bean curd skin, Chinese sausage (that's 4), and 6 other tasty ingredients, also available as a soup. Next, #97, the House Special Rice and Egg Noodle (available dry or as a soup), a gigantic steaming bowl of noodles, shrimp, pork, quail egg, and ground pork. If you're still hungry, choose #86, thin sliced charbroiled pork chops over buttery red rice. More? Number 143, bean curd skin with shrimp vermicelli served with bean sprouts, fresh basil, mint leaves, and a side of cucumbers in fish sauce. Drinks? Number 229, a strangely satisfying pickled lime drink and #234, the delicious, supersweet coffee with condensed milk. The rest is up to you! Open daily for lunch and dinner from 10 a.m. (Call first because the hours tend to change).

CORE Kitchen + Wine Bar, The Ritz-Carlton Dove Mountain Resort, 15000 N. Secret Springs Dr., Marana, AZ 85658; (520) 572-3000; ritzcarlton.com/dovemountain; American; $$$. Skip the highway and take the back roads to CORE. You'll drive past soaring saguaros, see hawks floating on the wind, and enjoy spectacular mountain and city views as you wind your way here. Don't be thrown off by the massive, rock-encrusted gateway that leads to the resort—you'll be waved through with a friendly smile. French-born David Serus is the executive chef here and his sophisticated, well-presented fare mirrors the elegant, luxury resort that has sprung up against the spectacular backdrop of the
Tortolita Mountains in this far corner of Marana.
Sample his American and Southwest fusion fare
in the cool, modern CORE where tables are
decorated with hand-thrown pottery sourced
from a local artist. A citrus grove is just
outside and the mountain tops are on view.
Chef Serus has made every effort to source local products (produce, eggs, beef, and pork come from local farmers) and to incorporate indigenous foods into his upscale menus. The seasonal menu is constantly changing to reflect what Chef Serus views as his quintessentially New American cuisine with influences from the Southwest and other parts of the United States. On the menu you might find

Maryland rockfish with caramelized salsify and smoked pecans in a white wine sauce, chile-lacquered New York strip steak with a corn-nopales salsa and avocado fries in a poblano pepper coulis, or pan-seared quail on a bed of tepary bean bacon stew. Clean, pure flavors are Chef Serus's goal and he achieves this masterfully with inspired combinations and platings. A 3-course prix-fixe menu is offered on select days showcasing seasonal ingredients and local purveyors. The Sunday Market Brunch should not be missed, offering a plethora of house-made baked goods, fresh seafood, hand-rolled sushi, and interactive chef stations serving everything from omelets to carved meats. Fresh juices are prepared *à la minute* by the "Orchard Mixologist" at the juice bar. Open daily for dinner from 6 p.m., brunch Sun from 10 a.m. to 2 p.m.

HiFalutin', 6780 N. Oracle Rd., Tucson, AZ 85704; (520) 297-0518; hifalutintucson.com; Steak; $$. Sometimes all you want is a simple steak, no fancy fixin's, just steak. If that's you, High Falutin' fits the bill. Family owned and operated, it's a family-friendly, easygoing spot that cooks up steak, barbecue, and seafood with a minimum of fuss. Servers in black cowboy hats come by quickly to take your order, your food arrives, and it's all simple and easy and tastes good too. Top sirloin, rib eye, filet, and flank steak are all cooked to order right in the open kitchen at the rear of the restaurant manned by more gallon-hatted cowboys and cowgirls at the grill. Want something different? You'll find super barbecue ribs, roast chicken, pot roast, salmon, sandwiches, soups, and salads too. Open for lunch and dinner daily from 11 a.m.

Kampai, 6486 N. Oracle Rd., Tucson, AZ 85704; (520) 219-6550; Asian; $$. Black and red, these are the primary colors that strike you when you come into this clean, modern sushi bar/restaurant. Owned by the So family, dad David is the sushi master, while wife Jennifer and son David handle the front of the house with great efficiency. While the sushi is fresh and well prepared, the daily Korean specials listed on the whiteboard are what make this place extra special. The Korean-born chef in the kitchen (his name is a closely guarded secret) decides what to offer each day so you never know what Korean delicacy you might be treated to. You might find *kalbi*—grilled short ribs marinated in soy sauce, garlic, and sesame oil, or spicy seafood noodle soup—a big bowl of rice flour noodles, shrimp, mussels, and squid, with mushrooms, carrots, peppers, and cabbage in a spicy kelp-infused broth. On the sushi side, the spicy tuna roll and the Playboy roll are customer favorites, but all the fish is top quality, well cut, and generously portioned. Open for lunch from 11 a.m. to 2:15 p.m. and dinner from 5:30 p.m., Mon through Sat.

Miguel's, 5900 N. Oracle Rd., Tucson, AZ 85704; (520) 887-3777; miguelstucsom.com; Latin; $$. Part of the adobe-style hotel La Posada Lodge, Miguel's was one of the first to bring Latin cuisine to Tucson with an adventurous Nuevo Latino menu. The modern Caribbean-style decor is warm and inviting, with lively music piped throughout the restaurant and out to the lovely outdoor patio with pool and mountain views. A semicircular bar with bamboo chairs hosts an extremely popular happy hour daily starting at 3 p.m.—hey it's five o'clock somewhere, right? There are over 100 varieties of tequila here and numerous specialty and exotic margaritas. The Hell's Margarita is a fiery concoction of pepper-infused tequila, Cointreau, and fresh lime juice; the sweet and sour Tamarindo Margarita combines tamarind, tequila, and fresh lime; and the Mango Margarita is made with fresh mango puree. Ooops, after all those margaritas I almost forgot about the food! You might too, but do try a few of the unique Latin fusion items on the menu. *Pollo a la brasa* brings a citrus-marinated, grilled chicken breast over creamy Oaxacan rice topped with a *mole verde* made with poblano peppers, toasted *pepitas,* and sesame seeds. Pan seared *cabrilla* (sea bass) is topped with pineapple salsa and napped with a citrus beurre blanc. Open daily, dinner starts at 5 p.m., happy hour at 3 p.m.

Noble Hops Gastropub, 1335 W. Lambert Ln., Oro Valley, AZ 85737; (520) 797-4677; noblehopspub.com; Pub; $$. Brothers Aric and Josh Mussman are the creative geniuses behind this place, Tucson's first official gastropub. Always on the cusp of culinary trends, they traveled to England and Spain (tough job, but someone's got to do it) to check out the concept and scope out menus before opening up their own place here. They clearly learned their lessons well, because this popular spot is contemporary and hip with modern furnishings (think leather, quilted banquettes, colored

Miraval Arizona Resort & Spa

Oprah, Giuliana, and Bill—these are just some of the celebrities that frequent Miraval, the award-winning luxury spa that's secreted away down a winding road off busy Oracle Road (5000 E. Via Estancia Miraval, miravalresorts.com). This oasis of health and mindful eating has been hosting famous and not so famous people since it opened in 1996. Mindful eating is the buzzword here and Miraval takes it seriously, creating healthy, scrumptious, beautifully plated dishes featuring seasonal and local products. You too can have a taste of what brings Oprah here with a spa day that gets you lunch at the lovely Cactus Flower Restaurant and all day access to the terrific smoothie bar (see recipe on p. 271). Yoga, meditation, massage, facials, fitness classes, all these are part of a wonderful day that will reinvigorate and restore you. Call (800) 395-6748 to make a reservation at least 30 days in advance, space is limited.

bottles, spot lighting), a 30-foot-long bar, lounge area, outdoor patio, and separate glassed-in keg room. There are 28 beers on tap and hundreds of bottles featuring handcrafted hops from local, regional, and microbreweries, along with keg wines available by the glass and bottle. An elevated comfort food menu offers a rotating list of selections and daily specials including appetizers (go for the house-baked Bavarian pretzels served with cheese sauce and champagne mustard), soup (try the beer bisque), salads (iceberg wedge with blue cheese dressing), burgers (the lamb and beef burger comes with red onion marmalade and *tzatziki*), and their version of shepherd's pie (lamb shank over mashed potatoes with sautéed vegetables.) Thanks guys! Open daily for lunch and dinner starting at 11 a.m.

The Parish, 6453 N. Oracle Rd., Tucson, AZ 85704; (520) 797-1233; theparishtucson.com; Cajun; $. Cajun cooking has come to Tucson courtesy of The Parish. Stuck onto the end of a strip mall in a dip in the road, this place packs people in for signature drinks and a taste of New Orleans, Tucson style. Stick with the Cajun-inspired items on the menu. Hush puppies are as big as golf balls, crunchy on the outside and soft and sweet on the inside with a great corn flavor—get them first. Move on to the bacon popcorn, cooked in bacon fat (what else?) and sprinkled with crunchy bacon pieces (hint: they fall down into the bottom of the bowl so you have to dig for them), it's a cholesterol festival. This is the only place in town to get frog's legs (yes, they taste like chicken), here wrapped in bacon and served up with a saucer of remoulade. The gumbo takes three whole days to make, no kidding! So popular you'll be lucky to find it on the menu if you go in late. The oysters on the po'boy are freshly shucked and well fried, so pull them out of the big slab of bread and enjoy them on their own. Touted as the "world's crispiest fish-and-chips" on the menu, this dish lives up to its claim. I'm not sure it's Cajun, but it's an extremely generous portion of codfish, excellently prepared, super-crispy as promised, and served with a huge side of highly seasoned fries. Don't forget those drinks—the Sazerac combines Hennessy, rye, and Peychaud's bitters with simple syrup (ask for rocks), and the La Verdad refreshes with house-infused cucumber tequila, agave nectar, fresh lime juice, and ginger ale. You'll be wearing Mardi Gras beads in no time. Open for lunch and dinner daily from 11 a.m.

Saffron Indian Bistro, 7607 N. Oracle Rd., Oro Valley, AZ 85704; (520) 742-9100; tucsonindianrestuarant.com; Indian; $$. Soaring ceilings, contemporary dishware, subtle colors, and traditional Indian flavors all fuse at this sophisticated, modern bistro. Owner Mintu Sareen, makes sure that the food here showcases his native cuisine of New Delhi. Start with crispy potato- and vegetable-filled samosas that arrive perched delicately on triangle plates with subtle cilantro and tamarind sauces. Thin, crunchy *papadums* (garlic, black pepper, and chile chickpea flour crackers) are nestled in wire baskets. Fresh-baked, warm breads come in a variety of flavors and fillings. The *aloo naan* (stuffed with spiced potatoes) and the *keema naan* (topped with ground lamb) are particularly good. Masala, vindaloo, korma—all entrees are delicately spiced (choose your own heat level) and generously laden with meat. There are many vegetarian options. Some of my favorites include the *chana masala,* a thick stew of chickpeas, tomatoes, onions, and garlic, and the *aloo matar paneer,* a mix of potatoes, peas, and homemade cheese spiced with cumin and cooked with garlic and onions. Among the dessert options is a milky rice pudding, fragrant with cardamom,

Local Chain: Sauce

Great name, casual space, quick service—pizza of all kinds are here, along with panini, chopped salads, soups, and pasta. Thin, artisanal-crust pies come with all sorts of toppings, sausage, pepperoni, and the oddly popular (to me) prosciutto and melon. If you want some special combo, just ask. It's nothing fancy but it is definitely a step above your standard pizza chain and everything but the pasta is made from scratch. Line up and place your order, have a seat, and before you can blink an eye the food arrives. Part of the Fox Concepts group of restaurants, they are extremely popular around town. Family-friendly and a magnet for teens who love to congregate here with their phones and their friends, it offers both eat-in or take-out options. 7117 N. Oracle Rd., (520) 297-8575; 5285 E. Broadway Blvd, (520) 514-1122; 2990 N. Campbell Ave., (520) 795-0344. Open daily at 11 a.m. for lunch and dinner. foxrc.com.

filled with plump golden raisins, and garnished with almonds and pistachios. A daily lunch buffet is generous and gives you a chance to try lots of things on the menu. Open daily for lunch and dinner from 11 a.m.

Wildflower, 7037 N. Oracle Rd., Tucson, AZ 85704; (520) 219-4230; foxrc.com/wildflower; New American; $$. This popular spot is consistently highly rated for its excellent New American fare and top-notch service. Part of the Fox Restaurant Concepts group, it is known for its innovative, seasonal dishes and comfortable, shabby-chic decor. Tucson is the only place in Arizona with a Wildflower and we're lucky to have it. Signature menu items include a miso-glazed black cod with edamame, dumplings, and Honshimeji mushrooms; scallops with forbidden rice, snap peas, lemongrass, and soy butter; and crispy calamari with mizuna, *yuzu,* and toasted sesame seeds. It may seem mostly Asian-inspired, but the menu changes frequently and is primarily influenced by seasonal ingredients. A spring menu might feature grilled artichokes with white truffle oil and a crescenza cheese fondue, or English pea tortelli over black kale with crisp bacon and a bright lemon-mint gremolata. Fall may bring warm Maine lobster salad with fingerling potatoes and a truffle vinaigrette. You'll always find inspired soups, unusual salads with house-made dressings, fresh pasta all made in house, sustainable seafood sourced from reputable purveyors, and hearty meat dishes on the menu. An award-winning wine list offers 80 labels by the bottle and 25 by the glass, including champagne. Desserts are all winners, and all made right here. The Bars of Sin are truly sinful—layers of praline cookies covered in chocolate with a light coffee flavor, you get two! I love the upside-down cheesecake, served in a jar with graham cracker crumbles and strawberry preserves on top. The light texture lets you eat it all even if you've indulged in some of the rich, filling entrees. Butterscotch pudding is another great choice. It's hard to find a good, truly scotchy pudding that isn't just another caramel. This one is just like Grandma's and you will love it. Open for lunch Mon through Sat from 11 a.m., dinner daily starting at 4 p.m.

Landmark

Tohono Chul Tearoom in Tohono Chul Park, 7366 N. Paseo del Norte, Tucson, AZ 85704; (520) 797-1222; tohonochulpark .org; Southwestern; $. Located in one of Tucson's most beautiful botanical gardens (established on the 37-acre grounds of the Wilson residence in 1985), this lovely restaurant has several great seating options. The best spot is on the gorgeous outdoor patio surrounded by lush trees, flowers, birds, hummingbirds, and butterflies. Next best is the inner courtyard, which is cool and shady and centered by a tinkling, moss-enrobed fountain. Indoors is lovely too, with intimate seating in an adobe-style house with low, wooden-beamed ceilings. Wherever you do sit, the Southwest-inspired menu offers up some great choices featuring native and indigenous ingredients sourced locally and picked à la minute from the Ethnobotanical Garden on the grounds, and they're all prepared with great finesse. The breakfast menu offers fluffy buttermilk and mesquite pancakes with prickly pear or Vermont maple syrup, addictive red velvet waffles (yes, same batter as the famous cake) with vanilla bean cream cheese, and several egg dishes. Try the unusual huevos Pancho Villa, a new twist on eggs Benedict; these are served in a tortilla cup, with beans, chorizo links, and blanketed with a deep red chile sauce. Pork lovers should not pass up the ham shank, sourced from heritage pork, hardwood smoked, seared, and served with several menu items or on its own as a delicious side order. Another great choice is the house made gravlax, cured with local citrus and layered on a toasted bagel with capers, onion, and lemon herb cream cheese on the side. Teas here are specially designed and blended by Tucson-based Maya Tea Company and are served iced or hot—the signature black tea with hints of Earl Grey and Arizona citrus is delicious and refreshing. Lunch brings a variety of choices from salads to burgers to hearty entrees. The steak salad here is not your standard fare—it features local greens, Dos Equis marinated steak, caramelized onions, roasted tomatoes, poblano chiles, creamer potatoes, sun dried corn, and crispy avocado, and is dressed with barrel aged balsamic, toasted vanilla bean, or chipotle mesquite honey vinaigrette—wow. Blackened ahi tuna, rubbed with a house made Sonoran spice mix of achiote, three different chile powders, and a touch of chamomile, and seared to perfect doneness, it is served with a rich, creamy garden herb risotto. Delicate blue corn crepes, with caramelized bananas, cajeta (thick, gooey, goat's milk caramel), and Kahlua whipped cream are a highlight of the dessert offerings. High tea brings scones with Devonshire cream and preserves and tea sandwiches. Weekend brunch is extremely popular, especially on the patio, so be sure to make a reservation. This is a great spot to bring out-of-town visitors who will get a taste of Southwest fare and a chance to learn about our native plants in a beautiful setting. It's a lovely place any time of day, and do plan to take a stroll through the beautiful grounds of Tohono Chul Park (there is a small entrance fee), where you'll see amazing cacti, all kinds of indigenous plants, sculptures by local artists, xeriscape gardens, and wildlife displays (a hawk viewing happens on select Wednesdays and reptiles are on display every Friday). Open for breakfast, lunch, and tea daily, brunch on Sat and Sun. Hours vary seasonally.

West

Beginning just west of downtown and spreading out to the scenic Saguaro Park West, this area encompasses open desert land, older residential communities, and several new developments and goes as far west as the Tohono O'odham Nation and Ajo (both part of Pima County). There's an interesting blend here; including drive-ins, Chinese and Mexican eateries, sophisticated, upscale casino and resort restaurants, brasseries, steak houses, and unique cafes.

Foodie Faves

Agustin Brasserie, 100 S. Avenida del Convento, Tucson, AZ 85745; (520) 398-5382; agustinbrasserie.com; French; $$. Tucked into the corner of the lovely Mercado San Agustin in the shadow of A Mountain, this super brasserie offers French-influenced fare in a terrific setting. Owner Glen Stosius has quite the pedigree—he worked at Jean-Georges in New York City and at top restaurants in

Tucson and Miami. The space is bright, light, open, and airy, with a white marble-top bar stretching along one side of the room, a long row of comfy banquettes under high windows on the other side, and a smattering of tables and chairs in the center. The bar is presided over by mixologist Pete Hoge, who shakes up some terrific handcrafted, classic cocktails. His signature French 75 "soixante-quinze" (a heady combination of gin and a fizz of champagne) and peach-infused Bellinis attract the young and gorgeous to the bar (along with the rest of us!). You'll find true bistro fare here, with house-made country pâté, niçoise salad, and a light, creamy vichyssoise all served up by extremely attentive waitstaff. The oysters on the half shell are the stars here. Sourced from British Columbia, they are plump and briny, served with spicy cocktail sauce and vinegary mignonette. Perfectly cooked mussels come in a big bath of white wine and shallots along with crispy french fries. The rack of lamb and juicy roasted chicken are winners too. Trout meunière, not seen too often this far west of Paris, brings you a whole sautéed trout, moist and flaky, with a bright lemon sauce and capers. Dessert options include profiteroles stuffed with locally made artisan ice creams and drizzled with chocolate sauce. Closed Mon, open Tues through Sat for lunch and dinner, Sun for brunch and lunch.

Desert Rain Cafe, Tohono Plaza on Route 19, Main Street, Sells, AZ 85634; (520) 383-4918; desertraincafe.com; Southwest; $. Far west on the Tohono O'odham Nation (about 60 miles west of downtown Tucson) this unique little cafe is an oasis of deliciousness. It's run by the nonprofit Tohono O'odham Community Action (TOCA), an organization that strives to reinvigorate culture and health on the Tohono O'odham Nation, with all proceeds from the cafe going into educational programming. The menu offers an opportunity to taste indigenous foods prepared in traditional and contemporary dishes based on recipes gathered from community elders and regional top chefs. You won't find many other places where you can taste cholla cactus buds (in the pico de gallo), white tepary beans (found in the hummus and the traditional short rib stew), and O'odham squash (the filling in the squash enchiladas). The beans, squash, and corn used in the cafe are grown locally on TOCA's farms and wild foods are purchased from community members who hand-harvest them seasonally. The staff is friendly and more than happy to offer tastings of unfamiliar ingredients. The tepary bean quesadilla is a top seller, stuffed with brown tepary beans, melted cheese, onions, and chiles. The sampler and combination plates are a great way to get a taste of everything. Thursday always features the extremely popular and affordable prickly-pear glazed pork rib special, served with a side of brown tepary beans, handmade wheat *gimet* (local tortillas), and a side salad with prickly-pear vinaigrette. Giant mesquite oatmeal cookies and a variety of unusual smoothies made with prickly-pear nectar, mesquite flour, and chia seeds are offered all day long. There is no signage on the main road, so be sure to Mapquest it or call for directions before you go. Open for breakfast and lunch until 3 p.m., Mon through Fri.

Dragon's View Chinese Restaurant, 400 N. Bonita Ave., Tucson, AZ 85745; (520) 792-3811; dragonviewrestaurant.com; Chinese; $$. Hidden away in the small neighborhood of Menlo Park, this place serves Chinese food with some very unusual specialty dishes you won't see elsewhere. The space itself is nothing fancy. Basic tables, chairs, and an empty fountain in the entryway won't inspire confidence, but the food is good and the variety of choices is amazing. Ask for the pink Chinese menu, where items are listed in both Chinese and English so you don't have to ask for a translation. If you do need help, gregarious owner Harry Gee will be happy to oblige. Lucky for me, on my first visit to Dragon's View I was joined by a foodie friend who is Chinese and who guided me through the menu (thank you Stephanie!). Our top picks are the shrimp paste *gai lan*, toothsome sautéed leafy Chinese broccoli in a salty, tangy, mildy fishy sauce; head on spicy salt shrimp, a wonderful combination of crunchy large prawns (be sure to eat the heads, they are sweet and flavorful) crusted with sea salt and sprinkled with jalapeño slices; bitter melon beef, a delicious mixture of thin-sliced beef, a light gravy, and wedges of soft bitter melon (if you're not used to bitter melon it might take a few bites to get accustomed to the flavor and texture, but it's really good). Peking duck is available both half and whole, and arrives with soft steamed buns, hoisin sauce, cucumber, and scallions. If you're not quite as adventurous, the regular menu offers more familiar items. If you want to mix it up a bit, the fusion menu offers some unusual combinations. As for me, I'll stick with the Chinese menu, it always satisfies! Open daily for lunch and dinner.

Little Abner's Steakhouse, 8501 N. Silverbell Rd., Tucson, AZ 85743; (520) 744-2800; abnersteakhouse.com; Steak; $$$. This unassuming, somewhat hokey steak house has been around since 1947. It's not easy to find, but it's worth it because they definitely know how to cook up a great steak. The interior is rustic and family-friendly, with low ceilings, dark wood, and lots of cowboy-themed paraphernalia.  Don't be put off by the pseudo out-houses in the main dining area, with their cartoonish cowboy and cowgirl signs, just close your eyes and concen-trate on your delicious steak. Their signature cut is the 1-pound rib eye and it is good; other choices include a 2-pound porterhouse and a 10-ounce top sirloin if you have a small appetite. Grilled to perfection over mesquite wood fires, steaks come with slices of toasted, buttered white sandwich bread and some pretty darn good cowboy beans. Steaming baked potatoes (really baked, not microwaved) with real sour cream are good, but cost extra. Laid-back waitstaff aim to please here, decked out in denim and aprons, and they take their food seriously—if your steak is not perfectly cooked, they'll whisk it away and keep bringing it back until you're satisfied, no questions asked and no dirty looks! If for some reason you're not a steak lover, they do some mighty fine barbecue ribs too. Open for dinner at 5 p.m. Mon through Sun.

Monterey Court Cafe, 505 W. Miracle Mile, Tucson, AZ 85705; (520) 207-2429; montereycourtaz.com; Continental; $. Part of the continued renaissance of this section of town, this lovely cafe used to be the office for the vintage motel built here in 1938. Lovingly restored and refurbished by owner Greg Haver, the space is a terrific blend of old and new, with the original motel rooms now home to art galleries and specialty retail shops. The interior of the Cafe has soothing chartreuse and apricot colored walls, small tables and chairs, and a cool poured concrete floor. A big picture window looks out onto busy Miracle Mile. The cafe offers an ambitious menu of starters, salads, sandwiches, and entrees along with a full bar featuring cocktails, beer, and wine. You can order your drink at the blue-tiled outside bar and have a seat in the courtyard around the stage that features local bands and musicians several days a week and live jazz on Sundays at brunch. Breezy and comfortable, it's a great spot anytime. Breakfast features french toast crostini with exotic fruit compote, maple syrup, and powdered sugar and (if you don't want something sweet) "chiliquiles," here layered with corn tortillas, salsa verde, casera and jack cheese, Anaheim chiles, and a fried egg. Lunch brings a cool green salad with melon, grapes, apples, kiwi, mint, and local greens all dressed up in a champagne lime vinaigrette, and a grilled fish of the day sandwich with napa cabbage, shredded veggies, and a yogurt cucumber sauce. Dinner? Braised chicken, house-made spaetzle, and seafood pasta are just some of the choices. Waiting for your check? See if you can find the original painted motel sign hidden in the brickwork. Open daily from 8 a.m. for breakfast, lunch, and dinner.

100 Estrella Restaurant and Lounge, 100 W. Estrella St., Ajo, AZ 85321; (520) 387-3110; American; $. You'll have to go way west to Ajo on the outskirts of Pima County to try the distinctive food offered here. Make it part of a day trip or a stop on the way to Organ Pipe National Monument or the beaches at Rocky Point. The lovely drive here from Tucson takes you on winding two-lane roads through the Tohono O'odham Nation with vistas of cactus and mountain ranges and will remind you of what the Southwest used to look like before development took over. The town of Ajo itself, although small, has an interesting history of copper mining and a growing community of artists and food lovers. Chef-Owner Mara Branson is definitely a foodie. Originally from Latvia, she brings her love of food and a green thumb to the menu here. Mara sources her beef from a local rancher and her pork from a specialty butcher in Phoenix. She has her own little garden out back where she grows herbs and vegetables. All these top-notch ingredients are transformed into a variety of juicy burgers, including ones made with veal, salmon, veggies, turkey, and chorizo. Her signature pork burger comes with homemade sauerkraut. The menu also offers an assortment of salads and pizzas. Specials are inspired by Mara's international background, and might include linguini with Adriatic clams or homemade ravioli in a pepper cream sauce—they change every two weeks. Husband Thomas is a self-proclaimed "beer geek" who offers one of the best selections of specialty beers in the area, both in bottles (15 different kinds of craft beers) and on tap (up to 10 selections with a focus on local breweries). The decor is colorful and features local artists' photography and paintings. Open for lunch and dinner, Mon through Sat Jan through Mar, Mon to Fri otherwise, and closed during Aug and Sept.

Pat's Drive In, 1202 W. Niagara St., Tucson, AZ 85745; (520) 624-0891; American; $. Get in your car, preferably a 1959 Buick Invicta convertible, throw the kids and the dog in the backseat, and drive to Pat's. In operation since 1961, it doesn't look like much, a red barn-like exterior with several windows across the front and pull-in parking spaces. Some folks call it vintage. You may need to wait, Pat's is packed day and night because people just can't seem to get

enough of these dogs! Everyone will love it—guaranteed! Who can resist a chili dog? And not just any chili dog. At Pat's the chile is homemade with beef, beans, and fresh chiles, and it can be HOT. You don't like dogs? No problem, there are burgers here too. Get the BIG PAT: double meat, cheese, chili, mustard, pickles, and lettuce. No to burgers? They fry up shrimp, chicken, and fish too. Don't forget to order the hand-cut, shoestring fries that go with everything. Grab a whole lotta napkins because you're going to need them. Get back into the car and get ready to eat because you are not going to get all the way home with this food—it smells and tastes way too good to wait. Open daily at 11 a.m. for lunch and dinner.

Primo, JW Marriott Starr Pass Resort & Spa, 3800 W. Starr Pass Blvd., Tucson, AZ 85745; (520) 792-3500; primo.jwstarrpassmarriott .com; Mediterranean; $$$. Soothing and sophisticated, über chef

Melissa Kelly's Primo is housed in the gorgeous Starr Pass Marriott Resort at the base of the Tucson Mountains. It looks like a little piece of Europe in here, with seafoam-green curtains, opulent table-cloths and table settings, and cushiony banquettes, Primo offers a welcome respite from the sometimes searing desert heat and bright sun. Local staff and an in-house pastry chef expertly produce Kelly's signature Mediterranean fare, with an occasional Southwest twist. The menu changes seasonally, but always features *primi,* pasta, mains, and *contorni* (side dishes). Pasta is the way to go: You might find cavatelli sauced with a rich Bolognese sauce of Niman Ranch beef and pork, with broccolini, blistered tomatoes, and a generous grating of Parmigiano-Reggiano cheese; or ravioli stuffed with Brown's Orchard lamb, English pea tendrils, and a dusting of pecorino. Main attractions include the seared diver scallops, some-times found atop parsnip puree and leafy arugula with a rich truffle vinaigrette, or crispy Hudson Valley Moulard duck breast and tender confit, with lentils, brussels sprouts, and local braised cabbage from Sleeping Frog's Farm. Hand-rolled cannoli, warm zep-pole tossed in cinnamon sugar, and the ever-delicious *affogato* espresso "float," here served with vanilla and chocolate gelato are dessert favorites. Open Tues through Sun for dinner only.

PY Steakhouse, Casino Del Sol Resort, 5655 W. Valencia Rd., Tucson, AZ 85757; (520) 324-9350; casinodelsol.com; Steak; $$$.

This upscale restaurant is secreted inside the gorgeous multimillion-dollar Casino Del Sol Hotel. No expense has been spared in the design of this sophisticated, intimate fine-dining space with black and white banquettes, thick carpeting, comfortable armchairs, modern chandeliers, and crisp white linens. Wine Director Kevin Brady has compiled an impressive wine list of over 3,000 bottles, accessible instantly at the touch of a finger on personal electronic tablets where you can look up ratings and pairing suggestions, or just ask one of the two full-time sommeliers, who are well  versed in the list. An open modern kitchen gives a glimpse of the hard work that goes into preparing the upscale, gourmet offerings on the menu, designed by Chef Erik Savin. For your appetizer, the crispy skin pork belly, braised in citrus and achiote for 17 hours, is served with a terrific homemade *guajillo* chile applesauce and is a great way to start the meal. Order anything with the crispy tobacco onions (deep-fried shallot rounds dusted with chile powder)—they are soooo hard to resist. Steak, of course, should be a first-choice entree, served on contemporary dishware with dangerously sharp wood-handled steak knives. Presentation is tops here, Chef Savin prides himself on his masterful plates and it shows with decorative swirls and garnishes on every dish. The 22-ounce T-bone (dry aged and cut to order) is incredibly tender and grilled and seasoned just right, with a nice crust on the outside and juicy pink on the inside. The menu also offers seafood, pork, veal, lamb, poultry, and tofu (mushroom-dusted in a red chile broth with truffle risotto) all accompanied by house-made breads and mesquite honey butter. Desserts are fanciful with the Cigar del Sol taking top honors for creativity—it's a frozen chocolate-chile tube filled with ice cream, dipped in cookie crumbles and served on a spun sugar "ashtray" with a white chocolate match book. So, if you are at the casino gambling or if you are looking for an upscale steak house, you can't lose with PY. The staff is as attentive and sharp as the steak knives, and management is extremely professional and on point, seeing to your every need and truly invested in making sure that you have a great meal. Watch for special wine events with prix-fixe menus held monthly. Open for dinner at 4 p.m. Tues through Sat.

Teresa's Mosaic Cafe, 2445 N. Silverbell Rd., Tucson, AZ 85745; (520) 624-4512; mosaiccafes.com; Mexican; $. Bobby Flay of the Food Network has been here for a throwdown. He won, but the food here is still a winner! You get homemade Mexican and a nice view at this family-run place, perched high on a hill, that's been in business since 1984. Cheerful, friendly, and casual with bright-colored furnishings and colorful tile mosaics, Teresa's uses their own recipes to create a variety of Mexican favorites. Some say they have the best *menudo* in town, others rave about the Oaxacan moles, still others laud the *machaca* with three kinds of chiles, and the chile rellenos. Bobby liked the huevos rancheros. Wash it all down with a cool glass of house-made *horchata,* the amazingly delicious rice-based, cinnamon drink. It's not fancy fare but it is all hearty and homemade. Open daily for breakfast, lunch, and dinner.

Todd's Restaurant, Ryan Field, 9700 W. Ajo Way, Tucson, AZ 85735; (520) 883-7770; toddsrestaurant.com; American; $. You might pass this place by as you speed past tiny Ryan Airfield just west of downtown on Route 86. Stop, you won't be sorry. Chef-Owner Todd Scott makes some tasty breakfasts and lunches that are not just for the pilots and passengers of the small planes that land and take off from here. It's clean and bright inside this small, homey place, decorated with model planes hanging from the ceiling and framed photos of pilots, planes, and family. Every seat is a window seat with a great view of the airfield and the mountain ranges beyond. It's fun to watch the planes taxi in and take off as you wait for your meal (pilots can enter the restaurant directly from the field, and they do). Breakfast is served all day and Chef Todd knows his eggs. Especially eggs Benedict. The lemony sauce is made from scratch and tops a perfectly poached egg. The "not so Benedict" version comes with a drizzle of prickly-pear syrup, tomatoes, and avocado. Giant waffles, original or buckwheat, are the size of a dinner plate and made from a specialty batter that comes in all the way from Michigan; the

homemade, hot apple-cinnamon topping and gobs of real whipped cream gild the lily. Chef Todd makes his own finger-licking barbecue sauce, a spicy, smoky combination of prickly-pear syrup, molasses, and chipotle peppers. You'll find it on ribs, chicken, and the Sloppy Barbecue Sandwich, a messy, yummy tangle of shredded pork, roast beef, or turkey piled on a toasted bun. There's lots more here—sandwiches, salads, hoagies, burgers, and omelets all made with love and care by Chef Todd. You won't pass by again without stopping in for a bite. Open daily for breakfast and lunch until 2 p.m.

Landmark

Ocotillo Cafe at the Arizona Sonora Desert Museum Restaurant, 2021 N. Kinney Rd., Tucson, AZ 85745; (520) 883-5705; desertmuseum.com; Southwestern; $$. Founded in 1952, the Desert Museum is one of Tucson's top attractions. A glorious combination of botanical and zoological garden, it is a great place to spend the day learning about our native flora and fauna. With 2 miles of pathways and hundreds of exhibits to explore, you just might get hungry, and the Ocotillo Cafe should be your destination. Set on the edge of the property near the entrance gate, it offers cool indoor seating and lovely outdoor patio seating amidst the cacti and trees. The menu features Arizona-Sonora regional cuisine with a focus on locally sourced ingredients. The warm focaccia bread with cilantro pesto dipping sauce will start you off on a great culinary trek here. Top starters include the shrimp and lobster flautas, generous portions of seafood tucked into corn tortillas, sauced with tangy tomatillos and topped with house-made salsa, and the *ensalada de camarones,* a hearty salad with jumbo shrimp perched on organic endive and greens, sprinkled with caramelized pecans and dressed with a cilantro-lime vinaigrette. On the entree side, the Sunset Trio is a great combination plate of crab, shrimp, and mushroom enchiladas, chicken and *nopales* (prickly-pear pads) enchiladas, and a mini chile relleno. Peruvian chicken gets you half a slow-roasted, herb-encrusted chicken served with a mustard lime *crema* you'll want to lick off the plate and the chef's signature green-chile au gratin potatoes—layers of creamy, rich goodness. Desserts vary seasonally, but if you need to replenish your calories after all that walking, go for the signature apple tart; caramelized, brandied Macintosh apples layered on top of apple pastry cream in a flaky crust, all topped with vanilla ice cream. Hours are seasonal, open for lunch until 3 p.m. only Dec through Apr, open for dinner only on Sat June through Aug.

East

This section of town spreads out quite a ways, skirting the lovely Saguaro Park East and extending to the edge of the Rincon Mountain Range. Home to ranches, housing developments, retirement and gated communities, older neighborhoods, and scenic vistas, there's a wide variety of restaurants here, from sophisticated fine dining and mom-and-pops to many chain and fast-food places.

Foodie Faves

The Bone In Steak and Smokehouse, 5400 S. Old Spanish Trail, Tucson, AZ 85747; (520) 885-4600; theboneinsteakhouse.com; Barbecue; $$. The Bone In is housed in a low adobe-style building just off the winding road, and inside you'll find saguaro-rib ceilings, whitewashed walls, and large picture windows framing lovely desert vistas. This is one of the only places I've found that carries my favorite specialty tequila, Almendrado, an artisan tequila flavored with almonds that makes a spectacular margarita. And they make great ones here, served in nice tall glasses. The best thing to have with the margarita is the bone-in pork wings (yes, pork wings!). These are plump bone-in pieces of pork, chili rubbed, smoked, and slathered with barbecue sauce. They come in a basket and are finger-licking good. Cow chips are better than they sound—house-made, super-crispy potato chips that you just can't stop eating. Smoked meats are done very nicely, with just the right flavor and texture. You can get one-third, half, and full racks of St. Louis–style ribs, pulled pork, pastrami, or combos with two different meats.

Sandwiches come with those wonderful cow chips; the Oklahoma Joe is a mouthful of smoked sirloin and pulled pork drenched with barbecue sauce. Steaks? Yes, there are steaks too (grilled tenderloin, New York strip, rib eye, and porterhouse), but the barbecue beats them all. Open Wed through Sun at 4 p.m.

Canyon's Crown Restaurant and Pub, 6958 E. Tanque Verde Rd., Tucson, AZ 85715; (520) 885-8277; canyonscrown.com; Pub; $$. This cozy, comfortable spot has brought some real English-style pub food to town. It feels slightly like a boudoir inside with low lighting, dark woods, low ceilings, and deep red banquettes offset by a busy central bar that puts out tankards of imported ales and brews (there are 20 selections on draft) and dart boards for those inclined. The menu includes items not often seen outside of the United Kingdom.

Scotch eggs—deep-fried, sausage-wrapped, hard-boiled eggs served with spicy mustard are a must try. Other top picks include Guinness pie, flaky crust over steak and mushrooms in a rich beer-based gravy and shepherd's pie made with ground beef and vegetables and topped with a cloud of mashed potatoes. The fish-and-chips are crispy, moist, and flaky. But the best part of all is the warm, sticky toffee pudding for dessert. This amazing concoction will keep me coming back every day. I don't know what it tastes like in good ole England but it is delicious here, creamy, rich, sweet, gooey, and you will want to lick the bowl. The vanilla ice cream on top just puts it over the edge. Open daily from 11 a.m. for lunch and dinner.

Eclectic Cafe, 7053 E. Tanque Verde Rd., Tucson, AZ 85715; (520) 829-5239; eclecticcafetucson.com; Eclectic; $$. Everyone on the east side of town knows Eclectic, in business since 1980. They do a bustling business day and night and especially at breakfast on weekends. The ambience is upscale diner with comfy booths and an outdoor patio. Service is efficient and quick. The extensive menu here really is eclectic—it's a sort of a crazy-in-a-good-way combination of diner food, deli, '60s favorites, Mexican-influenced food, and health food all in one. You'll find familiar items like homemade chicken rice soup, bagels and lox, tuna salad sandwiches, and burgers, and unusual ones like Sonoran black bean *torta* (an Eclectic original), tahini eggplant salad with mesquite bacon, and chicken and chorizo pasta. The breakfast here is very popular, with lots of choices including omelets, bagels, and giant, yummy whole-wheat pancakes. For lunch, get the classic quiche lorraine, creamy with lots of bacon and served with a nice side salad, always fresh and garnished with sprouts and vegetables, or the pastrami and corned beef sandwiches, each with a generous quantity of meat. For dinner, I like the spinach and mushroom crepes that take me back to the days of the Magic Pan (anyone remember this chain?), and the signature black-bean *torta,* swimming in a lickable jalapeño cream sauce. Burgers never disappoint. You really have to eat here to get a sense of the variety and it's easy to do so: Eclectic coupons are to be found in the newspaper weekly and in mass coupon mailings that come right to your mailbox. Open Mon through Fri from 11 a.m. for lunch and dinner, and Sat and Sun from 8 a.m. for breakfast, lunch, and dinner.

Dry River Company, 800 N. Kolb Rd., Tucson, AZ 85710; (520) 295-5555; dryriverco.com; Italian; $$. Neapolitan-style pizza and pastas made from scratch are on order here. It's casual and kind of self-serve: You order what you want at the counter and take it to go, have a seat at the bar, or seat yourself at the few tables and chairs scattered about inside and out front where your order will be delivered to you. Lots of people rush in and out getting pizza to go so it can be a dizzying experience to eat in, but it's fun to watch the pizzas cooking in the wood-burning oven that's right in the front of the restaurant. Dough made in house is transformed into super-thin-crust pizzas *a la Napoletana*. Sauce is made here too, and it's pure tomato. If you like heavy, sweet tomato sauce and thick crusts, go elsewhere. The bar has some great bottled craft beers, lovingly and carefully selected by owners K.C. Combs and Brendan

O'Brien. The Blue Moon ale was a favorite; served with a fresh slice of orange, it was a perfect match for the Margherita pizza, which is small enough for just one person and a nice combination of crunchy crust, light sauce, fresh basil leaves, and mozzarella. There are some unusual pizzas offered here too; sliced potato with onions and fresh rosemary is a traditional and tasty classic Neapolitan combination, while the tomatillo (tomatillo sauce, chicken, caramelized onion, cheddar, and jack cheese) is definitely not from anywhere in Italy.

Pasta, available only at dinner, is handmade in house. You can choose the style and the sauce. Cheese ravioli and fettuccine are available daily and can be tossed with garlic and oil, pesto, Alfredo, marinara, or Bolognese sauce. Closed Mon, open Tues through Fri at 11 a.m. and Sat and Sun at 11:30 a.m.

Happy Rooster Cafe, 1114 S. Sarnoff Dr., Tucson, AZ 85710; (520) 298-1752; American; $. Big barn-like space, big patio, big kitschy murals, big breakfast. It's hard to find this popular breakfast place, off the beaten track on a side street off 22nd Street. Look for a combo of cars, trucks, and motorcycles in the packed parking lot. This is a real neighborhood hangout serving up the kind of food you might have had on a road trip with Mom and Dad in the '50s: chipped beef on toast, pigs in a blanket, egg salad, French dip, pork chops and eggs, fried chicken with homemade mashed potatoes. This is what you'll find at the Rooster along with banana and pecan pancakes, waffles, eggs, omelets, burgers, fries, and all kinds of overstuffed sandwiches. Bring your vintage Lone Ranger lunchbox for leftovers, 'cause the portions are generous. Open from 7 a.m. to 2 p.m. daily.

Jonathan's Cork, 6230 E. Tanque Verde Rd., Tucson, AZ 85715; (520) 296-1631; jonathanscork.com; American; $$$. Chef/hunter Jonathan Landeen is passionate about food, particularly game meats, which are his specialty. Not only does he know how to cook them perfectly, he also knows how to hunt them, and his many hunter friends (and other meat lovers) were delighted when he took over the Cork in 1994 (it's been open since 1966). You'll find his classy, handsome place just around the bend at the intersection of Pima and Tanque Verde Roads. The subtly lit, intimate interior is decorated with Native American art, Western-themed oil paintings by local artists, and the occasional animal head. Beehive fireplaces are in the corners of several of the dining areas and a there is a lovely side patio. Award-winning Chef Landeen (Copper Chef, Iron Chef Tucson) has a big personality—almost as big as his signature handlebar mustache—and an impressive pedigree: He trained with the legendary Paul Prudhomme, executive chef of Commander's Palace in New Orleans. His classic menu features game meats, seafood, and top-quality beef. On the game-meat side, ostrich steak and venison can be had char broiled, sautéed, or blackened, and tender bison is wrapped up with jalapeño bacon. Prime rib is offered in 9- or 16-ounce slabs, along with filet mignon and New York strip. Alaskan king crab, Australian lobster tail with drawn butter, and an oven-poached salmon top the seafood selections. The Southwest chicken is so good that is has been on the menu by popular demand since the restaurant opened—ask for it. When Chef Landeen is not busy cooking at the Cork, he cooks for two pheasant-hunting groups, the Rocky Mountain Elk Foundation and the Wild Turkey Foundation. This is a chef who loves his work! Dinner from 5 p.m. Mon through Sat, closed Sun.

Le Buzz Caffe, 9121 E. Tanque Verde Rd., Tucson, AZ 85749; (520) 749-3903; lebuzzcaffe.com; American; $. You'll find lots of people having breakfast here, especially bicyclists still in racing gear and funky bicycling shoes. Extremely popular for their vast array of homemade breakfast pastries, Le Buzz offers a full breakfast and lunch menu too. For breakfast, tempting croissants, muffins, scones, and coffee cakes are on full view at the counter, and you can order omelets, oatmeal, scrambled eggs, and pancakes. Everything here is counter service, just get in line and order and they will deliver to your table. Lunch choices (served from 10:30 a.m. all the way up to 5 p.m.) include homemade soups that change daily and salads (the Sonoran with chicken, black beans, and tortilla strips and the Le Buzz with dried apricots, corn relish,

candied walnuts, and a poblano lime dressing are the most popular). The orange poppy-seed dressing is delish, ask for extra. You'll also find hot and cold sandwiches (top pick is the LA), most available on the house-made breads and flaky croissants. There are also six different kinds of quiche, all made in house, a to-die-for chicken pot pie, and lots of specials. Step around the bicycles and come on in! Open daily from 6 a.m. for breakfast and lunch.

New Delhi Palace, 6751 E. Broadway Blvd., Tucson, AZ 85710; (520) 296-8585; newdelhipalacetucson.com; Indian; $$. If you are looking for basic Indian comfort food, not too spicy, not too exotic, this is the place to come. A comfortable, open, and serene space, here you can try specialty dishes from West Bengal and signature *karhai* style dishes all prepared carefully with subtle flavors and respect for the Western palate. The gentle staff here is happy to help you navigate the menu. Stuffed eggplant fritters, spinach and lentils cooked with cumin, fenugreek and mustard seeds, and a wonderfully flavored chicken in a sauce with poppy seeds, peanuts, cloves, fennel seeds, and cardamom are some of the unusual Bengali specialties, all served with fluffy basmati rice that comes to the table in a lovely silver urn. Cooks here use deep, thick, two-handled pots to make several signature dishes referred to on the menu as the aforementioned *karhai* style. These include lamb, chicken, and shrimp *fraizee,* all cooked in a thick, rich tomato sauce with onions and bell peppers. They come to the table steaming hot in a decorative copper *karhai* pot. You will find many familiar options on the extensive menu— samosas, biryani, tikki masala, curries, and vegetarian dishes like *aloo goobi* and dhal. The breads are particularly good here, especially the whole-wheat naan that arrives hot and buttery and the puffy *kulcha* stuffed with onions. All desserts are homemade, and there is quite a selection: *kheer* (rice pudding), *gulab jamon* (sweet fried dough balls flavored with rosewater syrup), and several flavors of *kulfi* (Indian ice cream), including coconut and mango. Be sure to take a handful of the crunchy anise-flavored colored candies to clear your palate after your meal. Open daily from 11:30 a.m. to 2 p.m. for lunch, and at 5 p.m. for dinner.

Poco and Mom's, 1060 S. Kolb Rd., Tucson, AZ 85710; (520) 325-7044; pocoandmoms.com; New Mexican; $. Plain brick exterior, concrete front patio, drive-through window on the side, dried-out plants, well-worn furnishings, these are the realities of Poco and Mom's, but do not be deterred, this small, divey place cooks up some of the best New Mexico–style food in town. Just close your eyes, imagine yourself in Taos, and dig in. When your eyes are open, you can see all the food prepared in the open kitchen that keeps the place noisy and fragrant. They have an incredibly extensive menu considering the place has only 12 indoor tables. Everything is made from scratch every day and they get their red and green chiles straight from Hatch, New Mexico. The red and green chiles are featured in New Mexico–style flat enchiladas made with blue or regular corn tortillas in all sorts of combinations—you can even get fried eggs on top. Friends (that's you, David) who have lived in New Mexico groan over the chile rellenos and burritos and ask for special "off-menu" items like the *carne asada* omelet with jalapeños and cheese topped with enchilada sauce, sour cream,

LOCAL CHAIN: RISKY BUSINESS

Opened in 1997 by Tucsonan Jon Alubowicz, these casual, friendly sports bars are extremely popular around town, painted with bright colors and peopled with young, cheerful servers and neighborhood folks. This a place where you can bring the kids (no one will notice if Junior is running around or hollering for more fries, the lively background music will drown him out), or come on your own to sit at the bar for a drink, watch sports on the big-screen TVs and have a cocktail or a beer. Basic food is well made, reasonably priced, and filling. The extensive menu offers something for everyone, from appetizers, soups, salads, burgers, pizza, to all kinds of entrees and desserts. It's family-friendly food here, not haute cuisine. For adults, appetizers and entrees are the way to go. The peel-and-eat shrimp come with a nice creamy spicy remoulade and the Risky Nachos bring a plate piled high with chips, melted cheese, black beans, olives, and chopped scallions, topped with pico and sour cream. The pork chops are consistently good. Boneless and tender, they're grilled, glazed, and served with nicely seasoned sautéed squash and tomatoes. Although this is by no means a steak place, the seasoned grilled rib eye, sirloin, and filet mignon are nicely done. For the kids, the usual mac and cheese, burgers, chicken fingers, and fries will keep them happy if they like that kind of thing. If they are more adventurous, there are specialty pizzas, overstuffed sandwiches, and all kinds of salad combinations. Everyone likes the huge slab of 6-layer chocolate caramel fudge cake, one of many generously portioned desserts on the menu. Three convenient locations are in the East, Foothills, and Central parts of town. Check riskybusinesstucson.com for details. Open daily for lunch and dinner.

and green chiles. Ask the waitstaff for it, they are super-friendly and helpful. Green chile pork stew is a winner here—topped with melted cheese, it's rich and full of flavor. Regular and breakfast burritos are massive—the red chile pork or beef and the chili verde are great (the breakfast versions have scrambled cheese in them), and you can customize them with your choice of sauce (red, green, or sour cream green chile). If for some reason some of your family members don't like Mexican food, the American Favorites menu will have something for them too. If you don't want to sit inside, or the wait is too long since it's always packed, there's the convenient drive-through, and you can call your order in ahead of time. Open Tues through Fri from 6 a.m. to 9 p.m., Sat from 7 a.m. to 9 p.m., and Sun from 7 a.m. to 2 p.m.

Landmark

Tanque Verde Ranch, 14301 E. Speedway Blvd., Tucson, AZ 85748; (520) 296-6275; tanqueverderanch.com; Southwest; $$$. This must be one of the most amazing dining rooms in Tucson. With soaring saguaro rib ceilings, huge windows, and rough-hewn wood dining chairs and tables, it just has to be seen to be believed. Hidden away at the very, very end of East Speedway Boulevard, the dining room is part of the historic Tanque Verde Ranch, which has been in operation since 1868 and has had various lives as a working ranch, dude ranch, and now upscale resort. The resort, still family owned, stays true to its ranching roots. The first thing you'll see as you pull into the parking lot are lots and lots of horses behind rustic wooden fences. The unassuming, low-slung, ranch-style buildings give no clue that such a lovely dining room is inside waiting for you. Chef Ben Drury, a graduate of the Texas Culinary Academy, presides over the kitchen here, producing both tasty ranch grub for the special dude ranch events (breakfast trail rides, outdoor cowboy barbecues, Mexican fiesta nights) and gourmet food for indoor dining and special events, all open to the public. Chef Drury's cuisine shines during the sit-down dinner hour and Sunday lunch, where he merges his interest in local and indigenous ingredients with his culinary experience in the Caribbean and interior Mexico. The menus are seasonal and change frequently, but you may find

inspired dishes like bourbon- and mint-spiked watermelon gazpacho, smoked duck and house-made duck sausage pan-zanella salad, house-smoked trout, chili-dusted mahi mahi with Arizona blood orange citrus salsa, or citrus-marinated roasted half chicken with Oaxacan *mole coloradito*, sweet potatoes, and wilted local greens. All the breads and desserts (pies, cookies, cake, bars) are made in the vast kitchen behind the dining room that looks like it could easily feed hundreds of hungry cowhands. Lunch and dinner are prix fixe; the trail rides plus breakfast and outdoor barbecue dinners are priced separately. Lunch is served daily from noon to 1:30 p.m., dinner in the dining room is available Mon, Tues, Thurs, Fri, and Sun from 6 p.m. to 8 p.m., and the outdoor barbecue dinners take place on Wed and Sat. Reservations required.

South & South Tucson

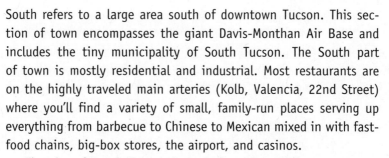

South refers to a large area south of downtown Tucson. This section of town encompasses the giant Davis-Monthan Air Base and includes the tiny municipality of South Tucson. The South part of town is mostly residential and industrial. Most restaurants are on the highly traveled main arteries (Kolb, Valencia, 22nd Street) where you'll find a variety of small, family-run places serving up everything from barbecue to Chinese to Mexican mixed in with fast-food chains, big-box stores, the airport, and casinos.

The city of South Tucson is an independent, mile-square area, home to residences, historic sites, and scenic barrios. There are lots of tiny mom-and-pop places, several family-owned restaurants that have been in business since the early 1950s, a few local and regional chains, and many roadside stands in this area of town, most serving up homey Sonoran Mexican fare in generous portions.

El Torero, 231 E. 26th St., Tucson, AZ 85713; (520) 622-9534; Mexican; $. To get here, look for the bullfighting mural on Fourth Avenue and take the next right turn onto 26th Street. Then watch for the square pink building set back from the street. El Torero is a longtime local favorite, open since 1956. It may not look like much on the outside, but inside is one busy and lively place serving up home-style Sonoran food and drink. It can be noisy in here, especially in the front bar area, but food is served quickly and efficiently in generous portions so hang in there! Start with a chile cheese crisp. This is Mexico's answer to the pizza. A deep-fried flour tortilla topped with tons of melted cheese and strips of green chiles, it's served on a pedestal as it justly deserves. *Carne seca* is popular here, big mounds of juicy shreds of beef come with rice and beans and warm tortillas to wrap it all up in. Turkey with a rich, deeply flavored mole is another favorite. The *topopo* salad is a tower of salad (shredded lettuce, avocado and tomato slices, cheese) atop a crispy corn tortilla. *The* only dessert to get here is the *almendrado,* a light, colorful (layers of red, white, and green for the Mexican flag!) meringue made with egg whites, sugar, and almond extract, then covered in a creamy almond sauce. I'm not sure where this dessert originated, but few restaurants here make it, and it is a delicious way to end your meal. Closed Tues, open Sat and Sun at noon for lunch and dinner, other days at 11 a.m.

Golden Phoenix Restaurant, 2854 E. 22nd St., Tucson, AZ 85713; (520) 327-8008; Chinese; $. Many local Chinese families frequent this low-key, simply decorated spot for reasonably priced, freshly made Cantonese and Mandarin food. Although there are many options and delicious-sounding dishes and combinations on the regular menu (which will be handed to you as soon as you sit down), ask for the special Chinese menu. Laminated and pink, this menu features most of the specialty dishes that the restaurant is known for in the Asian community. (Thank you for sharing this secret, Mike Lee and the ladies at the Chinese Cultural Center!) Top picks are the honey walnut shrimp, which arrive lightly battered, crunchy, and moist, topped with a sweet sauce and surrounded by amazingly delicious candied walnuts; black mushrooms with Chinese greens are served in a light sauce with perfectly wokked bok choy. Chow fun is basic and has a nice smoky flavor and lots of meat. Pork with salty fish, if available, is another one to try along with house panfried noodles with seafood and black mushrooms (Mike's mom's favorite). If you're used to heavily flavored dishes with thick, glutinous sauces, you will be disappointed. The food is simple, clean, and straightforward, and you won't have that bloated feeling or MSG headache after eating here. If you sit near the vast back kitchen, you can catch glimpses of the chefs working their woks and chopping fresh greens with their cleavers. Open daily from 11 a.m. for lunch and dinner.

Las Brasas Mesquite Grill, 2928 E. 22nd St., Tucson, AZ 85713; (520) 881-6077; lasbrasastucson.com; Mexican; $. If you weren't looking for this place, stuck in the middle of a nondescript strip mall on busy 22nd Street, you might just pass it by. Don't. It's small, busy, and family-run and offers up some great grilled meats. You order at the counter here where you will see the big, wood-fired grills sizzling with beef, chicken, and pork. Stick with the grilled

meats: The beef is tender and slightly charred with a great mesquite smoke flavor, the chicken is moist and crispy, and the marinated pork sweet-spicy and juicy. You can get the meat to go by the pint and lots of people do, taking it home to wrap into a warm flour tortilla with fresh salsa and guacamole. Be sure to order the heavenly grilled green onions too, available as a side order. If you do stay in, the Skillet La Parrillada for two is a big portion of three meats (chicken, beef, pork *adobada* or *tripitas*), served on a skillet with grilled green onions and jalapeños. It comes with 10 tortillas and you'll need them! You can get *raspados* here for dessert; the refreshing fruit ices come in a variety of flavors. Closed Sun, open other days at 10 a.m.

Nimbus Brewing Company, 3850 E. 44th St., Tucson, AZ 85713; (520) 745-9175; nimbusbeer.com; Beer; $. Way, way off the beaten track, this industrial-size brewpub has been in operation since 1996 and is the largest brewery in the state of Arizona, producing over 45,000 kegs of beer a year. Not easy to find  (it's off South Palo Verde Road in a warehouse district), it's known for its craft-brewed ales, live music, and basic comfort bar foods. To wit: curly fries (get them sprinkled with Cajun seasoning), ranch fries with ranch dressing and crumbled bacon, wings, burgers, hot subs, and sandwiches. They are famous for the fried bologna sandwich, a 4-ounce slab of grilled bologna (definitely not Oscar Meyer) on a bun with pickles, onions, and mustard. The Beef on Weck is as authentic as you'll find outside of Western New York, served on real kummelweck rolls encrusted with coarse salt and caraway seeds and dipped in jus. You really feel like you're in a factory here—the cavernous space, with exposed and very notice-able ductwork, houses three 30-foot-tall fermenters that hold about 15,000 gallons of beer. Signature Nimbus beers include Nimbus Ale, a light, clean brew with a hint of honey (killer bee honey from Bisbee is a secret ingredient), Nimbus Pale Ale, Red and Brown Ales, dark Oatmeal Stout, and the 8.2 percent alcohol Old Monkey Shine, all made and served here and shipped all over the country. Open at 11 a.m. daily.

Original Mr. K's BBQ, 6302 S. Park Ave., Tucson, AZ 85713; (520) 792-9484; Barbecue; $. Ray Kendrick puts out some mighty fine food here, family style and finger licking good. It's not a pretty or fancy place but it packs in the 'cue lovers day and night who can't get enough of that smoky meat. Order what you like at the counter and your order will arrive in basic Styrofoam. Meats are dry-rubbed, smoked, and slathered with sauce so be sure to grab reams of paper towels from the rolls conveniently located on each table. Choose from tempting sides including creamy potato salad, coleslaw, collard and turnip greens cooked with pork, candied sweet potatoes, and corn on the cob. Mmmmhmmmmm. Open Tues through Sat from 10:30 a.m. to 6 p.m.

The Silver Saddle Steak House, 310 E. Benson Hwy., Tucson, AZ 85713; (520) 622-6253; thesilversaddlesteakhouse.com; Steak; $$. Please do not expect anything fancy here, just good old grub in a rustic, saloon-like atmosphere next to the Lazy 8 Motel on the frontage road off busy Benson Highway. A longtime favorite with neighborhood residents, this place is always packed. Servers and the hostess are friendly and attentive and all the steaks are grilled before your very eyes over real mesquite fires contained within the grill in the main dining area. They take their meat seriously here, advising patrons not to order their steak well done since it'll dry out over the flames no matter what the cut or weight. Order a side of homemade onion rings to start, thick-cut and batter-dipped, they come with house-made creamy ranch dressing. Follow this with a trip to the salad bar, with lots of choices and nice chilled plates! As for steak, there are lots of cuts

Local Chain: Mariscos Chihuahua

You can't miss these bright blue buildings with lively ocean-themed murals painted on the outside walls. Founded as a little roadside stand, there are now multiple locations in Tucson, including several in the South and South Tucson. Why on earth are they called Mariscos Chihuhaua? The *mariscos* (seafood) part makes sense but the chihuahua? A reference to a family pet perhaps? No, it's even simpler than that. The original stand that served up ceviche and shrimp in Nogales, Arizona, was set up right next to a fruit stand called Fruteria Chihuahua. Locals started referring to the seafood stand and the fruteria in one phrase and the name stuck. Each of these clean, colorfully painted restaurants serve up fresh seafood scooped from the Sea of Cortez. Each restaurant in the chain is locally owned and operated, so the menus may vary slightly but they offer a wide range of options. My favorite is the whole fried fish (*pescado frito entero*), lightly floured and dunked into a vat of boiling oil, it comes to the table head and all and is a crispy, flaky delight. They are known for their shrimp, which are served up in ceviche, tostadas, cocktails, soups, and tacos, deep fried, sautéed, grilled, deviled, and stuffed. Their signature shrimp dish is the *camarones culichi,* a platter of sautéed shrimp served in a creamy cilantro green sauce. You'll also find sautéed octopus (*pulpo*) on the menu and fresh local oysters on the half shell. Check the website, mariscoschihuahua.com, for the location near you; they are all open daily.

to choose from, including a 21-ounce porterhouse and a 16-ounce T-bone, but my meat-loving friends go for the king cut rib eye, a humongous slab of beef. (Ask for the end cut larded with fat.) Choose the huge, fluffy, foil-wrapped baked potato to go with it. Classic steak-house mud pie is for dessert. With layers of chocolate and vanilla ice cream atop a chocolate cookie crust and drizzled with chocolate sauce, it's huge—share it! Open Mon through Fri at 11 a.m. for lunch and dinner, Sat and Sun at 1 p.m.

South Tucson: Foodie Faves

El Guero Canelo #1, 5201 S. 12th Ave., South Tucson, AZ 85706; (520) 295-9005; elguerocanelo.com; Mexican; $. This gussied-up road stand serves up some of the best Sonoran hot dogs around. What is a Sonoran hot dog, you ask? It's a mouthful of deliciousness, and Guero Canelo's are famous around town. A Sonoran hot dog starts with a very soft, oblong bun (some like it grilled, purists like it plain). Thick bacon slices are wrapped around a hot dog and the whole thing is grilled till the bacon is crispy. The bacon-wrapped dog is nested in the soft bun and topped with yellow  mustard, pinto beans, diced onions, grilled onions, diced tomatoes, and mayo in a paper dish with a freshly grilled yellow jalapeño on the side. Press the sides of the bun together, close your eyes, and take a bite. It's just the best combo ever. There is also a terrific salsa bar with three types of salsa, chopped cucumber, sliced radishes, and pickled red onions. Grilled green onions and whole jalapeños are available in a warmer to the side of the salsa bar. You can top your dog with some, all, or none of these. They do have other things to eat here: tacos, *caramelos,* quesadillas, and burros, but the hot dog is the way to go. This is El Guero Canelo's original location and it's definitely not fancy. Order at the window and you can take your food to go or sit in the outdoor covered patio at red, white, and green tables and benches with the working folks and the very occasional tourist who wanders in. You'll sometimes find a live guitarist on site, playing lovely Mexican folk music. This area of town can be somewhat daunting at night if you're not from the neighborhood, so lunch or an early dinner might be the way to go. Open daily from 9 a.m. for breakfast, lunch, and dinner.

El Indio, 3355 S. 6th Ave., Tucson, AZ 85713; (520) 620-0504; Mexican; $. With real home-cooked food, no muss and no fuss, this busy diner-like spot is clean and quick with experienced, hard-working waitstaff who will still take the time in between rushing from tables to kitchen to answer questions about the menu. I like to come here for breakfast because they have the most wonderful huevos rancheros. A big plate of two fried eggs on top of crispy fried corn tortillas and topped with your choice of green or red sauce, they come with the creamiest of refried beans and slices of avocado.

Wonderful and incredibly filling. Of course there are lots of other things on the menu, but I just never get to them, I just order the huevos rancheros over and over again. My frequent dining companions (thank you, Terrol), however, have tried most of the other menu items. Top picks are the *chile verde* with pork, a thick stew with big chunks of sautéed pork and the chile Colorado, beef chunks in a mild, flavorful red chile sauce. All are served with rice and those wonderful refried beans. You'll also find chimis, tacos, burritos, flautas, grilled steaks, and excellent fajitas on the extensive menu. And you can get a bowl of those marvelous refried beans (have I mentioned these?) as a side order any time. The place is always crowded, especially on weekend mornings when lots of families come in for breakfast. Open Wed through Mon for breakfast, lunch, and dinner starting at 7 a.m.

Los Portales, 2615 S. 6th Ave., Tucson, AZ 85713; (520) 889-1170; Mexican; $. Huge, heavy doors invite you in to experience the good, solid, home-cooked Central Mexican food from Jalisco that's featured here. The interior is pleasing with light yellow, blue,

and orange walls, Saltillo tiled floors, heavy wooden chairs and booths, and displays of attractive, hand-wrought metal sculptures of mariachi musicians. The *sopas* (soups) here are the way to go. Hearty, homemade, and filling, Cocido de Res is the one to choose. A big bowl of bone-in beef ribs in a light broth with a big piece of corn on the cob, a wedge of cabbage, garbanzo beans, potatoes, green beans, and thick-cut zucchini and carrots, it will keep you satisfied all day. Other choices include pozole, a hearty blend of pork, hominy, and vegetables in a red chile broth; *caldo de*  *queso,* a creamy, rich cheese soup, kind of like a Mexican fondue; and *albondigas,* full of delicious rice-filled beefy meatballs and lots of veggies and also available in a seafood version made with shrimp meatballs in a seafood broth. The *sopes* are also worth trying—you don't see them on many local Mexican menus. The tasty cakes are made from masa, shaped into a saucer and deep fried. They are the perfect edible container and here they come filled with your choice of moist shredded chicken or beef and a side of rice and pinto beans. Don't forget to eat them too! Specialties of the house include the *Parrillada Los Portales* (grilled, marinated flank steak, chicken, and tripe) and *Higado Encebollado* (sautéed beef liver and onions). Limeade, available by the pitcher, is made with fragrant, juicy Mexican limes, or you can have a glass of house-made *aguas frescas*. The dense apple cake is a house special dessert, served with a scoop of vanilla ice cream. Creamy chocolate flan is another popular choice or you can pick up a beautiful candied apple coated in sugar, tamarindo, and chile powder at the front desk to go. You will exit the *portales* well fed after a meal here. Open daily from 7 a.m. to 7 p.m.

Mi Nidito, 1813 S. 4th Ave., Tucson, AZ 85713; (520) 622-5081; minidito.net; Mexican; $. Bill Clinton ate here in 1999, and ever since then it's become a dining destination, even though it's been open since 1952 when Clinton was only six! Mi Nidito is located in a lovely area with restored adobes, hand-painted murals, winding streets, and desert landscaping. Eating at Mi Nidito is a great way to visit this attractive part of town and is a bit of a rite of passage for newbies looking for an introduction to basic Sonoran Mexican cuisine. Service is brisk, helpful, and friendly, and you'll often find a line out the door. Food here is basic and plentiful, and they are well known for their menudo. A classic soup made with beef tripe, it's reputed to cure hangovers. Here you can order it plain or in a spicy red chile broth, both served with chopped onions, cilantro, and slices of lime. Other Sonoran specialties include chile rellenos, flautas, *birria* (spiced shredded beef), chimis, and enchiladas all served with lots of rice, refried beans, and shredded lettuce. The *nopalitos* (prickly-pear cactus pads) with chile is an unusual combo plate choice,  served with beans, rice, and flour tortillas. If you're interested in what the president ate here for lunch, order the President's Plate and you will find out. Open Wed through Sun for lunch and dinner starting at 11 a.m.

Taqueria Pico de Gallo, 2618 S. 6th St., Tucson, AZ 85713; (520) 623-8775; Mexican; $. It may look small and unimpressive, but Pico de Gallo has the very best shrimp tacos in town. Publicity from food writers Jane and Michael Stern, *Gourmet* magazine, and a host of other food publications hasn't changed a thing here, thankfully. It's still friendly, small, and slightly cramped with faded photos of menu specials hanging on the walls. You order and pick up your food at the counter where you can get a glimpse of ladies making the corn tortillas from scratch, kneading the masa, rolling it into balls, and pressing it into perfectly round little tortillas. Get the shrimp tacos. Get a double order because three just aren't enough and you will want more. In just a few minutes, a set of perfectly cooked shrimp tacos, simply garnished with shredded cabbage and fresh limes, is ready for pickup. Condiments are on the tables in squeeze bottles. There's a friendly buzz of conversation, lots of people coming in for takeout, and families seated at the scattering of tables under rotating ceiling fans. I love to bring visitors here for the simple, delicious tacos, not the fancy ones or the specialty ones you might see elsewhere. This is homey, family food, made fresh day after day. There are other options—check the menu or look at the pictures on the walls (by no means an indication of the fresh food you'll end up with). Daily homemade soups, deep-fried fish, and tacos with other fillings are all available. There are other options, but to my mind nothing outdoes the shrimp tacos. Dessert should be Pico de Gallo, a big cup filled with fruit spears sprinkled with chile powder and a squeeze of fresh lime. Open daily at 9 a.m.

Downtown

Downtown is an urban area clustered around Congress Street that is home to residential lofts, tall buildings, parking garages, small retailers, museums, courthouses, and several unique historic areas. This section of town is rapidly becoming a top dining destination, with many restaurants found right on Congress, in the warren of little side streets, tucked under parking garages, on the edges of barrio neighborhoods, and in a historic hotel and train depot.

Foodie Faves

Cafe a la C'art, 150 N. Main Ave., Tucson, AZ 85701; (520) 628-8533; cafealacarttucson.com; American; $. Hidden away inside the courtyard of the Tucson Museum of Art, this family-run cafe has been pleasing museumgoers and downtowners since 1998. Chef-Owners Judith Michelet, her son Mark, and his wife Shirley take lots of pride in their food, and it shows. The long narrow space is bright and cheerful, with a quaint European feel, flower pots, and leafy vines line the outside patio and inside is comfortable and intimate with small tables and big windows looking out on the museum grounds. Most popular at lunch, the outdoor patio is the place to sit and dine on sandwiches like the highly popular and delicious gingered apricot almond chicken salad on a flaky house-baked croissant and the meaty Sonoran brisket, a super combo of braised beef, roasted red peppers, and pepper jack cheese on a toasted kaiser roll. Salads (try the Southwest Caesar), burgers (the burger and blue is a top pick, topped with gobs of Gorgonzola cheese), and homemade soups of the day round out the menu. Everything here is made in house, from the salad dressings to the tangy, refreshing lemonade. You'll find ladies who lunch along with families and businesspeople at the closely spaced tables. Take a stroll after your meal and enjoy the lovely courtyard and fountains on the surrounding museum grounds. Open daily for breakfast and lunch until 3 p.m., dinner is served Thurs through Sat from 5 p.m. to 9 p.m.

Cafe 54, 54 E. Pennington St., Tucson, AZ 85701; (520) 622-1907; cafe54.org; American; $. A meal here does a lot of good, both for your stomach and for the nonprofit organization, Coyote Taskforce, Inc., that runs this cute little cafe. It's designed as a training ground for people who are in treatment for mental illness and are seeking to reenter the workforce, and the chefs and staff here take their food and their mission seriously. The space itself is simple and welcoming, with big floor-to-ceiling windows looking out on busy Pennington Street, high ceilings with exposed, colorful ductwork, and a revolving art exhibit of works by local artists. The menu is amazingly extensive given the small staff, and it changes quite frequently. You order at the counter, and trainees working hard to succeed and move their lives forward deliver your meal to you with a smile. Rolls are made from scratch daily and come warm to the table, scented with rosemary and shiny with a brush of melted butter. Everything is made from scratch in the back kitchen using local produce. Soup, sandwiches (try the house-made corned beef), Greek salad, and entrees like butternut squash lasagna and Southern Arizona Wagyu beef burgers are all available on the menu along with vegan, gluten-free, and vegetarian options. Dessert is made by budding pastry chefs and overseen by professional culinary instructors, and it can be delicious and creative—try the green tea olive oil cake or the blueberry jalapeño pie if they're available. There may be the occasional serving stumble or repeated order, but remember that this is a teachable moment. The staff welcomes constructive feedback in their efforts to replicate real-world experiences. Open for lunch only from 11 a.m. to 2 p.m. weekdays.

Cafe Desta, 758 S. Stone Ave., Tucson, AZ 85701; (520) 370-7000; cafedesta.com; Ethiopian; $. Smack in the middle of Five Points (at the intersection of Stone Avenue and Sixth and 18th Streets), this little gem of a place is cooking up authentic Ethiopian food. The small, streamlined space is spare but inviting, with distressed-wood tables, big picture windows, a high ceiling, and exposed brick walls decorated with large-scale, artsy, black-and-white photos interspersed with whimsical wood carvings. The back of the menu will tell you all you need to know about the unique ingredients used to create a variety of unusual dishes. *Kibe* (purified, spiced butter), *teff* (a gluten-free grain indigenous to Ethiopia), *injira* (pancakelike, stretchy bread made with *teff,* sorghum, and wheat flours), these all form part of the meat and vegetarian dishes offered here. The *injira* here is a dusky purple, thin, crepe-like pancake with hundreds of tiny, perfectly spaced bubbles (a sign of a good *injira* maker, and not an easy feat). The best way to experience the food is with a combination plate, served on a huge round ceramic platter atop a bed of *injira*. The presentation is lovely, the brightly hued foods look like a painter's palette—almost too pretty to eat. But do eat. Use your hands (they don't even provide silverware unless asked) to rip off a piece of *injira* and fold it over your food. Try the *kik,* a soft mash of yellow split peas cooked with onion, turmeric, and herbs. Lamb, fish, and chicken are available cooked in the traditional deep red *berbere* (hot chili powder mixed with spices) and homemade cheese (*ayeb*) is available as a side order to accompany your entree. If you have any questions not covered by the menu, owners Brooke and Telahoun Molla are experts, so ask away. This must be healthy food, the patrons here are lean and attractive and dig in with great enjoyment and concentration. Drinks are listed on the big chalkboard above the counter, the *yekeman shai* (black tea) is fragrant with cinnamon and cardamom and served hot or cold.

There's coffee too—the coffee beans are sourced only from Ethiopia (of course!). Open daily, 11 a.m. to 9 p.m.

Cafe Milano, 46 W. Congress St., Tucson, AZ 85701; (520) 628-1601; caffemilano.com; Italian; $$. You will feel like you are in Milan in this bustling cafe where owner Carlo Borella greets you with a friendly "ciao" when you come in. Originally from Milano, Carlo and wife Laura make all their sauces from grandma's recipes and their own gnocchi. Lunch brings in local business people, lawyers, and clerks from the courthouse and jurors looking for a bite to eat on break. They were making panini here way before they became popular and they are really good. The breads are specially made by a local Italian baker and are filled with a variety of delicious meats and cheeses. My favorite is the Duomo, a crispy melt of prosciutto, smushy mozzarella, roasted peppers, and pesto (ask them to leave out the lettuce). There are 14 other choices so I'm sure 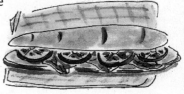 you too will find a favorite. Antipasto plates, salads, pasta, soups, and excellent espresso fill out the lunch menu. The cafe transforms itself for dinner, with low lighting, Italian contemporary music, and an intimate feel. Dinner options are more extensive and feature a variety of homemade pastas, including the excellent bacon-strewn spaghetti *alla carbonara,* cooked perfectly al dente, and jumbo-size house-made gnocchi. If you're not sure what to order, Carlo will be happy to make suggestions, in between greeting and serving. He does it all up front while Laura works the kitchen! *Affogato al caffè* is the choice for dessert, served Italian-style in a tall glass with a handle, a scoop of vanilla ice cream, and a generous pour of hot, bitter espresso. There's a limited wine list and a great selection of Italian fashion magazines and newspapers if you're dining solo or just looking to brush up on your Italian. Open Mon through Fri for breakfast and lunch until 3:30 p.m., dinner Thurs through Sat, starting at 5:30 p.m. Closed for a month during the summer, generally mid-June to mid-July when Carlo and family head to Italy for new culinary inspirations.

Cafe Poca Cosa, 110 E. Pennington St., Tucson, AZ 85701; (520) 622-6400; cafepocacosatucson.com; Mexican; $$$. Chef-Owner Suzana Davila, a native of Guayamas, Sonora, is a powerhouse. She runs this longtime and very popular restaurant with great energy and enthusiasm. One of the first people to showcase haute Sonoran Mexican cuisine, her personal style is reflected in the modern, striking decor. Tucked underneath the Pennington Avenue Garage, it's a long, narrow space with cushy, black-and-white banquettes, tables, fire-red walls, and contemporary art. The menu changes twice daily and is presented to you tableside on a tiny chalkboard by your enthusiastic black-garbed server. Feel free to ask lots of questions about the unusual dishes on the menu and the different combinations you can order. Most people go for the Plato Poca Cosa, a combination plate of the chef's choosing because it can be so hard to select from the many interesting dishes on the menu. The combo brings you three mini servings of select entrees surrounding a large mound of salad greens and gives you a taste of Suzana's creativity. I prefer to taste the complexity of her moles and explore her imaginative cuisine with individual entrees, which are generous portions accompanied by inter-  esting sides. For dessert, you can stay with the combo concept and opt for the dessert trio, or just choose one of the delicious vegan cupcakes made by Davila's daughter, Shanali Zeballos—the chocolate mole is to die for. Open Tues through Sat for lunch and dinner starting at 11 a.m.

Casa Vicente, 375 S. Stone Ave., Tucson, AZ 85701; (520) 884-5253; casavicente.com; Spanish; $$. Big, busy, noisy, delicious. Casa Vicente is a sprawling space with multiple levels and a large outdoor patio that offers the best Spanish tapas in town. Take your time with the menu, there's a lot to absorb and choose from and it's all good. The complimentary *patatas bravas* that arrive at your table as soon as you are seated are amazing. The little chunks of potato have a crunchy exterior, creamy interior, and come in a pool of rust-colored smoky paprika sauce with a delicious garlicky aioli. These get eaten up fast and the waitstaff will bring more, so keep yourself in check because there are many, many more tapas to come. It's nice to bring a big crowd with you here so you can order lots and lots of tapas and pass them around. *Croquetas de jamon* are a real crowd pleaser. The deep-fried orbs of mashed potatoes filled with chopped, cured ham and creamy béchamel sauce disappear fast. Marinated octopus, sautéed garlic shrimp, white asparagus, and lots more all come on easily passable little plates just made for sharing. Skip the paellas and go for some of the more unusual choices including *fabada Asturiana* (fava bean and chorizo soup), *bacalao a la Vizcaina* (a Basque dish of pan-seared cod in a rich tomato sauce), and *conejo Casa Vicente* (rabbit stew with chestnuts and prunes). White sangria is the drink of choice, brought to the table in pitchers if you like, filled with apple slices, oranges, and green grapes, although if you prefer wine, there are many good Spanish, Portuguese, and Italian labels to choose from, as well as cocktails expertly prepared at the bar. The flourless chocolate cake, served with a brandy and coffee ganache, is my go-to dessert here (if I have any room left after eating all those potatoes and tapas). Select weeknights feature live guitar music that adds to the din in a good way, and Friday and Saturday bring live flamenco to the center stage with lots of stomping and clapping (for a small extra charge). Open Tues through Sat for dinner only starting at 4:30 p.m.

Downtown Kitchen + Cocktails, 136 S. 6th Ave., Tucson, AZ 85701; (520) 623-7700; downtownkitchen.com; Fusion; $$$. Chef-Owner Janos Wilder is definitely one of the most creative chefs in town (see his recipe on p. 274). He uses his creativity and love of global flavors and international cuisines to create a highly original atmosphere and menu here. Jetson-like furnishings, handmade ceramic plates with colors created especially for Janos by a local ceramic company, and kitschy touches like a huge boulder wall held in by chicken wire join upscale lighting, contemporary ceiling fans, and exposed brick, and it all works just fine! Downtown is Janos's culinary playground, a place where you never know what will be on the seasonal, highly eclectic menu that springs from his fevered culinary brain. If you have an adventurous culinary spirit, this is the place to eat. Take, for example, pounded green papaya salad with a sprinkling of toasted peanuts, serrano chiles, lime, and basil, inspired by Janos's friend from Laos, or crispy calamari with mango and candied ginger. Janos is always seeking to challenge your palate and introduce new flavor combinations. Who else would dare to combine quinoa with roasted pineapple and almond mole or cold somen noodles with roasted squash and olive oil? The staff is professional and extremely knowledgeable about the menu and Janos's culinary philosophy, and will be by your side throughout your meal making sure that you too become a Janos-phile. Cocktails are equally adventurous, the Cuban Sunset combines habañero-infused vodka and passion-fruit juice served with a cilantro garnish, while the Death+Taxes will make April 15th a breeze, with a hit of white whiskey, apple juice, cinnamon bark, Punt e Mes, and bitters. The bar menu offers items not found on the regular dinner menu. The Downtown burger should not be missed—hand-ground beef with *foie gras,* mushrooms, bacon, and Manchego cheese comes with purple potato chips (see what I mean?). Open for lunch Mon through Fri from 11 a.m. to 2 p.m., happy hour from 4 to 6 p.m. daily, and dinner daily from 5 p.m.

LOCAL CHAIN: EL CHARRO CAFE

The first thing people will tell you about El Charro is that it's the oldest restaurant in Tucson. Established by Monica Flin, it has been in continuous operation by the family since 1922. The downtown location on Court Street (originally Monica's home) has been open since 1968. Most Tucsonans and visitors have been directed to this landmark restaurant (now with five locations around town) to experience Sonoran Mexican cuisine. Current Chef-Owner Carlotta Flores (Monica's great niece) keeps tradition alive with a menu full of her family recipes and specialties. Carlotta is not only a chef, but also an expert on Mexican cuisine and culture—she is the co-author (along with Jane and Michael Stern of *Road Food* fame) of the *El Charro Cafe Cookbook* and keeps the family culinary flame burning. The downtown location on Court Street is my favorite. The front of the restaurant looks like a diner from days gone by, and the inside is a packed with a collection of chairs and tables in a busy, bustling atmosphere. Head to the back room, which is dark and relaxing with cozy leather banquettes, windows looking out onto the inner patio, and brightly colored walls decorated with paintings, Talavera pottery, and traditional Mexican *papel picado* banners (intricate, lacy paper cuttings). The service here is brisk and efficient, with waiters who can explain the many choices on the menu that may not be familiar. My picks come from the specialty family recipes that made El Charro famous in the first place and have kept it growing and successful. This is hearty family fare prepared well and served up in generous portions. All of the El Charro locations are family-friendly and great spots for gathering with large numbers of family and friends for a meal or a celebration. Start with the signature margaritas, thick and icy with a rim of salt and a slice of lime. Tamales are all handmade by the El Charro kitchens and are also shipped nationwide, they're so good. You'll find all sorts of tamale choices, some not seen elsewhere, like pork carnitas and the *tamales supremas* topped with house-made brisket. El Charro is also known for its *carne seca* (dried, shredded beef) and chiles rellenos that come with a choice of several homemade sauces. A dessert sampler will give you a taste of their most popular items—moist, homemade *tres leches* cake, caramel flan, and warm cinnamon rice pudding. Kids will find lots of options from a plain quesadilla to a tasty grilled-fish taco. Happy hour at all locations is a great deal along with lots of weekly and daily specials and kids-eat-free days. El Charro Cafe, The Original, 311 N. Court Ave., Tucson, (520) 622-1922; El Charro Oro Valley, 7725 N. Oracle Rd., Oro Valley, (520) 220-1922; El Charro El Mercado, 6310 E. Broadway Blvd., Tucson, (520) 745-1922; El Charro Ventana, 6910 E. Sunrise Blvd., Tucson, (520) 514-1922; El Charro Sahuarita, 19920 S. Rancho Sahuarita, Sahuarita, (520) 325-1922. All locations are open daily from 11 a.m. for lunch and dinner; elcharrocafe.com.

El Minuto Cafe, 354 S. Main Ave., Tucson, AZ 85701; (520) 882-4145; elminutocafe.com; Mexican; $. Home cooking is what you will get here, simple, homemade Sonoran Mexican food. El Minuto has been a mainstay of the downtown scene since 1939 and their homey, hearty food keeps people coming. It's not fancy here but it's clean and fun, with wandering mariachi players, paper cutouts dangling from the ceiling, and lots of large groups and families laughing, chatting, and eating heartily. Kids love the famous cheese crisps, deep-fried tortillas topped with melted cheddar and served on a pizza rack. Parents love the rich tortilla soup, full of chicken chunks, avocado slices, fresh vegetables, strips of corn tortillas, and a nice blob of melted cheese at the bottom (scrape it up!). Burros, chimis, enchiladas, quesadillas, tacos, tostadas, frosty beers, they are all filling and good. There are no fancy airs here, just hard-working servers and cooks whose food pleases year after year. Open Mon through Sat for lunch and dinner starting at 11 a.m.

Empire Pizza & Pub, 137 E. Congress St., Tucson, AZ 85701; (520) 882-7499; empirepizzapub.com; Pizza; $. All the way from New York, slices of true pizza have arrived downtown thanks to Empire. The front of the place, with its tiny eat-in patio and takeout counter, doesn't look like much, but the back room surprises and delights. High tin ceilings, tables and chairs, and a big bar with a huge TV usually set to a sports channel make it a great space to sit down with your slice (or whole pie) and have a glass of beer or wine. Order up front and the low-key bartenders will bring your

pizza back when it's ready so you don't even have to get up. There are lots of combinations (pineapple, ham, sausage, salami, mushroom, pesto, meatball, barbecue) but I confess to being a purist when it comes to pizza and the plain old cheese is the one for me here—the crust has just the right texture and the sauce is just right, not too much and not too little, and the cheese is not fancy, not hand-pulled or made from buffalo milk, it's just mozzarella, good mozzarella, and that's good enough for me. In addition to pizza, you can get subs (eggplant, meatball, chicken parmigiana) and salads (Greek, chef, garden, spinach). Open daily for lunch and dinner from 11 a.m.

Hub Restaurant and Creamery, 266 E. Congress St., Tucson, AZ 85701; (520) 207-8201; hubdowntown.com; American; $$. Owner Kade Mislinski has transformed Congress Street almost singlehandedly, taking a block that used to be run-down and dingy and creating a destination restaurant and club. The Hub is the center of this successful revitalization effort—succeeding in both design and degustation. The interior really has to be seen to be appreciated. Soaring ceilings, exposed brick walls, and wide plank floors are the setting for a long, narrow room of contemporary banquettes, tables, and floor-to-ceiling curtains for private dining areas. Even the bathrooms are beautiful, with etched glass and funky toilets and sinks. Be sure to make reservations here because it's almost always packed. On the bar side, there's a cozy lounge, in reds and blacks, where the bartenders mix up top-shelf liquor into a variety of classic drinks—like cosmos, stingers, and Manhattans. The menu is full of comfort foods expertly prepared. Pot pies come to the table steaming hot, packed with veggies and meat in a creamy béchamel inside a dense, flaky crust. Plus there are sandwiches (try the porchetta hot off the rotisserie on ciabiatta with caramelized onions), soups (hearty minestrone), and salads (the Picky Farmer is loaded with roasted corn, asparagus, beets, radishes, and cucumbers). If you have a hearty appetite, you can't beat the rotisserie roast chicken and house-cured corned beef served up with potatoes and braised cabbage. For dessert, the homemade ice cream in 23 flavors that rotate daily is the only way to go. Open daily from 11 a.m. for lunch and dinner.

Landmarks

Cup Cafe, 311 E. Congress St., Tucson, AZ 85701; (520) 798-1618; hotelcongress.com; American; $$. Housed in the historic Hotel Congress (built in 1919, this was where the Dillinger gang famously holed up in 1934 under aliases on the third floor before being captured by cops), this ever-popular cafe serves up an eclectic menu of goodies for breakfast, lunch, and dinner. The ambience alone is enough to keep you coming back. The hotel lobby harks back to days gone by (check out the old-fashioned phone booth and antique phone console) and features a terrific bar if you want a drink (alcoholic or otherwise) while you wait for a table at the busy cafe. This is a very popular spot for breakfast inside or alfresco at the little tables that skirt the outdoor plaza, home to live music and special events at night. Neighborhood folks like to read the paper and sip a cup of coffee here while they breakfast on homemade baked goods and the signature Eggs and Gunpowder, an explosive and delicious combination of roasted red potatoes, eggs, chorizo, and jack cheese. On the lighter side, the Frutopia brings a big bowl of fresh-cut fruit, house-made granola, and agave-sweetened creamy yogurt. Lunchtime is busy with international students (the hotel is also a hostel), tourists, and businesspeople digging into salads like the Depot, a  big dish of beef medallions, greens, tomatoes, avocados, and crispy onions with a creamy shallot dressing; sandwiches (try the Queer Steer); and slices of homemade pies and cakes (all on view spinning around in the refrigerated case). Dinnertime attracts more tourists, locals relaxing after work, and a whole slew of fun folks who come for the fisherman's stew, tamales, pasta, and fish-and-chips, all made with the Cup Cafe special twist (pecans with your salmon, gingersnaps in your mashed potatoes, curry in your fish stew). It can get full fast here (see note about the bar above). Open daily for breakfast, lunch, and dinner.

Cushing Street Bar and Grill, 198 W. Cushing St., Tucson, AZ 85701; (520) 622-7894; cushingstreeet.com; American; $$. **Built as** a private residence in 1869, this place is known more as a historic bar than restaurant, but it has been serving up both libations and food since 1971. Located in the historic barrio district, it sits on the corner of Cushing and Meyer Avenues. You have to look closely to find it, as it blends in with the low-key, adobe-style buildings in the neighborhood. The interior reminds me of a Victorian parlor. With low lighting, antiques, wooden wainscoting, cozy tables and booths, along with a piano and a huge silvered mirror behind the bar, it's a great place to have a relaxed meal and a great drink in a lovely ambience. The bar is a convivial spot where you can chat with your friends or make new friends while you enjoy a number of specialty drinks made up by skilled bartenders (German chocolate cake martini, anyone?). A full menu is available at the bar, or you can sit in the outdoor patio (my first choice) at tiny metal tables and chairs surrounded by whitewashed adobe walls and fragrant orange trees under twinkling white lights. The small menu offers a combination of haute and home cooking with meat loaf, seared ahi with a ginger and jicama slaw, and an excellent shrimp quesadilla stuffed with large grilled shrimp, generous amounts of cheese and poblano peppers, and grilled just till crispy on the outside. Desserts include a rich, homemade chocolate mousse pie. There is no rush here, a trio playing light live jazz fills up the space on select Saturday nights and the patio is often the setting for special music events under the stars. Open for dinner Tues through Sat from 5 p.m.

La Cocina, 201 N. Court Ave., Tucson, AZ 85701; (520) 622-0351; lacocinatucson.com; American; $. They are really cooking at La Cocina, with lots of live entertainment and a menu full of excellent food. Owner Jo Schneider has turned this space inside the historic Old Artisans complex (built on the site of the original fort, El Presidio San Augustin del Tucson, established in 1775 by the Spanish), into a hopping, happening, attractive restaurant. The way in is through the little house that leads you into the heart of the space—the open-air courtyard. Plastic patio chairs and tables and garden benches surround a plant-filled pond and large outdoor stage roofed with corrugated iron. Old-growth mesquite trees roped with white Christmas lights make for a shady, restful space. Indoor seating in the cantina consists of about 10 metal-topped vintage tables and wooden school chairs amid low lighting in a space that also houses the bar. Opt for the outside if you can—this is a busy venue that fills up fast with live music four nights a week, featuring local bands and musicians. The eclectic Asian-inspired menu is full of terrific vegan and vegetarian options. While all sorts of beer, wine, and signature cocktails are on tap, I opt for the house-made ginger soda. A refreshing fizz of seltzer with fresh pureed ginger root and a not-too-sweet simple syrup, you will want several refills, it's delicious. Start off with the spring rolls, served with a yummy peanut sauce for dipping, they are some of the best I've had, full of cellophane noodles and big slices of avocado, lettuce, jicama, and carrots (in addition to your choice of tofu or chicken). The quinoa plate is equally good; a fluffy mound of quinoa is surrounded by sautéed spinach and onions, your choice of protein (chicken is tender and flavorful), and garnished with pickled carrots. Sandwiches, salads, pot roast, tacos, salmon, pizza, pasta, nachos, hummus, and bruschetta are all offered here too. Desserts are all homemade—the spicy hot fudge sundae is a great mix of hot and cold sure to keep your feet tapping to the music. Open Mon 10 a.m. to 3 p.m., Tues through Fri 10 a.m. to 10 p.m., Sat 9 a.m. to 10 p.m., Sun 9 a.m. to 3 p.m. The bar is open until 2 a.m. Wed through Sat.

Maynards, 400 N. Toole Ave., Tucson, AZ 85701; (520) 545-0577; maynardsmarkettucson.com; French/American; $$$. Housed in the gorgeously renovated historic train depot built in 1941, Maynards is a real dining destination both for its food and ambience. Chef Addam Buzzalini's seasonal menus feature the very freshest, locally sourced ingredients, many culled from the Saturday Farmers Market at his doorstep. Step inside the restaurant and it's like walking into a private railcar. Windows offer a view of the train tracks where passenger and freight trains whizz past day and night. Soft lighting, heavy drapes, and dark woods soothe you as you review the menu, and highly professional staff hover to answer any and all questions about where the food comes from and how it's prepared. Salads feature locally grown greens, and the occasional wild green (think dandelion, amaranth) with delectable house-made vinaigrettes (hazelnut and smoked maple). For hors d'oeuvres, try the

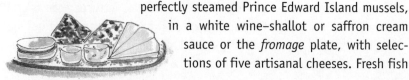

perfectly steamed Prince Edward Island mussels, in a white wine–shallot or saffron cream sauce or the *fromage* plate, with selections of five artisanal cheeses. Fresh fish is always sustainable, and prepared *à la minute,* ask your server about the day's catch. The chef's French influences can be seen in his entrees: coq au vin, choucroute garni, and bouillabaisse are a few of the several choices. Small portion sizes let you try everything without feeling stuffed. Chef Buzzalini is always creating new specials inspired by the season and availability of local products. Don't miss the Sunday Farmers' Market Suppers, held monthly, where he and his talented staff use their creative juices to create a seasonal special multicourse dinner including wine pairings and served family-style. Open Mon through Sun starting at 11 a.m. for lunch and dinner.

U of A
& Fourth Avenue

When people say "University" they are generally referring to the area around the University of Arizona, bustling with students during the school year and with limited street parking. There are loads of restaurants here along the main drag (University Avenue) that starts just outside the main entrance to campus. Eateries are mixed in with coffee shops, retail stores, parking garages, and a high-rise hotel. Fourth Avenue is a north/south busy street that intersects with University. This multi-block area is an eclectic combination of bars, coffee shops, vintage and thrift stores, a bookstore, tattoo parlors, and restaurants of all shapes and sizes. While University is mostly packed with students, Fourth Avenue has a bit of a gritty, bohemian ambience.

Athens on 4th Avenue, 500 N. Fourth Ave., Tucson, AZ 85705; (520) 624-6886; athenson4th.com; Greek; $$. This upscale restaurant serving traditional Greek cuisine straddles the corner of 4th Avenue and Fifth Street. Owned by the Delfakis family, who have operated it since 1994, this 4th Avenue mainstay has a lovely, cozy dining room and a private inner courtyard where you may see a whole lamb turning on a spit. Owner Andreas Delfakis, originally from Dara, Greece, prides himself on offering authentic Greek cuisine prepared with top-quality ingredients including olive oil and cheeses imported from Greece. Service is attentive and very helpful if you are not sure what to order from the extensive menu. *Oretika* (appetizers) include taramosalata (one of my favorites). The addictive, creamy, salty spread made with olive oil, lemon juice, and carp roe is served with warm pita bread. The sampler plate is a good way to try a variety of appetizers; it's filled with cheeses (feta, kefalotiri), olives, and grape leaves. House specialties include a braised lamb shank in a stew of tomatoes and spices, served with flat beans and rice; and *gleekthakia,* tender seared sweetbreads with garlic and scallions. Traditional dishes available on the menu include a hearty, rich pastisio with layers of béchamel, pasta, and ground beef; and flaky spanakopita here made with spinach and herbs. There are many seafood dishes to choose from. Check with your server for the fresh fish of the day, prepared with garlic, white wine, and herbs, and order it with the wonderful roasted potato wedges. *Milopita,* cinnamon spice apples baked in layers of phyllo dough is a dessert not seen elsewhere and a great way to end your meal. Closed Sun. Open for dinner Mon through Sat at 4 p.m.

B-Line, 621 N. Fourth Ave., Tucson, AZ 85705; (520) 882-7575; blinerestaurant.com; Southwest; $. Sleek with large picture windows looking out at 4th Avenue, B-line was a top pick for Rachael Ray when she breezed into town with the Food Network some years ago. You can sit inside at the counter along the windows or head up a few steps to several cozy dining areas. Known for their homemade baked goods and Southwest-style bistro food, this is a popular spot for breakfast and lunch. For breakfast, try the signature crepe cakes. These huge, thin pancakes are topped with a chunky pecan butter and served with a little pitcher of real maple syrup. Bagel sandwiches and breakfast burritos are also on the menu, and they're easy to grab and go along with a great cup of coffee if you're on your way to work and don't have time to sit. Lunch and dinner are casual sit-down affairs, with giant salads (get them all with the house-made raspberry vinaigrette), upscale versions of tacos, burros (try blackened ahi ahi), quesadillas, soups, sandwiches, and big bowls of specialty pastas. Desserts here are amazing, all made from scratch by pastry chef Terri La Chance and impossible to resist. The pies,

 made daily (many berry combinations and peach) are served warm or cold with real whipped cream, and the peanut butter cookies and brownies are so good you will want to buy dozens to take home—I do! Open daily at 7 a.m.

Boca, 828 E. Speedway Blvd., Tucson, AZ 85716; (520) 777-8134; bocatacos.com; Mexican; $. Duck, ostrich, cuttlefish, all these ingredients find their way into the incredibly inventive tacos created by Chef-Owner Maria Jose Mazon, whose creative mind tosses together all sorts of amazing things and slaps them on her homemade corn and flour tortillas. You might pass this place by as you race along Speedway, there's nothing to the bland concrete building set back from the road, marked only by the tall sign sporting sexy red lips and the word *boca*. Your *boca* will be extremely glad if you do stop here. Up to 18 different kinds of tacos, homemade salsas, and over 40 tequilas await you inside the tiny space with only four tables and a counter. Everything is cooked to order, so be prepared to wait a bit—these are not fast-food tacos. Tacos are priced individually and are small so you can order a whole bunch of them to try. The *rajas* tacos, filled with expertly sautéed poblanos and onions, are a great choice; octopus tacos are filled with chewy, flavorful little chunks of octo on a smear of house-made sauce and topped with chopped cabbage. All tacos come with three sauces, but beware of the innocent-looking strawberry sauce—a super-spicy combo of fresh strawberries and habañeros, it will definitely make your *boca* burn. Open Mon through Sat at 11 a.m., Sun at noon.

Brooklyn Pizza Company, 534 N. Fourth Ave., Tucson, AZ 85705; (520) 622-6868; Pizza; $. Solar pizza anyone? All the pizza ovens here are powered by the solar panels at the parking lot next door.

You'll find all sorts of folks here, from dreadlocked, skateboarding students to young families and retirees. Pizza makers are on view right in front of the oven, throwing large disks of floury dough into the air, catching them expertly, saucing them on the countertop and flinging them into the heat on massive wooden pad-

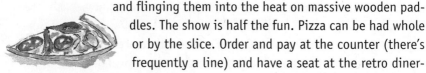

dles. The show is half the fun. Pizza can be had whole or by the slice. Order and pay at the counter (there's frequently a line) and have a seat at the retro diner-style tables and they'll call your name when it's ready. Pizza here is thin crust, with a smear of sauce and generous hand-fuls of cheese. There are lots of different toppings: vegans and veg-etarians will find artichoke hearts, broccoli, eggplant, mushrooms, and potato, and carnivores can choose from Italian sausage, bacon, chicken, meatballs, and pepperoni. They even deliver within the area, a boon for UA students but not so hot for those of us living outside the nabe and craving a slice. Open daily at 11 a.m.

China Pasta House, 430 N. Park Ave., Tucson, AZ 85719; (520) 623-3334; chinapastahouse.com; Chinese; $. You will have to look really, really hard to find this place. It's a nondescript concrete building stuck back from the busy corner of 6th and Park. Teeny tiny inside with only a few tables and chairs, it serves up some amazing noodles. And that's all you should get here. Oodles and oodles of ramen noodles, made by hand in the back behind the curtained doorway. The servers don't speak much English so don't expect lengthy descriptions of the food and the cooking methods. Just order the noodles. Any noodle dish with pork is delicious—the noodle texture is soft and stretchy and the broth rich and flavorful. Noodles come steaming to the table in plastic bowls with a spoon and maybe some chopsticks if you ask. Slurp away, no one cares about manners here, just great flavors. There is absolutely no decor, some Chinese calendars and a few posters but you won't care because you will be transported to a small village in China where mom has placed a simple pot of homemade noodles on the table for the family. Open Mon through Fri at 8 a.m., weekends at 11 a.m.

Delectable's, 433 N. Fourth Ave., Tucson, AZ 85705; (520) 884-9289; American; $$. Originally built in 1946 as a Harley-Davidson showroom, Delectable's has been an anchor restaurant on Fourth Avenue since it opened in 1973. Owner Diana DiFiore serves up homemade super salads, soups, and sandwiches along with a slew of tasty entrees and vegan and vegetarian specials. This is a popular spot to hang out and chat, especially at the intimate dog-friendly outdoor patio that hugs the side of the building. An open dining area with semicircle of big windows offers a great view of the avenue, and unique local art lines the walls. The salads here are legendary, served in super-large bowls brimming with fresh ingredients. The signature salad here is the Chef's Salad, chock-full of romaine leaves, turkey, artichoke hearts, peperoncini, cabbage, olives, cucumber, hard-boiled egg, feta cheese, and tomato wedges, dressed with Thousand Island, blue cheese, citrus vinaigrette, or dill ranch. The 201 Sampler makes for a great starter, featuring hummus, quiche, and brie served with baguette slices and fresh fruit. The entrees have an international flair: You'll find selections from Italy (pasta puttanesca), France (quiche), Mexico (enchiladas), and the good ole US of A (build your own burgers). It's very family-friendly here, with a large kids' menu sure to please any kid (PB&J, spaghetti, melted-cheese sandwich, burger, all served with fresh fruit). Drinks are kid-friendly too, with Shirley Temple and Roy Rogers on the kiddie drinks menu. Open Mon through Sat at 11 a.m., Sun at 10 a.m.

Frog and Firkin, 874 E. University Ave., Tucson, AZ 85719; (520) 623-7575; frogandfirkin.com; Beer; $. The Frog, as it is commonly referred to, is always packed with lots of college students laughing, drinking, and eating at outdoor tables that are crowded onto the outdoor patio right on University. It's a good place to meet friends for a casual meal and great beer—there are over 75 imported beers available here. Loud music, live or recorded, plays night and day, keeping the vibe upbeat and active. You'll find lots of lagers, ales, wheat, porter, and stouts on the extensive beer menu, both on tap and in the bottle. On the menu, lots of beer-friendly food. Popular appetizers are the Frog Bites, sliced baguettes topped with garlic, pesto, and a raft of melted mozzarella, and the Pile o' Fries, topped with melted cheddar (yellow fries), pesto and brie (green fries), or tomato sauce and mozzarella (red fries). You'll also find other things that go well with beer here: burgers, a huge selection of pizzas, sandwiches, and fish-and-chips—all frogilicious. A jukebox, darts, and a pool table, it's all here to keep you entertained. You can even buy "Frog gear" (T-shirts, hats) to remind you of the hopping good time you had here. Open daily at 11 a.m.

Gentle Ben's Brewing Company, 865 E. University Blvd., Tucson, AZ 85719; (520) 624-4177; gentlebens.com; Brewpub; $. Located just down the block from the U of A's Main Gate, this friendly brew pub has been brewing beer and drawing crowds since 1991, way before the microbrewery and gastropub craze hit nationwide. There are lots of seating options here—outside under a wooden-beamed covered porch, upstairs in the large dining space, upstairs on the outdoor vine-covered deck, or at the dining room and bar downstairs. Wherever you decide to sit, the beer is the thing here and you can even see it being brewed in the glass-enclosed vats inside. Tucson Blonde is a signature brew, light and crisp. Ask your server or a bartender to make some recommendations—there are so many different choices, and they can help you pair your beer with whatever you plan to order from the menu. To eat?

Lots of hearty comfort foods. Start off right with an order of "beer sponges," house-made soft pretzels that come with a zesty beer mustard. They are justly famous for their wings here. Crispy, hot, and tossed with your choice of hot or hotter sauces, they come with cooling buttermilk ranch on the side. The pizza dough gets its yeasty flavor from a hit of Tucson Blonde,  with tons of toppings to choose from. I usually go for a stromboli to soak up the suds. This is a giant crescent of house-made dough, filled with just about anything you want, brushed with red sauce and garlic oil, dusted with cheese, and baked till crusty. I like the Original, a mix of capocollo ham, pepperoni, salami, mozzarella, provolone, and mustard. It is guaranteed to fill you up and keep you thirsty. Salads, sandwiches, pasta, and lots of daily specials round out the menu. Dessert? The beer float, of course! A tall glass of Nolan Porter beer with scoops of vanilla ice cream, has there ever been a better combination? Open Mon through Sat at 10 a.m., Sun at noon.

Joel's Bistro, 806 E. University Blvd., Tucson, AZ 85719; (520) 529-7277; French; $. This little treasure box is hidden away in Geronimo Plaza. Step up into a quaint, adorable dining room with a French provincial feel and menu. Chef-Owner Joel Suira has created a real culinary oasis here away from the hustle and bustle of busy University Avenue. He makes a mean breakfast, with delicious crepes filled with a variety of fresh fruit or just adorned with cinnamon and sugar. Breakfast burritos, scrumptious eggs Benedict, french toast, and perfect omelets (try the supreme, filled with lobster) all come with addictive roasted potatoes and fresh fruit on the side. Quiche is made from scratch with a buttery crust and custardy fillings featuring anything from shrimp and crab to spinach and herbs. You can also sit outside at a few little tables sprinkled around the front steps, but I prefer the adorable dining room. Open Mon through Sun from 8 a.m. to 3 p.m.

La Indita, 622 N. Fourth Ave., Tucson, AZ 85705; (520) 704-9240; lainditarestaurant.com; Mexican; $. A Tucson original, La Indita has been offering homemade regional Mexican cooking on Fourth since 1983. Beautiful, large-scale, hand-painted murals of rural Mexico along with primitive art grace the walls of this gem, which consists of two separate high-ceilinged dining areas and an outdoor patio. This family-run spot serves a mixture of indigenous Mexican dishes and no pork products. There are unusual dishes here, some influenced by Michoacan, Tarascan, and O'odham cuisines. Things to try include the Tarascan tacos, chicken mole, flat enchiladas, chicken enchiladas with green sauce, and fry bread. The Tarascan tacos are more like empanadas, with thick handmade corn tortillas folded over a variety of fillings (spinach, beef, chicken, bean, *carne seca*) and deep fried. Not at all greasy, they are hearty and filling, and the mild spinach/nut filling is different and tasty. Chicken mole brings chicken breast smothered in a thick black mole sauce made with chocolate, peanuts, prunes, ancho peppers, and spices. It's not a pretty plate but the mole has serious depth of flavor with a strong cumin overtone. The flat enchiladas are made with layers of homemade corn tortillas topped with red chile sauce and a vinegary carrot and potato mixture that adds a welcome hit of acid to the dish. Chicken enchiladas with green sauce are soft and comforting, with a shredded chicken filling and creamy sauce on top. Lots of people come here for fry bread (also known as popovers). Although it's not an indigenous O'odham food, it is strongly identified with native people who used commodity foods provided by the government to create this ingenious "native pizza." Here disks of dough are deep fried till crispy and topped with beans, beef, red chile, lettuce, and grated cheese. It's definitely home-style cooking here, hearty and filling. Open Mon, Wed, Thurs, and Fri from 11 a.m. for lunch and dinner, Tues from 11 a.m. to 1 p.m. for lunch only, Sat at 6 a.m. for breakfast, lunch, and dinner and Sun at 9 a.m. for breakfast, lunch, and dinner.

Lindy's on Fourth, 431 N. Fourth Ave., Tucson, AZ 85705; (520) 207-6970; lo4th.com; Burgers; $. It may look like a take-out window from the sidewalk, but Lindy's is a sit-down burger joint with loud rock music, brushed metal walls, a small  countertop, and tables all dressed up in black and red and reflected in large mirrors hung from the walls. Lindy's special burger sauce is spicy and so is its menu, with the tag line "battling anorexia one cheeseburger at a time" prominently displayed. But don't let that stop you, the burgers are awesome here. Owner Lindy Reilly is known for his wacky sense of humor and his ginormous burgers. The king of them all is the omfg burger: three pounds of meat, with mushrooms, onion rings, cheese, Lindy's sauce, lettuce, tomato, and onion between two grilled cheese sandwiches. Even Adam Richman of *Man v. Food* couldn't eat it all. For those of us with smaller appetites, every burger on the menu can be had with one, two, or three patties. All the patties are a third of a pound of good beef, cooked just right, and sandwiched inside a soft bun. There are several funky burger choices on the menu—some I've never heard of or even imagined. Take the Ninja with pineapple, provolone, and wasabi aioli, or the Kush with raspberry jam, green chiles, blue cheese, and bacon. Sides include fries and tots, plain or smothered in hot sauce and ketchup, or bacon, cheese, sour cream, and chives. Everything is over the top here, including the humor. Open Mon from 11 a.m. to 4 p.m., Tues through Sat from 11 a.m. for lunch and dinner, Sun from noon to 5 p.m.

Pasco Kitchen and Lounge, 820 E. University Blvd., Tucson, AZ 85719; (520) 882-8013; Farm to Table; $$. Chef-Owner Ramiro Scavo brings his farm-to-market concept alive here, with all ingredients sourced from regional farmers. Seating is available on a large front outdoor patio, indoors at tables scattered around the casual, low-ceilinged dining area or outside at the edges of the lovely Geronimo Plaza with its shady trees and fountain (my pick). The menu features fresh, local ingredients transformed into upscale comfort food and drinks. Cocktails are innovative and delicious, made with fresh-squeezed juices, syrups, and mixers made in house and handmade garnishes (candied grapefruit, brandied cherries). The Harlem Renaissance features house-made limoncello, house-made rosemary syrup, and fresh lemon; the Father Kino blends tequila, muddled cucumber and cilantro, and jalapeño-spiced agave nectar. Water is served in Ball jars and the atmosphere is casual chic. The Asian Salad is one of my favorite things on the eclectic menu. A delectable combination of organic greens, fried wontons, chives, orange supremes, fresh pineapple chunks, radishes, bok choy, and sesame seeds in a light vinaigrette, it's a meal in itself (you can order a half portion). Vegetarian friends love the Quinoa Super Food Bowl and fish lovers enjoy the fish and grits with fried okra and braised greens. The menu tends to change with different entrees offered seasonally that reflect what the chef has found at local markets and received from local purveyors. Thankfully the dessert that doesn't change is the amazing, melt-in-your-mouth beignets, deep-fried, chocolate-filled orbs served atop a spicy cayenne-infused caramel sauce. Don't skip them, and let's hope they are never, ever taken off the menu. Open daily from 11 a.m. for lunch and dinner.

1702, 1702 E. Speedway Blvd., Tucson, AZ 85719; (520) 325-1702; 1702az.com; Beer; $. You'd never know that what looks like a casual pizza parlor at first glance is really home to hundreds of innovative craft beers. If you've been searching for that special beer brewed only by monks in Bavaria, chances are you'll find it here with over 50 specialty imported beers and many, many more domestic craft beers on draught and by the bottle. The vast selection changes frequently and the choices are listed on long typed lists available at the counter that give details about each beer—where it's from, flavor profile, and alcohol content. They are so serious about their beer here that it's even served in specific styles of glassware to enhance the flavor and aroma. This place is a real U of A grad student hangout, with well-used tables and chairs and UA sports paraphernalia. Red and black are the theme colors of the casual "decor." If you are a beer lover, this is a perfect spot to sample some unusual brews along with a slice. Pizzas are available whole or by the slice with tons of different toppings, from the standard cheese and pepperoni to the more unusual chorizo with green chiles and barbecue chicken with pineapple. They also offer wings (ask for them with the specialty sauce of the moment) and salads (go for the PHS, with pepperoni, ham, salami, green peppers, tomato, and mozzarella) and an unusual garlic cheese bread served up with fresh leaf hops strewn over top. Even the ice cream (all made here) has a beery twist—a special beer-infused selection is available daily, check the small list at the counter or ask your server (note: you have to be 21 to order this!). Closed Sun, open Sat at noon and all other days at 11 a.m.

The Tasteful Kitchen, 722 N. Stone Ave., Tucson, AZ 85705; (520) 250-9600; thetastefulkitchen.com; Vegetarian; $$. Sisters Keanne and Sigret Thompson have brought raw, vegan, and vegetarian fine dining to Tucson, and we are grateful. This slip of a place is hard to find, wedged into an industrial area just north of downtown. There is no noticeable signage so keep your eyes peeled. Sigret creates all the signature dishes here. She is a self-taught chef and very serious about her flavors, seasonal ingredients, and the sustainable sources of her all her foods. Keanne (a dead ringer for Talia Shire) handles the front of house with zen-like concentration. The decor is not much to speak of; soft lighting, local artwork on the walls, and basic tables and chairs all coexist in a simple orange-hued space. The prix-fixe tasting menu will give you a great sense of all the healthy and delicious goodness being served here. Freshly pressed juices in unusual combinations (pineapple, beet, and red pepper) kick off the meal, followed by soup, salad, and your choice of several entrees. Soups are beautifully presented in small white bowls and garnished with local herbs. You might find a miso-ginger consommé sprinkled with scallions or a creamy carrot avocado with house-made kale chips on the menu. The house salad is a mélange of mixed greens, jicama julienne, and orange segments tossed in Sigret's special **Apple-Cumin Vinaigrette** (see her recipe on p. 272), it's light, crisp, and refreshing. Entrees can range anywhere from enchiladas (corn tortillas filled with a surprisingly meaty combination of spinach, mushroom, millet, and cilantro-pumpkinseed pesto topped with salsa verde) to a spring vegetable risotto with roasted tomatoes and a vegan cream sauce. Sigret is always experimenting with new combinations and recipes so the menu changes quite frequently. The desserts are winners too, especially my absolute favorite of all time, the gluten-free orange cake. Served ice cold, it's an intensely orangey, dense but spongy cake that I just cannot get enough of. It's usually served with a drizzle of house-made vegan chocolate sauce, but it really doesn't

 need a thing, it's perfect. If you want to learn more about vegan and raw cuisine, Sigret offers hands-on classes on a regular basis, check her Facebook page or website. Open for dinner Wed through Sat from 5 p.m. and Sun at 4.

Tooley's Cafe, 29 S. Park Ave., Tucson, AZ 85719; (520) 623-3735; tooleyscafe.com; Mexican; $. I adore this funky place smack dab in the middle of the Lost Barrio. Finding the Lost Barrio can be a challenge so take your time and don't get frustrated when Park suddenly dead-ends into Broadway and you have to go around again (it's probably just me, even with mapping functions on my car and phone, I still seem to get lost). Here since 1989, Tooley's may like being lost but you will be sooo happy that you've found it—it's the only restaurant here amidst curio, antiques, and furniture shops and an industrial laundry service. The wide patio is a super spot for any meal, quiet, tree lined, and decorated with simple tables and chairs. Inside is quaint and spacious, with lots of charm and no pretentions. Good, inexpensive food arrives for breakfast and lunch, served all day. Delicious corn pancakes with black beans and a spicy jalapeño syrup, chipotle pork hash, the Starving Artist (2 eggs, rice, and grilled veggies with salsa), and a cup of espresso or cappuccino make for a terrific breakfast. House specials not to miss are the turkey enchiladas in a rich mole sauce, and the Aris special, a big bowl of black beans, rice, sour cream, and salsa with a flour tortilla so you can scoop it up or roll it into your own burrito. Quesadillas, tacos, and burros all come stuffed with Tooley's turkey in all sorts of guises. They march to the beat of a different drummer here. Service can be very laid back so don't stop by if you're in a big hurry—it's not always open when it says it is, and they never answer the phone so you'll have to take your chances. But when you do find it open, it's worth it! Published hours are Mon through Fri 9 a.m. to 4 p.m., Sat and Sun till 3 p.m. Hand-lettered signs on site tell a different story (Mon to Sat 9 a.m. to 3 p.m.). Cash only.

Wilko, 943 E. University Blvd., Tucson, AZ 85719; (520) 792-6684; wilkotucson.com; American; $$. This inviting barn-like space is like being in a big country kitchen with warm, dark woods, exposed ductwork, an open kitchen, and a long wooden bar. Sit at communal, heavy wood tables, or on your own along the wall of windows with a view of University Gate, where you can watch the UA world go by while you peruse the drinks menu. There is a wide variety of amazing specialty craft cocktails mixed up here. Consult your server or the ever-changing list at your table to see what the crafty mixologists have created from herbs, spices, infused syrups,  and top-shelf liquors. For starters, graze on the artisanal cheese plate, three selections of domestic specialty cheeses with baguette slices and sour, crunchy cornichons, or the charcuterie plate of delicately sliced artisan-cured meats including sopressata and salami. The soups are yummy (curried carrot is especially delish), and salads are generously portioned and inventive. The Asian salad brings an enormous bowl of shredded napa, fennel, and sesame seeds in a sweet ginger dressing (get it topped with a moist filet of wild caught salmon). Comfort-food choices on the small entree menu include mac and cheese, burgers, sandwiches, pizzas with unusual toppings (the Murcia has pine nuts, Drunken Goat cheese, and fresh mint leaves), pasta, and seafood. Open daily from 8 a.m. for breakfast, lunch, and dinner.

Landmark

Caruso's, 434 N. Fourth Ave., Tucson, AZ 85705; (520) 634-5765; carusoitalian.com; Italian; $$. It seems like Caruso's has been here forever, wait, it *has* been here forever. Set back from the sidewalk and surrounded by a tall, wrought-iron fence, it can escape your notice as you walk by but it has been serving homey American-Italian food since the 1930s. Owned and operated by the Zagona family since the beginning, it has a large, open dining area and a lovely covered outdoor patio inside the gate. Decor is low key with checked red-and-white tablecloths and casual furniture. Caruso's is a dying breed of Italian restaurant that showcases the recipes that people brought with them from their homeland and found a way to cook in a new land, sometimes improvising with the ingredients (there was a time when the olive oil, canned tomatoes, and Parmesan cheese in the grocery store were not imported from Italy). The vibe here reminds me of my own grandma's kitchen, a warm gathering place where there was always a pan of tomato sauce on the stove and a pot of water merrily boiling, ready for a handful of pasta. Going to Caruso's is like taking a step back into time and should not be missed. Longtime waitstaff bring over the menu and wait patiently for drink and food orders. This is not Euro fusion

Italian but immigrant Italian fare, where sauce is called gravy, pizza is pizza-pie, and food is prepared with gusto by hardworking cooks. The hearty baked pastas are the way to go here: lasagna, stuffed shells, manicotti, cannelloni, rigatoni, all covered with mamma's homemade sauce (also known as Caruso's sauce). Another good choice is the homemade meat and cheese ravioli that can be had with meat, garlic-mushroom, Alfredo, butter, or pesto sauce. For dessert, opt for the spumoni, a rainbow of ice cream sauced with almond cream, *buonissimo*. Open Tues through Sun at 11:30 a.m.

Regional Gastronomic Info

Specialty Stores, Gourmet Shops & Purveyors

Some people like to shop for shoes or clothes or furniture. Me? I love to shop for food, and one of my favorite things to do is to visit specialty food markets. I can spend hours wandering down the aisles full of exotic foods, scanning the funny literal translations on the labels. No matter how many times I visit, I always learn something new and run across an ingredient or product that I've never heard of. In addition to featuring many ethnic markets, Tucson is home to food co-ops and locally based stores carrying local and unusual regional products. There are quite a lot of choices here, from the giant warehouse to the tiny mom-and-pop, all with shelves full to the brim. I hope you enjoy them as much as I do!

Alejandro's Tortilla Factory, 5338 12th Ave., Tucson, AZ 85706; (520) 319-2279. A busy and unassuming market, Alejandro's is a bakery, butcher, and take-out restaurant. Almost everything you need to make delicious Mexican food is here, from the ingredients to the equipment. Shelves are full of many different kinds of chile powders and hot sauces (25 different kinds at last count!). A refrigerated section offers *nixtamal,* salsa, guacamole, and a small selection of seasonal produce. Equipment includes tortilla presses, *molcajetes,* hot-chocolate stirrers, citrus presses, and tamaleras for steaming your very own tamales. The butcher carries beef cheek, seafood, pork fat, chorizo, *chicharrones,* and carnitas too. If you want something already cooked to go, the counter inside (also known as La Cocina de Lorena), offers chile Colorado, *menudo,* and *carne asada* by the plate, gallon, quart, or pint. Alejandro's supplies tortillas to many area grocery stores, but you can get them from the source right here along with pastries and rolls. Open Mon, Tues, Thurs, and Fri 7 a.m. to 8 p.m.; Wed 7 a.m. to 7 p.m.; Sat 6 a.m. to 8 p.m.; Sun 6 a.m. to 7 p.m.

Anita's Street Market, 849 N. Anita Ave., Tucson, AZ 85705; (520) 882-5280. This teeny tiny market is really hard to find, hidden in the lovely Barrio Anita. Run by the third generation of the Soto family, it offers homemade tortillas and tamales that sell out fast. You'll find salsas, grandma's pickled green chiletepin peppers,

Local Chain: Bashas' Family of Stores

Founded by brothers Eddie and Ike Basha in 1932, this family-owned grocery chain owns and operates numerous food stores throughout Arizona. Locally, these consist of the eponymous Bashas' found citywide, the upscale AJ's in the Foothills, and Food City stores with several locations around town. If you are looking for high-end foods and household goods, AJ's is the place for you with a deli, sushi bar, coffee and pastry bar, hundreds of specialty items, a full butcher and fish counter, fine-wine section, and gorgeous produce. Bashas' offers standard grocery-store fare, while Food City features lots of Mexican and Hispanic ingredients and produce (prickly-pear pads, roasted agave, raw chickpeas, epazote, bulk pinto beans) with butchers, bakeries, and delis at some locations and lively in-store Mexican music so you can dance while you shop—I do!

spices, and snacks along the aisles. Closed Sun. Open Mon and Sat 8 a.m. to 5 p.m., Tues through Fri 8 a.m. to 5:30 p.m.

Babylon Market, 3954 E. Speedway Blvd., Tucson, AZ 85712; (520) 232-3700; wwwbabylonmarket.com. This well-stocked, busy store is chock-full of every Middle Eastern ingredient imaginable. This is the place to get fresh lamb. The small butcher section carries shanks and large and small legs, and the friendly butcher will cut to please. The shelves are lined with jarred and canned spreads, dips, vegetables, juices, oils, olives, cookies, pastries, mixes,

spices, herbs, grains, and lots more, many sourced from Syria, Iraq, and Lebanon. Freezer sections offer pita bread, filo, and a wide variety of packaged products. A small refrigerated area is home to homemade yogurt and cheeses. Don't miss the pastry housed at the front counter—ask for the "ladies arm," a homemade dessert of filo pastry filled with mild cheese and drizzled with sugar syrup. If you want to host your own Arab-themed feast, you can buy giant metal platters of all sizes, tra-ditional dresses, Turkish coffeemakers, cups,
rugs, and hookah pipes here too. If you have any questions, super-friendly owner Feras Rashid and his wife Raghad Ismail, originally from Iraq, are more than happy to help. Open every day, 9 a.m. to 9 p.m.

Caravan Mid Eastern Foods, 2817 Country Club Rd., Tucson, AZ 85716; (520) 323-6808. Small and fully packed, Caravan has one of the best selections of olives in town. Oil-cured, Syrian, spicy green, they are all waiting for you in bins in the refrigerated section, just grab a plastic bag and start filling it up. Canned goods including hummus, baba ghanoush, *fool medames,* and *harissa* line the shelves along with a selection of packaged items. A dairy case holds the addictive thick Lebanese yogurt *labni,* a variety of real feta cheeses from Bulgaria, yogurt drinks, and Syrian cheeses. There are bins full of dried fruit and nuts (my favorite are the roasted chickpeas). Couscous and bulgur wheat, ground coarsely or finely, are available bulk or packaged along with a nice selection of dried spices and herbs including dried mint. You'll find a wide assortment of teas and Arabic coffees, plus cups and coffeemakers too. They will grind coffee beans especially for Turkish coffeemakers—ask them to add cardamom pods to the grind for an authentic flavor. You will find short-grain Egyptian rice behind the counter, the best to use for stuffing grape leaves (they have these too!). Open Mon through Fri 10:30 a.m. to 7:30 p.m., Sat and Sun 10 a.m. to 6:30 p.m.

El Herradero Carniceria y Panaderia, 4211 E. 22nd St., Tucson, AZ 85711; (520) 881-3715. Clean and neat, you'll find fresh seafood, including shrimp from the Sea of Cortez, oysters, and freshly made ceviche here along with a full-scale meat counter offering tripe, skirt steak, tongue, and beef liver along with chicken, pork, and many cuts of beef. The best part of buying your meat here is that they will cook it too! Take it out to the parking lot where you'll find a few chairs surrounding a wood-fired grill. Hand over your meat, have a seat, and soon you will have beautifully grilled meat to go at no extra charge. An in-house bakery puts out freshly  made cookies, rolls, empanadas, fruit filled chimis, and a variety of brightly colored cakes. The round sweet bread made with *piloncillo* (cane sugar) is a unique specialty. Grocery items include many Mexican packaged products along with more unusual items including whole tamarind pods and candied *visnaga* (barrel cactus). They also carry bags of mesquite charcoal if you want to get that distinct mesquite flavor from your own grill. Open Mon through Sat 7:30 a.m. to 9 p.m., Sun 7:30 a.m. to 8 p.m.

European Market, 4500 E. Speedway Blvd., #36, Tucson, AZ 85712; (520) 512-0206. Russia, Croatia, Georgia, Bulgaria, Lithuania, Poland, Latvia . . . these are just a few of the countries that supply the many imported foods, beers, spirits, and wines that you'll find on the shelves here. Sausages, specialty cheeses, fruit syrups, jams, chocolates, pickles, and herbs join nesting dolls, lacquer boxes, and hand-embroidered linens in this cozy shop. You'll find dark rye bread, blintzes, crepes, pierogis, and strudel in the freezer, and specialty vodkas and beers in the cooler. There's a tiny, homey, indoor cafe in the back hosted by owner Olga (she tells me her last name is too long to include) who grew up in the Ukraine. Go for the items from the Russian menu; stuffed cabbage rolls, *vareniki, pelmeni,* blini, and borscht are great choices. Open Mon through Sat 9 a.m. to 8 p.m., Sun 9 a.m. to 3 p.m.

Food Conspiracy Co-op, 412 N. Fourth Ave., Tucson, AZ 85705; (520) 624-4821; foodconspiracycoop.com. The only food co-op in town, this natural foods market in the heart of the University area is small in size but big in spirit. It carries a huge selection of over 500 bulk items including grains, rice, beans, nuts, dried fruit, granola, teas, and herbs along with a limited selection of organic produce. Tall shelves are lined with mixes, sauces, condiments, snacks, cookies, chips, and many, many gluten-free, vegan, and vegetarian items, all healthy and PC—no GMO (genetically modified foods) products are sold here. Frozen meats and fish are all from sustainable sources. You don't have to be a member to shop here, but membership has its benefits—discounts, a newsletter, and a voice in products sourced for the store. Open daily from 8 a.m. to 10 p.m.

G&L Import, 4828 E. 22nd St., Tucson, AZ 85711; (520) 790-9016. Huge and cavernous, this is one of the oldest Asian markets in town. Ignore the sign outside that indicates dim sum is here—it's long gone, but what you will find are wide aisles filled with food and goods from all over the continent of Asia. You can easily get lost here, there is so much to see. Aisles are mostly organized by geographic area (Vietnam, India, Thailand, Japan), but also by type of ingredient—for example there is an aisle labeled "starch," and it doesn't refer to laundry. Canned, refrigerated, and frozen items predominate with huge freezers full of fish (whole, balls, filets), meats (pork snouts and feet, duck necks, oxtail, and a variety of intestines), leaves (tamarind, screwpipe, pandan, jute), fruit (coconut milk, grated coconut, sliced coconut, durian). Fresh items include a selection of produce and herbs, including bok choy, bitter melon, fresh water chestnuts, and duck eggs. Equally fascinating are the aisles full of cooking implements. They carry my favorite hard-to-find vegetable peelers along with giant woks, dumpling presses, spoons, plates, cups, teapots, soup bowls, steaming baskets, stackable metal steamers, clay pots, and an electric fish roaster that I'm saving my pennies to buy! Open Mon through Sat 9 a.m. to 8 p.m., Sun 10 a.m. to 6 p.m.

India Dukaan Fine Food Market, 2754 N. Campbell Ave., Tucson, AZ 85719; (520) 321-0408. Small, clean, and neat, this is the only market in town that sells refrigerated Indian sweets, nicely packaged and ready to eat. You'll also find several varieties of basmati rice, dhal, lentil flour, jarred chutneys, packaged curries and sauces, spices, and teas. A small freezer holds frozen samosas, naan, rotis, and dosas. A few of the more unusual items here include coconut-milk flour, jaggery, and whole grains used for ceremonial purposes. Open Mon through Fri 10 a.m. to 2:45 p.m. and 4:30 to 8 p.m., Sat and Sun 10 a.m. to 8 p.m.

India Food & Gifts, 863 E. Grant Rd., Tucson, AZ 85719; (520) 624-2474. Tucked away in a little corner of a strip mall, this tiny store has been in operation since 1997. I love this place because it always smells good. Although his store is small, owner Pradip Kedia has carefully stocked the well-organized shelves with quality items. And if you want personal attention, or have questions about a specific ingredient, Indian cuisine, or restaurants, he has the answers. A wide variety of *pappadums* (plain, black pepper, garlic, cumin), many varieties of flour including *irad* and rice flours, rices, and a wide selection of frozen items are available here. Unusual spices, whole and ground include, *supari, methi, saunf,* and *kali*—ask Mr. Kedia what they are! They also sell a huge selection of Bollywood movies, incense, and some lovely bangles and cotton shirts. Closed Mon. Open Tues through Sat 11 a.m. to 8 p.m., Sun noon to 8:30 p.m.

Joy Asian Market, 6261 N. Oracle Rd., Tucson, AZ 85704; (520) 531-1121. Specializing in Korean ingredients, this little place is small and manageable and the ladies who work here are very helpful. There is a nice selection of teas, spices, and mixes, and a large bank of freezer chests full of sushi-grade fish along a side wall. What sets this market apart is the handmade sushi, prepared fresh on select days, that can be ordered from a window in the back of the store. If you want to learn how to make your own, sushi-making classes are offered for a minimum of two people. Not publicized but highly popular, on Saturday afternoon they make traditional Korean dishes from scratch in the little back kitchen; the *jap chae* is delicious. Open Mon through Sat 9:30 a.m. to 7 p.m., Sun 2 p.m. to 6 p.m.

Kimpo Oriental Market, 5595 E. Fifth St., Tucson, AZ 85711; (520) 750-9009. At the entrance of this small but fully packed store, don't be intimidated by the odd display of mechanical toilet seats. Head on in and try to wend your way through the tiny aisles stuffed with products from Korea, Japan, and China. You'll find shelves of food, toiletries, and kitchen equipment here. A refrigerated section has seaweed salads, glutinous rice balls, and a variety of homemade and commercial kimchees I haven't seen elsewhere. Aisles hold seaweed, snacks and cookies, teas, lots and lots of bagged beans of all kinds, and rice. Open Mon through Sat 9 a.m. to 8 p.m., Sun 1 p.m. to 6 p.m.

Lee Lee Market, 1990 W. Orange Grove Rd., Tucson, AZ 85704; (520) 638-8328; leeleesupermarket.com. The biggest of them all, this market is one of three in the state of Arizona, and Tucson is lucky to have it! In the northwest section of town, it offers what has to be the largest selection of Asian food in town. One of the best features here is the seafood: a huge selection of live, frozen, and refrigerated fish and shellfish. Dungeness crab, mussels, lobster,

oysters, baby octopus, Manila clams, yellow carp, I could go on and on. . . . Even better, the expert butchers behind the counter will pull a live fish out of the tank before your eyes and clean and filet it for you on the spot. An equally large meat counter offers many, many meats and unusual (for me) things like pork blood, duck gizzard, black chicken, pork neck, and chicken feet. I won't even try to describe the aisles full of products—canned, bottled, boxed, bagged, frozen, dried, there is everything here. A very nice refrigerated produce section has herbs, vegetables, shredded green papaya, yucca root, tiny eggplants, and lots more. Drinks, packaged pastries, breads, and cookies, along with many Asian newspapers and a special section of medicinal herbs are also available. You can stay here for days and not get through it all, so wear comfortable walking shoes because you will be putting on the miles just looking around. What don't they have here? If you come up with something, let me know! Open 9 a.m. to 9 p.m. daily.

Maynard's Market, 400 N. Toole Ave., Tucson, AZ 85701; (520) 545-0577; maynardsmarket.com. Upscale and attractive and set up like an old-fashioned country store, this is the place to find all kinds of locally and regionally produced products. There

are over 40 vendors who supply the market with mesquite flour, ice cream, cheesecake, heirloom beans, bars, breads, jams, salsas, olive oil, tubs of local honey, and chocolates. Maynard's also sells its own brand of pickled veggies, sauces, dressings, jarred whole fruit, and fruit butters. They also do a brisk to-go lunch and breakfast business, serving up tasty soups, baked goods, salads, cheese plates, and sandwiches. Open Mon through Sat 7 a.m. to 10 p.m., Sun 7 a.m. to 8 p.m.

Nur Market International Foods, 3565 E. Speedway Blvd., Ste. 171, Tucson, AZ 85716; (520) 881-6333. Don't judge a book by its cover—this may look like a concrete block, but inside you'll find an assortment of African, Mediterranean, and Indo-Pakistani products. The selection is not huge, but there are some unusual things to be had here. Foremost among them is fresh goat meat. Somali owner Mohamed Osman sources goats from a local rancher and will have one slaughtered just for you by special request; orders must be placed on Monday for pickup on Thursday. You can purchase a whole goat or pieces, just let Mohamed know what you need. All meat is halal. The store also sells locally made *injira,* a spongy bread available in large rounds. Open daily from 9 a.m. to 8 p.m.

Rincon Market, 2513 E. 6th St., Tucson, AZ 85716; (520) 327-6653; rinconmarket.com. Somewhat of a Tucson landmark, this neighborhood grocer near the U of A campus has been in operation since 1926. This is a real watering hole for neighborhood folks who linger over coffee and shoot the breeze throughout the day. There are two sections to this market: a small produce, refrigerated goods, baked goods, deli, salad bar, to-go area, and a larger supermarket-style section down a small ramp. On the deli side you'll find sand-wiches, hot items, and a big salad bar.  The small bakery case offers pastries (the chocolate éclairs are a good choice as are the peppermint brownies made only at Christmas). The to-go winner here is the roasted chicken, cooked to perfection on a rotis-serie and held hot in paper bags, not sweating in plastic. It is the best chicken in town. The fish and meat counter offers top-of-the-line seafood and meats, extremely fresh and presided over by local personality and fish monger Yuri Rabiyev, who will give you the provenance of every bit of protein in the case. Open Mon through Fri 7 a.m. to 9 p.m., Sat 7 a.m. to 8 p.m., Sun 8 a.m. to 8 p.m.

Roma Imports, 627 E. 6th St., Tucson, AZ 85719; (520) 792-3173; romaimports.com. The challenge is finding this market. Set back in a residential and somewhat industrial area, it offers a big selection and variety of frozen Italian pastas, cheeses, and meats. Those of you craving home-style Italian-American food without the cooking will find homemade oven- and microwave-ready meals like lasagna, baked ziti, meatballs, sauce, and more, all on display in freezers along the wall. Sausage is made here from scratch, flavored with a good amount of garlic and fennel and available in mild, medium, and hot. A smattering of shelves offers a small selection of imported canned and packaged goods while a deli and bakery put out fresh breads and highly addictive cannoli. Hot and cold to-go sandwiches feature Italian meats like mortadella and Genoa salami layered with *giardiniere* (chopped pickled veggies), provolone cheese, and a zesty vinaigrette. Closed Sun. Open Mon through Thurs 9 a.m. to 6 p.m., Fri and Sat 9 a.m. to 8 p.m.

17th Street Market, 840 E. 17th St. Tucson, AZ 85719; (520) 792-2588; seventeenthstreetmarket.com. Do not try to find this market without detailed directions or mapping on your GPS. Housed in a warren of warehouses, this barn-like market is chock-full of ethnic foods (over 70 varieties of noodles alone), locally made products, produce, meats, fresh fish, and a music store full of instruments and CDs. Do not be afraid—you access the market through a bustling commercial food service business, part of the reason the prices are so competitive. You'll find the biggest selection of organic produce in town here. Bring a coat because the huge produce area is nicely chilled (a great spot on hot August days) and you'll want to spend quite a bit of time looking at the beautifully organized displays of gorgeous fruits and vegetables, including local and regional products and specialty items. Closed Sun. Open Mon through Sat 10 a.m. to 6 p.m.

Sun Oriental Market, 2205 S. Craycroft Rd., Tucson, AZ 85711; (520) 790-6945. Question: What do whole frozen octopus, a foot massager, and a tofu maker have in common? Answer: They are all for sale at this cozy south side market owned by Korean native Keun Soo Lim and his lovely wife. I have never seen such a large selection of seaweed and I sure wish I knew what to do with it. It's available here frozen, dried, roasted, shredded, chunked, rolled, in huge planks, and as long rolls on shelf after shelf in this neatly organized store. If you want to make your own kimchee, this is the place for you with all sizes of bags and containers of all kinds of red pepper powders. Freezers along the walls hold an assortment of fish, including octopus, along with frozen pot stickers and dumplings. There's an interesting selection of roasted teas—corn and barley—and puffed corn and rice crackers. A display of clay cooking pots and teapots, rice cookers, and household items round out the shelves. Open Mon through Sat 9 a.m. to 7:30 p.m., Sun 2 to 6 p.m.

Santa Cruz Chili & Spice Company

Every type and style of chili (sic) powder lines the shelves at this small family-owned shop in Santa Cruz County, about 50 miles south of Tucson. Located on the side of a scenic country road, this is a popular destination for locals and visitors alike. A tiny cookbook section offers books by local authors and a bit of history about the region. Some of their products are also available at grocery stores in town. 1868 E. Frontage Rd., Tumacacori, AZ 85640; (520) 398-2591; santacruzchili.com. Closed Sun. Open Mon through Fri 8 a.m. to 5 p.m., Sun 10 a.m. to 5 p.m.

Time Market, 444 E. University Blvd., Tucson, AZ 85705; (520) 622-0701; timemarket.lbu.com. Market, pizzeria, coffee bar, beer hall, this small-scale store has multiple personalities.  Although the space is limited, they do source a variety of specialty foods including artisan chocolates, salsas, artisan pasta, sauces, mixes, and dairy products. You can also get a slice of pizza, a sandwich, glass or bottle of beer, and an espresso on site. What better way to reward yourself after shopping? Open every day from 7 a.m. to 10 p.m.

Butchers

Carnicerias, various locations. There are numerous *carnicerias* (butcher shops) here, most in Hispanic areas of town at major intersections and in small strip malls. They tend to be very basic with little decor and lots and lots of meat displayed in glass cases,  from chicken to pork to beef along with innards and some cooked products. You can get just about any cut of beef from flank to ground here, and they will cut to order as well. Each *carniceria* has its own distinct personality and neighborhood vibe so you will have to scope out your area and pick your favorite.

Dickman's, 7955 E. Broadway Blvd., Tucson, AZ 85710; (520) 885-8020, and 6472 N. Oracle Rd., Tucson, AZ 85704; (520) 229-9777. Rattlesnake, kangaroo, alligator, buffalo, elk—it's all available here. Owner Jan Dickman has been providing Tucson with exotic game since 1997, along with fish (walleye, perch), prime and choice beef, and homemade sausages. Most of the exotic products are wrapped in butcher paper and stacked in big glass freezer cases along the walls. Jan will special order just about anything, and the shops will even process your own game meat; no need to call ahead, just bring in your bounty and their expert butchers will grind, chop, and slice to order. Open Mon and Sat 8 a.m. to 6 p.m., Tues through Fri 8 p.m. to 7 p.m., and Sun noon to 5 p.m.

Sausage Shop Meat Market, 1051 W. Prince St., Tucson, AZ, 85705; (520) 888-1701. Do you love sausage? This family-run (Dad and daughter) deli and butcher carries 200 different kinds of sausages, all made right here, the old fashioned way. Brats, sweet Italian laced with fennel, kielbasa, Hungarian kolbasz—whatever kind of sausage you are craving, you will find it here, all laid out in the glass cases. The space is small but the sausages are big in flavor, and people travel from all over town to get them. With fresh ground meats, spices, and secret recipes, they've been grinding and creating sausages since they opened in 1984. You'll also find specialty sausages not found anywhere else. Delta dogs are Louisiana  hots filled with onion and jalapeños and wrapped in pepper bacon; bull dogs are Polish dogs stuffed with with jalapeño and onion and wrapped in jalapeño bacon; and Grill dogs are quarter-pound all-beef hot dogs stuffed with peppers and onions and wrapped in bacon. If you don't want sausage, The Bacon Explosion is a meatloaf filled with sausage, peppers, onions, marinara sauce, and blanketed in bacon you can cook up at home. They also sell dry-aged beef, cut to order, and smoked meats (all smoking is done in-house) and bacon. The deli side offers 53 kinds of sandwiches with a different 8-inch sub special daily. Open Mon through Sat 8 a.m. to 5 p.m.

University of Arizona Meat Sciences Laboratory, 4181 N. Campbell Ave., Tucson, AZ 85719; (520) 318-7021; ccgameats.com. The name conjures up visions of lab coats and classrooms, and that is just exactly what you see here. Part of the university's College of

Nan Tian BBQ

It's not really a butcher, but the teeny tiny independent store within a store, Nan Tian BBQ (1990 W. Orange Grove Rd., 602-697-0894), is located inside giant Lee Lee Oriental Supermarket. You can buy whole and half roasted Peking ducks, whole cooked chickens, cooked duck feet and pig snouts, and order an entire 45-pound roasted pig. Closed Tues. Open all other days from 10 a.m. to 7:30 p.m.

Agriculture and Life Sciences program, this is a full USDA processing facility that serves as a lab and classroom for demonstrating meat-processing techniques. Student projects here become the meat products available for sale. You can buy beef, pork, and lamb products at the facility, mostly ground and steaks. If you want a special cut, you need to place your order in advance either via e-mail or by phone. Payment is by cash and check only and meat is sold only on specific days and times (usually Fri from 3 to 5 p.m.), so call or check the website first.

Bakeries

Beyond Bread, 6260 E. Speedway Blvd., (520) 747-7477; 3026 N. Campbell Ave., (520) 322-9965; 421 W. Ina Rd., (520) 461-1111;

beyondbread.com. One of Tucson's largest bakers, this locally owned bakery has three glorious locations. The very best part is the centrally located bins of free (yes, free) samples of sliced bread and creamy unsalted butter at each store. While you wait in line to place your order, be it for bread or pastries to go or one of the many soups, sandwiches, and desserts offered here, you can munch on the bread to your heart's delight. You'll find crusty multigrain, white, ciabatta, focaccia, scones (orange currant is a winner), croissants, cakes, tarts, giant cookies (death by chocolate and ginger are tops), brownies, coffee cake, and seasonal treats like house-made panettone (that addictive eggy, raisin-studded Italian holiday bread) and more, all available here. Open Mon through Fri 6:30 a.m. to 8 p.m., Sat 7 a.m. to 8 p.m., and Sun 7 a.m. to 6 p.m.

Frog's Organic Bakery, Casas Adobes Plaza, 7109 N. Oracle Rd., Tucson, AZ 85704; (520) 229-2124; frogsorganicbakery.com. This is the spot for delectable pastries and some pretty darn good baguettes. Macarons of all colors and flavors (even gluten-free), to-die-for lemon meringue tarts, chocolate éclairs bursting with pastry cream, giant muffins, bready croissants, fruit tarts, and it's all organic too! Pastry chef Jean-Luc Labat has worked in many top-rated restaurants in France and his elegant touch is everywhere, from the quality ingredients to the lovely garnishes. Closed Mon and Tues. Open Wed through Fri 7:30 a.m. to 4 p.m., Sat 8 a.m. to 4 p.m., and Sun 8 a.m. to 3 p.m.

Gourmet Girls Gluten Free Bakery, 5845 N. Oracle Rd., Tucson, AZ 85704; (520) 408-9000; gourmetgirlsglutenfree.com. Finally, a place where you don't have to ask—it is gluten-free? Everything here is! You can indulge your craving for pastry and breads with crumbly cookies (peanut butter is super), baguettes, muffins, challah, bagels, English muffins, quick breads, and cakes, all made in house from scratch. Owners Mary Gibson and Susan Fulton have spent years experimenting with specialty gluten-free flours, adapting recipes, and tasting countless experiments to come up with their signature items. They're happy to fill special orders for birthday cakes, cheesecakes, pies . . . whatever your heart desires. Closed Mon. Open Tues through Sun 7 a.m. to 3 p.m.

La Baguette Bakery, 1803 E. Prince Rd., Tucson, AZ 85719; (520) 322-6297; ghiniscafe.com. True to its name, this small-scale storefront contained within Ghini's Cafe in midtown offers up a variety of delicious baguettes—but that's not all. Homemade pound cakes of all flavors, chocolate croissants, fruit- and cheese-filled Danish, loaf breads, sliced breads, rolls, pies, tarts, they're all on the shelves and in the cases. There are two distinct styles of baguette made here. Hand-rolled baguettes have a slightly denser texture and are ideal for toasting and dipping into hearty soups, while their signature baguette is crusty, airy, and perfect for sandwiches. Do not miss the seasonal *bûche de Noël,* ethereal sponge cake soaked with simple syrup, slathered with buttercream and covered with chocolate frosting. Closed Sun and Mon. Open Tues through Fri 6:30 a.m. to 6 p.m., Sat 6:30 a.m. to 4 p.m.

MADE HERE: SMALL PLANET BAKERY

Small Planet (520-884-9313; smallplanetbakery.com) has been baking distinctive, artisanal organic breads since 1975. They produce hundreds of loaves a day in many familiar (whole wheat, raisin) and unusual (curry, tomato basil) flavors. Fans follow the breads to farmers' markets and seek them out in select area grocery stores, markets, and in restaurant breadbaskets because that's the only place you'll find them as they primarily sell wholesale.

La Baguette Parisienne, 7851 E. Broadway Blvd., Tucson, AZ 85710; (520) 296-1711. Bread, bread, bread. This extremely busy bakery is located in a strip mall in the southeast part of town. The active bakery section of the store is visible through a large glass window and you will see just how hard the bakers work to make a wide variety of baked goods. Loaves of bread are the main draw here: seeded and non-seeded rye, marble rye, white, pumpernickel, black are just some of the selections. You'll also find baguettes, rolls, and a variety of pastries. Breads sell out very quickly and the lines can be long, so get there early in the day. Open Mon through Fri 7:30 a.m. to 5 p.m., Sat 7:30 a.m. to 3 p.m., Sun 7:30 a.m. to 1 p.m.

La Estrella, 5266 S. 12th Ave., Tucson, AZ 85706; (520) 294-3675; laestrellabakeryinc.com. This small, homey bakery specializes in traditional Mexican baked goods and supplies many retail stores in Tucson. If you've never had a churro, the highly habit-forming cinnamon sugar pastry, this is the place to get one. They have plain, cream, and fruit-filled versions and they are super. Family owned for over 35 years, they know what they are doing here and will be happy to explain the names and flavors of the many items in the bakery cases. The red, white, and green pastries made from masa (corn dough) are a real winner, with a unique flavor and soft texture. Kids will love the *marrinitos,* pig-shaped cookies made with brown sugar and molasses. Dense doughnuts, plain and cinnamon sugar, are top sellers. Other choices include *pan huevos* (egg bread), fruit-filled empanadas, and soft rolls. A small countertop satellite branch is located at Mercado San Agustin but all baking is done here. Open Mon through Sat 6 a.m. to 7 p.m., Sun 6 a.m. to 2 p.m.

La Mesa Tortillas, 7823 E. Broadway Blvd., Tucson, AZ 85710; (520) 298-5966; lamesatortillas.com. Best tortillas in town, hands down, and you can quote me on that! These thin, slightly floury, flavorful tortillas are wonderful. Available in several flavors and sizes, they are used by top resorts and spas around town that appreciate the artisan style and consistent quality. You won't find these mass produced and sold in retail or grocery stores—the only place to get them is at the retail/bakery locations and they sell out fast, especially the whole-wheat variety. Your best bet is to get to the store early when the tortillas have just been made and are warm and

Made Here: Cheri's Desert Harvest

Jalapeño jelly, pomegranate chews, margarita morsels, cactus marmalade, and Old Pueblo pecan bread mix—these are just a few of the many products made right here at Cheri's Desert Harvest. Owner Cheri Romanoski started out small, making homemade jams from local fruits right in her kitchen. Now she oversees a small production facility in town where local citrus, cactus, and other products get processed, jarred, bagged, and shipped all over Arizona and beyond. I like to give Cheri's products as house or holiday gifts—the unusual combination of citrus and cactus makes for a memorable gift and supports our local producers. Two of my favorites are the pecan bread mix, which is easy to make, moist and delicious, and the red chile pepper jam, spicy sweet and great as a spread on sandwiches or dumped on top of cream cheese. All the products along with attractive prepackaged combinations of quick breads, jam, jellies, and syrups are available from her website or at select local retailers and airport shops. Check cherisdesertharvest.com or call (520) 623-4141.

pliable. You can call ahead the day before to pre-order if you want to be sure to have some available. Each location has its own bakery and offers a small lunch menu too. There's an additional location at 3923 E. Pima Rd. (open Mon through Fri 9 a.m. to 5 p.m., Sat 9 a.m. to 3 p.m.). The Broadway location is open Mon through Fri 9 a.m. to 5:30 p.m., Sat 9 a.m. to 3 p.m.

Mona's Danish Bakery, 4777 E. Sunrise Dr. #113, Tucson, AZ 85718; (520) 579-1959. The baker and owner of this small sandwich shop, Steve Hafshemi, is originally from Aarhus, Denmark, where he trained as a pastry chef. He rises every day at 4 a.m. to create his handmade breads and pastries, specializing in unique Danish products including *kringles* (filled coffeecakes), *danske rugbrød* (dark pumpernickel rye), and crusty Danish rolls. Breads here are made using natural leaveners, no fats or sugar and only unbleached, unbromated, hard wheat flour. The dough is transformed into a wide selection of breads, with a different "daily bread" available each day. Customers come all the way from Phoenix for the *kringles,* and locals love the almond croissants, dense with almond paste and sprinkled with sliced almonds. Open Mon through Fri 6 a.m. to 5 p.m., Sat 7 a.m. to 5 p.m., Sun 7 a.m. to 3 p.m.

Nadine's Bakery, 4553 E. Broadway Blvd., Tucson, AZ 85711; (520) 326-0735; nadinesweddingcakes.blogspot.com. You'll find an eclectic mix and wide variety of baked goods for sale here at this longtime, family-owned and -operated shop founded by Len Parker in 1979 and still the only kosher bakery in town. The industrial-style shop bakes off specialty pastries like hamantaschen and rugelach, breads including challah and seeded rye, along with cakes (rum custard and carrot are the top sellers), breakfast pastries, and cookies. Special orders for tiered wedding cakes and birthday cakes are welcome, and they go out of their way to design one-of-a-kind confections for special occasions. Closed Sun. Open Mon through Fri 7 a.m. to 6 p.m., Sat 7 a.m. to 5 p.m.

Viro's Real Italian Bakery, 8301 E. 22nd St., Tucson AZ 85710; (520) 885-4045; virosbakery.com. Viro's is the Little Italy of Tucson. Rose and Vito Croce have been baking here since 1985 and produce some of the most authentic Italian pastries in town. You'll find cannoli, sfogliatelle, tiramisu, biscotti, and the amazing *cassata Siciliana* (layers of cake filled with cannoli cream). Everything is made by hand and with lots of *amore*. Their sesame cookies are a real winner—crumbly and generously sprinkled with seeds, they are just like Nonna's. Pine nut cookies, another Sicilian specialty, can be special ordered and should not be missed. Breads include *casareccio* (a dense whole-wheat loaf), and focaccia. Not only do they bake desserts here, but the shop is also a small cafe where you can get savory goodies like homemade lasagna, pasta, and sausage either to eat in or take home. *Bravi!* Closed Mon. Open Tues 9 a.m. to 6 p.m., Wed through Sat 9 a.m. to 8 p.m., Sun 8 a.m. to 3 p.m.

Village Bake House, 7882 N. Oracle Rd., Tucson AZ 85704; (520) 531-0977; villagebakehouse.com. Located in Oro Valley, this busy bakery owned by Paulette Griggs has been supplying quality baked goods to the northwest part of town since 1996. There's not a large selection up front but the actual baking takes place in a huge space in the back, where breads, cakes, and pastries are all made on site. A top pick is the multigrain bread, a hearty oblong-shape

OUT OF TOWN

Get your daily bread at the Holy Trinity Monastery in St. David, about 50 miles east of Tucson (Highway 80, between milepost 302 and 303, 520-720-4016). An Olivetan Benedictine monastery, the lovely grounds are home to monks, sisters, and lay oblates. Members of the monastery community make an amazing dark seven-grain bread full of raisins, pecans, and cranberries. It's available daily at the gift shop, and bread lovers have been known to drive all the way here just to buy a loaf, it's that good. Open Mon to Sat 9:30 to 11:30 a.m. and 2 to 4 p.m., Sun 11:30 a.m. to 1 p.m.

loaf made with a mix of bran, oats, sesame seeds, rye flakes, wheat berries, and pumpkin and sunflower seeds. Customers line up for rich sour cream fruit muffins (blueberry is a hit), bear claws fly off the shelves, and kids and adults clamor for the raspberry shortbread bars and New York–style black and white cookies. Paulette is known for her custom wedding cakes; the pink champagne cake (available in all shapes and sizes) is a favorite with local brides to be. Open Mon through Sat 7 a.m. to 6 p.m., Sun 8 a.m. to 2 p.m.

Coffee, Tea & Dessert

Tea- and coffee-making is an art—there is no quick dipping of the bag or sprinkling of freeze-dried grounds at these single-location shops where they take their craft seriously and have a distinct personality.

Tearooms

Chantilly Tea Room, 5185 N. Genematas Dr., Tucson, AZ 85704; (520) 622-3303; chantillytearoom.com. This enchanting tearoom is a real treasure. You'll find this oasis off busy Oracle Road just north of River. Put on your finest clothes, vintage lacy gloves, a monocle perhaps (!), and get ready to be transported back to an earlier era when ladies lunched and afternoon tea was not just a once in a lifetime experience. Lovingly decorated by owner Tamara Read, tiny tables are decorated with starched tablecloths and set with vintage silver. A little shop full of beautiful china, teas (of course), and collectibles is at the entrance to the dining area. Inside there are several seating areas, including a private table and back room for special occasions (it's a popular spot for bridal showers). The outdoor patio is a lovely choice; shaded and with a little fountain, it's perfect in the spring. You can choose your own teacup from the collection of antique and fine china on racks all along the walls. The tea selection is vast, from silky bags to loose leaf, herbal to caffeinated. Sourced from around the globe, there are lots of unusual selections (chocolate mint, rose-scented, chamomile lavender). The friendly and attentive servers are intimately familiar with the flavor profiles and happy to make recommendations—they are so knowledgeable they are like tea sommeliers. Tea comes to the table in beautiful flowered china teapots, with endless refills. You can easily while away the whole afternoon here, with the soothing atmosphere and lovely surroundings. There is food too! The menu offers scones, soups, salads, and a selection of entrees and rich desserts all prepared in house. Specialty high teas (Victorian, Duchess) are available with a 24-hour advance reservation. Closed Mon and Sun. Open Tues through Sat, breakfast from 8 to 10 a.m., and lunch and tea from 11 a.m. to 3 p.m.

Scented Leaf Tea House & Lounge, 943 E. University Ave., Tucson, AZ 85719; (520) 624-2930; thescentedleaf.com. **Tea lovers**

Shane and Adrienne Barela, who want to make tea accessible to everyone—from the connoisseur to the beginning sipper—own this laid-back tea lounge. You can get a cup to go, or have a seat on the giant 13-foot couch or at the groupings of small tables. Get ready to try a wide variety of whole-leaf teas sourced from China, South America, South Africa, Sri Lanka, Japan, and India. Tea is served in ceramic, glass, or cast-iron pots, depending on the variety, and you can also get a bite to eat from the small menu of pies, soups, sandwiches, and, on special days, chocolate fondue! If you like what you taste, the teas are sold retail here as well. Open daily, 10 a.m. to 10 p.m.

Seven Cups Tea House, 2516 E. 6th Ave., Tucson, AZ 85716; (520) 881-4072; sevencups.com. The ancient art of tea is celebrated in style here. Look for the green awning squirreled away on a strip mall in the University area, and enter the land of tea. Certified Tea Master and owner Zhuping selects and brews the wide variety of specialty teas available for tasting and purchase here. The tiny, intimate tearoom features lacquered tables, Chinese lanterns, and a calming, zen vibe. The extremely knowledgeable staff will guide you through the many choices and styles of tea sourced directly from tea growers in China. Asian sweets including mooncakes and pastel-colored Japanese *wagashi* are imported from specialty bakeries in Phoenix and a small selection of interesting savory snacks (spiced tea

High Tea

On select days from November through the end of January, Loews Ventana Canyon offers an afternoon tea in their comfortable Cascade Lounge. Enjoy a 4-course tea service with complimentary champagne (!), delicate finger sandwiches, scones, and a selection of holiday pastries. Tea service starts at the civilized hour of 2:30 p.m. and ends at 4 p.m. Available Nov and Dec, Mon through Sat; Jan, Thurs through Sat. Not offered Nov 24–30, Dec 24–26, Dec 31–Jan 4. Reservations required, call (520) 615-5496.

eggs boiled in spices and tea, steamed rice dumplings) are available to eat along with your tea. You can also schedule an authentic Chinese tea ceremony and try the teas at free tea tastings held every Friday from 3 to 3:30 p.m. Open Mon through Sat 10:30 a.m. to 8 p.m., Sun 11:30 a.m. to 6 p.m.

Tohono Chul Tearoom, 7366 N. Paseo del Norte, Tucson, AZ 85704; (520)797-1222; tohonochulpark.org. Afternoon tea is available daily at this lovely spot inside Tohono Chul Park. You can sit inside the rustic rooms or outside on one of two patios surrounded by trees and visited by the occasional hummingbird. Tea service here is presented tableside with a modern twist—instead of a china teapot, you are presented with a glass French press. Pick a blend of leaves (created by tea experts from the local Maya Tea Company) from the tea cabinet and watch as the leaves are added to the hot water, bloomed, pressed, and steeped right before your eyes. Homemade scones (delish!), orange, strawberry, and tomato marmalade, and delicate finger sandwiches make for a lovely meal. Plan to make an afternoon of it and save time to tour the beautiful grounds (there is a separate fee to enter the park). Afternoon tea is served from 2:30 to 5 p.m., Mon through Sun, June through Sept, summer hours and availability during July and Aug vary so call first.

Coffeehouses

Bentley's House of Coffee and Tea, 1730 E. Speedway Blvd., Tucson, AZ 85719; (520) 795-0338; bentleyscoffeehouse.com. You'll find all sorts of people at Bentley's—most of them with their heads buried in their laptops! This unpretentious spot is a favorite with UA students, families, and freelance writers. It's a great place to plug in your computer during the day when you just have to get out of the house. As long as you order something (even a measly cup of coffee), the cool staff never pressures you to give up your table (thank you, thank you!). Run by locals Jo Anne and her son Ben, the friendly, low-key space is furnished with lots of tables and local artists' work on the walls. Their rich, full-flavored coffee is served in bottomless cups and finds its way into cappuccinos, lattes, mochas, espresso drinks, smoothies, and shakes. (Caffeine junkies should take note of the triple espresso shake.) A tasty menu offers breakfast (toasted bagels with lox are generous), sandwiches, homemade soups (cool cucumber avocado refreshes), and desserts with lots of vegan and vegetarian options. If you want to know what's happening around town, check out the double bulletin boards that line the back hall where you'll find flyers for everything from ayurvedic yoga to roommates wanted to avant-garde music and art openings. I just wish they would stay open later (are you listening, Ben?). Open Mon through Sat 10 a.m. to 6 p.m., Sun 8 a.m. to 6 p.m.

Cartel Coffee Lab, 2516 N. Campbell Ave., Tucson, AZ 85719; (520) 225-0437; www.cartelcoffeelab.com. The baristas here are dead serious about their coffee. Engage one in conversation and suddenly you will learn more about how to brew coffee than you ever thought you wanted to know. Training is a must for their staff who spend weeks learning the proper ways to roast, grind, tamp, and drip before they even pour you a cup. And the training shows, because the coffee here is divine. Deep, dark, and smooth, their brews are made with beans they roast themselves in a facility in the Tempe area. Choosing a coffee here requires deep thought—beans are sourced from single growers from around the world, and the history and provenance of each bean is outlined in great detail. Winners are the frothy, creamy cappuccino and the cold-brewed iced coffee. Food choices include pastries and all sorts of inventive sandwiches (try the Digby at breakfast, a super combo of bacon, spinach, tomato, pesto aioli, and two sunnyside up eggs on ciabatta), salads, dips, and snacks (try the spicy house made chex mix). Enjoy your java at long wood tables and benches in the industrial-style interior with its exposed ductwork. Open Sun through Wed 7 a.m. to 10 p.m., Thurs through Sun 7 a.m. through 12 a.m.

Chocolate Iguana, 500 N. Fourth Ave., Tucson, AZ 85705; (520) 798-1211; chocolateiguanaon4th.com. Warning! Don't bring your kids to this candy and coffee land—they'll want to buy and eat everything in sight! Teeny, tiny, this espresso bar, sweet shop, and cafe aims to please with shelves packed full with gourmet chocolates, candy, cards, and gifts. The Conklin family has definitely had fun decorating and stocking this little place. Coffee lovers will find mochas, lattes, and espressos along with eclectic gourmet sandwiches (chicken salad is combined with water chestnuts and green onions and served with sprouts on multigrain bread), soups du jour, and salads, all to go. There's no indoor seating, but a little group of tables and chairs is gathered outside so you can sit and watch the scene on Fourth while you indulge your caffeine and sweets cravings. Open Mon through Thurs 7 a.m. to 8 p.m., Fri 7 a.m. to 10 p.m., Sat 8 a.m. to 10 p.m., and Sun 9 a.m. to 6 p.m.

Crave Coffee Bar, 4530 E. Broadway Blvd., Tucson, AZ 85711; (520) 445-6665; cravecoffeebar.com. Sleek and modern, with a shiny steel bar and stools, couches, and banquettes, this is a nice space to grab a cup of joe. Owner Fatmir Morina is originally from Kosovo and he uses only Illy coffee and a special Zoka blend of beans for his signature espressos and cappuccinos. Caffeine lovers rejoice—you can pick your number of espresso shots—up to six for a serious cup of coffee. You'll find homemade pastries, including baklava and unique honey biscuits (made from a traditional Kosovar recipe) and a selection of panini for lunch. Expats are often found here, reading international newspapers and wheeling and dealing on their cells. Open daily 6 a.m. to 11 p.m.

Epic Cafe, 745 N. Fourth Ave., Tucson, AZ 85705; (520) 624-6844; epic-cafe.com. A Tucson mainstay, Epic has been grinding beans and pouring coffee and tea since M. Twofeathers opened the place. Comfortable and well-worn, brightly colored walls, high ceilings, and soft couches invite you to come in and stay a while. The outdoor tables and chairs on the avenue are the closest thing to coffee bars in Europe, attracting conversations, guitar players, and readers. There's a real mellow vibe here—you order at the counter where you'll see a selection of homey casseroles, quiche, cakes, pies, and pastries in the refrigerated case and a huge blackboard of drinks, soups, and sandwiches (there are lots of vegan, gluten-free, and vegetarian options). Breakfast is served all day here. The couscous with fruit, granola, and yogurt is a hearty, healthy way to start the day. Homemade waffles are great any time of day, available hot with fruit compotes, ice cream, or syrup on top. House-made rugalach sell out within the first hour. Coffee beans come from local roaster XO, and you can order them brewed in an espresso, au lait, latte, iced, shakes, and cappuccinos. The sinful "Naughty/Noddy Toddy," a decadent blend of coffee concentrate, half and half, and vanilla is the most highly caffeinated thing on the menu and will keep you from nodding off anytime soon! Open daily 6 a.m. to midnight, also Thurs through Sat from midnight to 6 a.m.

Le Buzz, 9121 E. Tanque Verde Rd., Tucson, AZ 85749; (520) 749-3903; lebuzzcaffe.com. A favorite hangout for cyclists seeking a caffeine and carb load before or after a daunting ride to the top of nearby Mt. Lemmon, Le Buzz is famous for its coffee and delicious pastries. They roast and brew their own beans and handcraft them into cappuccinos and espressos to go along with buttery croissants, to-die-for cinnamon buns, sweet scones, an amazing coffee cake, addictive fruit-filled flaky turnovers, all kinds of tarts, quick breads, and gooey lemon bars oozing a tongue-tingling sour-sweet filling. People come from across town for their famous house cookie (a chewy combo of chocolate chips, Heath Bar, pecans, and oatmeal) and it sells out daily. You can also get a full breakfast and they also serve up inspired salads, soups, and sandwiches for lunch in or to go. Outdoor tables are the top picks, with lots of dogs and people vying for spots. Open daily 6 a.m. to 5 p.m.

Raging Sage, 2458 N. Campbell Ave., Tucson, AZ 85719; (520) 320-5203; ragingsage.com. Devotees of this spot come for the coffee and the amazing baked goods—especially the scones. The bad news—the scones sell out fast. The worst news—you can only buy six bakery items at a time. The good news—you can buy as much coffee as you want. The best news—it's delicious! Owners Roger and Julie Sliker are committed to quality. Beans are sourced from environmentally responsible growers, air roasted, and *never* pre-ground. You will see lines out the door here and people jockey for a seat inside at small, closely packed tables or on the lovely outdoor side patio. Don't even think about using your cell phone here, because there is a strict no-cell policy and no Wi-Fi (horrors!), which creates a calm, convivial atmosphere where conversation is encouraged (imagine that!). Open Mon through Thurs 6:30 a.m. to 9:30 p.m., Fri and Sat 6:30 a.m. to 11:30 p.m., Sun 7 a.m. to 7 p.m.

Revolutionary Grounds, 606 N. Fourth Ave., Tucson, AZ 85705; (520) 620-1770; facebook.com/Revolutionary.Grounds. This tiny shop is squished into a space on Fourth Avenue and it's hardly big enough to turn around in, with just a few little tables and chairs. In this comfy spot that is more like a reading room, you'll find well-read copies of the *New York Times* along with a selection of progressive political, literary, Spanish, gender studies, and children's books on the shelves that line the walls. All the books are for sale but you are welcome to browse as long as you like. Owner Joy Soler makes everything here. The unusual lavender walnut coffee cake is light and cinnamony, and not at all like potpourri, so give it a try! There are always at least three vegan and gluten-free choices, including a chocolate cake and chocolate tartlets. The top

seller here is the carrot cake. Made with a
whole orange, it's moist and tasty with
a rich cream cheese and orange
zest frosting—it sells out immediately whenever Joy makes it.
You'll also find soups, salads, and
sandwiches here. Che's Fave is the
most popular on the sandwich board,

with vegan turkey slices, avocado, spicy sriracha vegenaise, vegan
cheese, peperoncini, lettuce, and tomato sandwiched between
sourdough bread slices. Direct trade, shade grown, organic coffee
beans come directly from growers in Chiapas, Mexico (there's no
middleman here). Open Mon through Thurs 8 a.m. to 8 p.m., Fri and
Sat 8 a.m. to 11 p.m., Sun 7 a.m. to 4 p.m.

Roasted Tea & Coffee Shop, 33 N. Stone Ave., Ste. 150, Tucson,
AZ 85701; (520) 624-8852; roastedcoffeeshop.com. Downtowners
love this sliver of a shop—it's an easy in, easy out on the way to
the courthouse or a downtown office. Owner Nikolas Ilka knows
everyone by name and has tons of repeat customers who come by
for his signature medium roast Sumatran house brew supplied by
a local roaster. He loves to try new brews and always features a
new and different daily special. Keep an eye out for the Red Eye,
guaranteed to keep you up for at least 24 hours! Food choices are
limited, with to-go packaged breakfast pastries, salads, and sandwiches. Open Mon through Thurs 7 a.m. to 3:30 p.m., Fri 7 a.m. to
2:30 p.m. Closed Sat and Sun.

Sabine's Cafe Passe, 415 N. Fourth Ave., Tucson, AZ 85705; (520) 624-4411; cafepasse.com. Busy, busy, busy, Sabine's is a top spot for aspiring writers and poets, musicians, and the bohemian Fourth Avenue crowd. There are lots of seating options here: out front at small metal tables, inside at large communal wooden tables, on the secluded red-velvet couch, or in several outdoor, plant-filled patios out back. Owner Sabine Blaes, originally from Germany, makes delicious desserts. Her scrumptious Black Forest cake is a family recipe made from scratch with a hint of cherry schnapps. Coffee is organic from Peru and Colombia and available in just about every combination. The Cubano is deep and delicious, a rich espresso sweetened with raw sugar and lightened with whipped cream. Fancy espresso drinks compete with all kinds of mochas on the extensive coffee menu. Breakfast offerings include bagel sandwiches, oatmeal, and organic granola. The grilled PB&J is super-duper, served on nine grain, ciabatta, or sourdough with banana and bacon! A variety of sandwiches and panini, vegetable platters, and salads round out the savory choices here. Open Mon through Fri 7 a.m. to 7 p.m., Sat and Sun 8 a.m. to 7 p.m.

Savaya Coffee Market, 5350 E. Broadway Blvd., Tucson, AZ 85711; (520) 747-3200; savayacoffee.com. You'll want to spend the day here at the long wooden bar with the attractive, chatty baristas who seem to have all the time in the world. There's no rush here, and they take their time to do things right, focusing on just the right water temperature, grind, drip time, and press time required to make the perfect cup of coffee or tea. They use a single-origin bean from Brazil to brew a super-dark, dense, bright cup of espresso that satisfies even the pickiest coffee drinkers. Also available here is Turkish coffee, made from beans sourced directly from Turkey by owner Burc Maruflu, who just happens to be Turkish. Coffee's the thing here, so don't expect any food—occasionally they'll have a bit of baklava or a packaged cookie to dip in your coffee. Relax and enjoy! Open Mon through Fri 7 a.m. to 7 p.m., Sat and Sun 9 a.m. to 6 p.m.

Sparkroot, 245 E. Congress St., Tucson, AZ 85701; (520) 272-8949; sparkroot.com. This newbie to the Tucson coffee scene, opened in 2011, is the brainchild of Ari Shapiro and features Blue Bottle coffee, sourced direct from San Francisco. Try the "Nola," iced and slightly sweetened, and you'll become a fan of this cool, smooth, deeply flavored, cold-brewed concoction. The soaring ceiling, funky furnishings, and Jetson-like upstairs lounge attract hip downtowners toting iPads and yoga mats who spend hours here sipping their drinks and grazing on the light fare. The tiny kitchen offers a limited but upscale menu of whole-grain toast spread with house-milled nut butter, jam, or marmalade (these are huge and satisfying with a nice smoky flavor); house-made granola; pressed cheese sandwiches on crusty ciabatta (double-cream brie marries well with apple slices, walnuts, and fig jam); and salads for lunch (roasted beet comes with arugula and orange slices and a tangy sherry shallot vinaigrette). There is no meat but you can order micro beers and wine by the glass and bottle. The vintage jukebox turns out tunes for free, and a great selection of fashion mags and a super view of Congress Avenue plus the amazing coffee will keep you coming back again and again. Open Mon through Sat 7 a.m. to 10 p.m., Sun 8 a.m. to 9 p.m.

Dessert

Allegro—il gelato naturale, 446 N. Campbell, Tucson, AZ 85719; (520) 207-1991; gelatoallegro.com. Some of the most interesting and delicious flavors of gelato and sorbetto are to be had at this popular spot. Cheerful, bright, and welcoming, the servers will give you a taste of everything and explain each and every flavor and technique in great detail. The display is almost as good as the gelato—colorful mounds of ice creams garnished with fresh fruit, spices, and herbs turn around and around in the circular displays. No artificial flavors, colors, or concentrates mar the clean, fresh taste of the products made right here. One of the best is the pineapple basil sorbetto, a refreshing not-too-sweet combo of pineapple with flecks of fresh basil leaves. Gelato aficionados opt for the dark chocolate mint and amazing pistachio. They are always experimenting with new flavors here—you might find anise or cucumber vodka among perennial favorites chocolate and *vaniglia*. Open Mon to Thurs and Sun 11:30 a.m. to 10:30 p.m., Fri and Sat 11:30 a.m. to 11:30 p.m.

Bing's Boba Tea, 2040 W. Orange Grove Rd., Tucson, AZ, 85704; (520) 270-8447. This little takeout place (there is one lone table) offers milk, slush (finely pureed ice), and snow (crushed ice) teas with or without boba (tapioca balls) in many different flavors. I love the almond slush, a milky sweet puree. The boba and other add ins are extra, but do get the boba. The chewy, little, black tapioca balls make the drink extra special, and the giant boba straws are half the fun—stab them through the clear cellophane cover and start sucking up the bobas along with the liquid. Choose from over seventeen flavors including kiwi, banana, lychee, mango, taro, and cantaloupe. Add ins include jellies (geometric

shaped, fruit flavored gelatins), prominently displayed on the counter, and caffeine powder. They also serve regular (green, jasmine, oolong) and unusual (blueberry, chocolate) iced and hot teas and smoothies (check out the avocado smoothie). Everything is available in 16- and 24-ounce cups. Open Mon through Wed 11 a.m. to 8 p.m., Fri through Sun 10:30 a.m. to 8:30 p.m., closed Thurs.

Blue Banana Frozen Yogurt, 12125 N. Oracle Rd., Ste. 121, Oro Valley, AZ 85737; (520) 989-3998. If you're a fan of frozen yogurt, the one and only Blue Banana is the place to go. Nestled into the sprawling Oro Valley Marketplace, it's a magnet for frozen yogurt lovers. Owners Rick and Linda Brady named their shop after the blue Java banana that actually tastes like ice cream! (Google it!) The decor is simple, with bright yellow sponged walls, high ceilings, and a whole wall of self-serve frozen yogurt spouts. Help yourself to a multitude of flavors—you'll always find chocolate, vanilla, and banana, but there are 53 different flavors that rotate in and out. Local faves include New York Cheesecake, Thin Mint Cookie, and Maple Bacon Donut. Tiny little paper cups let you sample them all before you make a final decision, but don't sample too much or you won't have room for the full serving. Once you've decided on a flavor, fill your cup and add toppings (you pay by the ounce). All the yogurt here is made from YoCream frozen yogurt and has live and active cultures so it's "healthy," but don't tell the kids. They'll be clustered around the counter full of toppings galore—three kinds of granola, lots of candies, nuts, and beautiful fresh berries. Rumor has it that the Mayor of Oro Valley is a regular customer, you should be too! Open Mon through Wed noon to 9 p.m., Thurs through Sun 11 a.m. to 10 p.m. (sometimes the hours change seasonally, so call first).

Brooklyn Pizza Company, 534 N. 4th Ave., Tucson, AZ 85705; (520) 622-6868; brooklynpizzacompany.com. It's hard to find Italian ice in Tucson, but you can count on getting it at Brooklyn Pizza. A true Italian ice is fruity, sweet, cold, and served in a little fluted paper cup—that's it, nothing fancy. Here you'll find a limited selection squeezed in next to the cash register but it's all good and they offer gelato as well as ices. The pistachio gelato is creamy and nutty but the lemon ice will always be my favorite (when they have it!). Open Sun through Wed 11 a.m. to 11 p.m., Thurs through Sat until 2:30 a.m.

Cafe Marcel, 344 N. Fourth Ave., Tucson, AZ 85705; (520) 623-3700; cafemarcel.biz. Savory, sweet, Swedish—no, I'm not talking about Ingrid Bergman but about the delectable crepes at Cafe Marcel. This tiny place on the east side of Fourth Avenue is easy to miss, but don't pass it by. Walk up the little steps and into a little piece of France. Crepes are expertly made by Chef-Owner Joe Frazier, who makes all the batter from scratch. His sweet crepes include a simple cinnamon sugar and a Nutella with fresh strawberries and bananas, all served with powdered sugar and whipped cream. A savory crepe top seller is the fresh spinach, tomatoes, feta, and pesto topped with Chef  Joe's secret creamy herb sauce. It's so good some people come in just for the sauce. Swedish crepes are spread with a variety of jams (including lingonberry) and folded into quarters for easy eating. You can mix and match your crepe fillings—co-owner/wife Michelle is happy to fill any special requests. There's a bit of a dining room and a patio out back if you care to eat in. Closed Sun. Open Mon through Thurs 8 a.m. to 5 p.m., Fri and Sat 8 a.m. to 7 p.m.

LOCAL CHAIN: FROST, A GELATO SHOPPE

Owners Jeff Kaiserman and Steve Ochoa were inspired to open Frost (as everyone calls it) after licking many a cone on a vacation trip to Rome! The equipment and ingredients come directly from Italy and so does the chef/gelato master Nazario Melchionda of Bologna. This is a sophisticated ice cream store, clean and crisp with loads of flavors showcased in decorative swirls under glass. Tastings are encouraged and there are so many choices you will need to try at least a few to experience the depth of flavor and texture of the gelato—richer, sweeter, and denser than "American"-style ice cream. The concept has proved so popular that it's now become a franchise with locations in Phoenix, Chicago, and Albuquerque. Locations locally are at 7131 N. Oracle Rd, (520) 797-0188; 7301 E. Tanque Verde Rd., (520) 886-0354; and 2905 E. Skyline Dr., (520) 299-0315; frostgelato .com. Open Mon through Thurs and Sun 11 a.m. to 10 p.m., Fri and Sat 11 a.m. to 11 p.m.

Frosty Jake's Frozen Custard, 3102 E. Grant Rd., Tucson, AZ 85716; (520) 319-8001. If you can figure out when this place is open it's worth a stop. It's attached to a water-supply store, and you order everything to go from a little window. They make thick, eggy, custard-style ice cream here and it only comes in two flavors—chocolate and vanilla. But don't despair, there are over 20 different toppings and syrups that be mashed into or poured onto your ice cream that put it way over the edge. You can also get shakes, floats, Sundaes and Mondaes, and their signature "concretes." Named for different states of the union, these high-cal delights blend ice cream with select toppings—the Illinois gets you vanilla ice cream with butterscotch sauce and roasted pecans. Why Illinois? I have no idea, but thank you Illinois! Closed Mon. Open winter 1 to 7 p.m., summer 1 to 9 p.m. Call first, hours tend to change without notice.

Hub Restaurant and Ice Creamery, 266 E. Congress St., Tucson, AZ 85701; (520) 207-8201; hubdowntown.com. You'll see lines out the door for the ice cream here. The little frozen case is smack in the middle of the restaurant Hub so you have to wend your way through the busy restaurant and get in line inside the velvet ropes to order. Check out the whiteboard for the day's choices. The ice cream is all made in house by three (yes three!) full-time ice cream chefs who churn out 23 interesting and delicious flavors. My all-time favorite is the salted caramel, others (like my son) adore the dirt chocolate (chocolate ice cream, Oreos, and chocolate chips). Other tasty choices include Nutella, red velvet, and bourbon almond brittle, but they change every day, so get in line! Open Sun through Wed 11 a.m. to midnight, Thurs through Sat 11 a.m. to 2 a.m.

Oasis Fruit Cones, 1002 St. Mary's Rd., Tucson, AZ 85745; (520) 792-6657. Don't be deterred—a chain-link fence surrounds this tiny

Where to Find Mexican Treats

A number of cool Mexican treats can be found at roadside stands, carts, and in small shops, primarily in the South side and in South Tucson.

Paletas are fruit- and milk-based popsicles, and they come in a variety of wonderful flavors including coconut, strawberry, lime, tamarind, and lemon. You can find them in refrigerated cases in Hispanic grocery and specialty stores, and sold from pushcarts on the street and in local parks—listen for the tinkly bell that signals the arrival of the cart.

Raspados (Sonoran Sno Cones) are shaved ice spooned into a cup and topped with any combination of macerated fruits, sweet syrups, ice cream, condensed milk, and wet nuts. These are cold and perfect for hot summer days when the thermometer hits the low hundreds.

Pico de Gallo is generally a cup full of spears of fresh fruit, usually pineapple, mango, melon, and coconut and occasionally vegetables like cucumber or jicama. It's sprinkled liberally with a bright red, granular chile powder (not spicy) and seasoned with a squeeze of fresh lime. Terrifically refreshing, the fruit juice accumulates in the bottom of the cup for a great finish. The name comes from the Spanish word for a rooster's beak.

roadside stand and it looks like it's closed but it's open and ready to serve you up some super desserts. There is absolutely no decor and the street noise on St. Mary's can be pretty loud, but the desserts are worth it. Take a close look at the menu up on the wall—there are descriptions and helpful pictures of all the things they offer here. If you're not sure, the folks at the window are super nice and helpful. You'll find *raspados* with and without ice cream and many different flavors of syrup including plum and melon. You can order a small, medium, large, or JUMBO if you're really hungry! Unusual choices include the *de chamoy,* which gets you a cup of mango topped with slightly sweet and spicy crunchy peanuts, salted plums, and candied fruit. *Escamocha* is a heaping plate of bananas, grapes, and melon topped with crunchy granola, surrounded with whipped cream and topped with a cherry. Banana split anyone? It's here too along with cones and sundaes. If you'd rather have something with fewer calories, order the *pico de gallo,* served here in a big cup with at least five different kinds of fresh fruit. Have a seat on the plastic chairs or at the picnic table under the olive tree or head back to your car and eat on the side of the road. There are two additional locations (4126 S. 12th Avenue and 1600 W. Valencia, inside the Chevron station), but I like this one because it reminds me of a shack on the beach. Open Mon through Thurs 10 a.m. to 9 p.m., Fri through Sun 10 a.m. to 10 p.m.

Something Sweet Dessert Lounge, 5319 E. Speedway Blvd., Tucson, AZ 85712; (520) 881-7735; somethingsweet-dl.com. This place is all about dessert. Cakes, pies, puddings, cookies, cobbler—there are over 30 desserts to choose from here, all homemade. And, best of all, they are open until 2 a.m. Fri and Sat . . . yes, until 2 a.m. Oh, did I already say that? It's just so great to be able to indulge your sweet tooth at such an ungodly hour. There isn't much to  look at here—it's a large room with a bunch of tables and chairs, kind of diner-like, but you really won't want to look at anything but your dessert anyway! Don't miss the "Sugar OD Challenge"— four brownies, four slices of cheesecake, four scoops of ice cream, chocolate syrup, whipped cream, and four cherries. If you manage to finish it in 45 minutes and stay alive, you will be added to the Wall of Fame—now that's an accomplishment to be proud of! Oh, and they have salads and sandwiches too, in case you need something other than dessert. Open Mon through Thurs 11 a.m. to 12 a.m., Fri and Sat 11 a.m. to 2 a.m.

Sonoran Delights, 921 W. Congress Ave., Tucson, AZ 85745; (520) 623-3020. It's nothing fancy, but here you will find a large selection of *raspados*/Sonoran sno cones in this no-frills space connected to a small mom-and-pop restaurant. The covered porch is home to freezer and refrigerator cases with buckets of ice, macerating fruit, brightly colored syrups, milky syrups, chopped nuts floating in dark syrups, and ice creams. Order from the ladies stationed behind the cases. Step one—start with the ice. Step two—choose your toppings (priced per topping). Step three—order optional ice cream to top it all off. Step four—alternately slurp and chop at the ice, doing your best to bring it all into your mouth for a great taste sensation, sweet and cold, cold, cold. Open daily from 8 a.m. to 10 p.m. They also have a counter called Sonoran Sno-Cones inside the lovely Mercado San Agustin (100 S. Avenida del Convento, 520-344-8470, mercadosanagustin.com) with more limited, but equally tasty, selections.

Farm Fresh

Tucson is blessed with numerous farmers' markets found in all parts of town. Some are small with just a few vendors, others are large and incorporate artisans and craftspeople into the mix, and each has its own distinct personality. Here is a description of some of the larger markets and what you'll find there.

Farmers' Markets

Green Valley Farmers' Market, Green Valley Village, 101 S. La Canada Dr., Green Valley, AZ 85614; (520) 490-3315; greenvalley farmersmarket.org. Slightly more crafts fair than farmers' market, this sprawling market covers the entire Green Valley Village square both inside the courtyard and out on the edges of the parking lot. There's much to be had here, from cooked food from local vendors to fresh produce from community gardens. Salsa, eggs, biscotti, artisan breads, kettle corn, and more are sold throughout the market. Don't miss locally made caramels from Untamed Confections (mesquite vanilla is creamy and delish) and the Arizona wild crafted honeycomb from Indigenous Nutrition. Many artists and crafters display their work here, from paintings to sculptures, along with locals selling Mexican pottery, jewelry, and fanciful metal works. You can even buy a whole saguaro cactus, roots and all, to plant in your garden. The market takes place on Wed from 10 a.m. to 2 p.m.

Oro Valley Farmers' Market, Oro Valley Town Hall, 11000 N. La Canada Dr., Oro Valley, AZ 85737; (520) 882-2157; farmersmarket tucson.com. This busy, friendly market takes over the lovely town hall. Inside and around the shaded courtyard, vendors offer coffee, tea, frozen to-go entrees, seasonings, meats, sprouts, produce, fruit, chutneys, mustards, dog treats, pastries, breads, and more. Local musicians serenade with everything from acoustic guitar to opera. Be sure to stop by Jim and Dolly Manley's table where they sell wild Alaska salmon and their own secret recipe salmon spread (ask for a sample, it's yummy). An unusual product sold only here is *dukkah*, a savory nut and spice blend made right in Oro Valley. You can taste it at the Victory Gardens

booth—it's different and delicious. The Van Haren Meat Company stand here specializes in lamb and goat meat, antibiotic- and hormone-free. Owners Tom and Stacy sell whole and half pieces, racks, chops, legs, kebabs, and shoulder cuts. Be sure to taste a sample from their steaming crockpot—you won't be sorry. A parking lot with covered and uncovered spaces is a treat and makes for easy access to the market. Open Sat 8 a.m. to noon May to mid-Oct, and 9 a.m. to 1 p.m. from mid-Oct to the end of Apr.

Rincon Valley Farmers' and Artisans' Market, 12500 E. Old Spanish Trail, Tucson, AZ 85641; (520) 591-2276; rvfm.org. Smaller scale and laid back, this combination artisan and farmers' market is located in a more rural setting on the far east side of town surrounded by fields, ranches, and mountain views. You really can't beat the setting. To find it, look for an old stable and a billboard with a covered wagon on it. The market offers produce stands, homemade fudge, holistic dog food, frozen lasagna and baked pasta to go, grass-fed meats, tamales, ceviche, granola, and handmade artisan breads, cookies, and pizza shells. Trescia Power of Power Ranch sells her heritage pork products here, including pork fat, along with all kinds of cuts of meat. If you're hungry, don't pass up a barbecue brisket sandwich from Smudgies' grill; tender meat is slathered with homemade smoky-sweet barbecue sauce and plopped into a soft bun. There's really no place to sit here, but you can perch on one of the straw bales while you balance your plate. The artisans' market is inside the stable among the stalls and on one side of the market and features all sorts of stuff from the kitschy to the sophisticated. Parking is mostly across the street—look both ways, it's a busy road. Sat 9 a.m. to 2 p.m. starting Oct 1st, 8 a.m. to 1 p.m. starting May 1st.

Santa Cruz River Farmers' Market, Mercado San Agustin, 100 S. Avenida del Convento, Tucson, AZ 85745; (520) 622-0525, x242; communityfoodbank.com. This is one of the largest farmers' markets organized by the Community Food Bank. It takes place in and around the attractive Mercado San Agustin, just below A Mountain on the west side of town. You'll get a terrific view of the downtown from this bustling market. Gourmet food trucks, produce stands, sprouts, heirloom plants, honey, and jams are all here for the purchase. The market takes place on Thurs 3 to 6 p.m. from Oct to Apr, and 4 to 7 p.m. from May through Sept, and is closed the last two weeks of Dec. The market accepts WIC vouchers and Arizona Farmers' Market Nutrition Program coupons.

Tucson Farmer's Market East, Jesse Owens Park, 400 S. Sarnoff Dr., Tucson, AZ 85710; (520) 882-2157; farmersmarkettucson.com. Referred to by everyone locally as the Jesse Owens market, this event features a group of tents and booths under shady trees next to a baseball field and swimming pool at Jesse Owens Park on the east side of town. There is ample parking and a relaxed vibe with picnic tables sprinkled around in case you want to eat some of your purchases! Local vendors sell produce, homemade jams, pickles and jellies, farm-fresh eggs, grass-fed beef, and baked goods of all kinds. Check out sweet potato pies and fruit cobblers from Willie  Mae's Southern Style Bakery, "handmade with love," and Richcrest Farms' selection of heirloom dried beans. Open 9 a.m. to 1 p.m. during the winter, 8 a.m. to noon in summer.

Tucson Farmers' Market at Maynards, Historic Depot at Pastor Plaza, 400 N. Toole Ave., Tucson, AZ 85701; (520) 882-2157; farmers markettucson.com. This small-size and highly popular market with the downtown crowd takes place in the courtyard of the historic train depot. You'll hear and see the freight and Amtrak passenger trains as they whiz by the booths and stands offering artisan chocolates, organic eggs, tea, artisan breads, handcrafted tortillas, and produce from local gardens and farms. Don't pass by the gorgeous display of artisan chocolates by Majorie Dewald of Monkey Flower Chocolates. She'll be pleased to give you a sample; they're almost too pretty to eat, but do so because they taste amazing. Vendors here are serious about their craft and love to share details about their gardening methods, baking styles, ingredients, and specialty products. The Zenhens table is particularly interesting, supplying detailed information about raising chickens while offering organic eggs and composted chicken manure for your garden for sale. Parking is at a premium here so be prepared. Free parking can be found on side streets and paid lots in the area and Maynards has a few spots in its small parking lot (you'll see meters but it's free on the weekends). The market takes place on Sat 9 a.m. to 1 p.m.

Tucson Farmers' Market at St. Philip's Plaza, St. Philip's Plaza, 4300 N. Campbell Ave., Tucson, AZ 85718; (520) 882-2157; farmersmarkettucson.com. The biggest market of all, the Sunday market at St. Philip's Plaza is busy and booming. Tents, booths, people, dogs, kids, food, plants, soaps . . . you'll find over 60 vendors spread out among two courtyards with tinkling fountains, along the streets, and around the perimeter of the courtyard. Plan to take your time and spend several hours, there are so many wonderful choices here from small mom-and-pop growers and food producers to large farmers and ranchers. You'll find trays of flourishing sprouts

of all kinds at Arizona Sprouthouse, croissants at Frogs Organic Bakery, apples from the orchards in Willcox, bright red hydroponic tomatoes, herbs and lettuces, local citrus, several varieties of goat cheese at Fiore de Capra (mascarpone and marinated herb are winners), seeds and indigenous foods, local honey, jams and jellies, scones, grass-fed meats, and lots, lots more. The unusual and tasty quinoa tamales are worth a stop at Treasures of the Sun's booth. Jojoba Beef Company sells tender, tasty beef that's been munching on jojoba bushes and nuts at their ranch in Kearny. The market takes place on Sun from 8 a.m. to noon, Apr through Oct, and 9 a.m. to 1 p.m., Oct through Apr.

Other Farmers' Market Locations:

A full listing of markets is available in the "The List" section of the "Caliente" insert in the Thursday edition of the *Arizona Daily Star*.

Friday Farmers' Market, Broadway Village, SW corner of E. Broadway and Country Club Roads, Tucson AZ 85716; (520) 603-8116. Fri 10 a.m. to 2 p.m. year-round (indoors).

77 N. Artworks and Marketplace, 16733 N. Oracle Rd., Catalina, AZ 85739; (520) 825-4427. Fri 9 a.m. to 2 p.m., Aug through May, Fri 1 a.m. to 12 p.m., June through Sept.

Bear Canyon Open Air Market, 8987 E. Tanque Verde Rd., Tucson, AZ 85749; (520) 982-2645. Sat 9 a.m. to 2 p.m., closed from Labor Day to Mother's Day.

Farmers' Market at the Shoppes at La Posada, 665 S. Park Centre Ave., Green Valley AZ 85614; (520) 603-8116. Mon 10 a.m.

to 2 p.m. from Nov through Apr, 9 a.m. to 1 p.m. from May through Oct.

Plaza Palomino Farmers' Market, 2970 N. Swan Rd., Tucson, AZ 85712; (520) 327-4676. Sat 10 a.m. to 2 p.m., from Oct through Apr, Sat 9 a.m. to 1 p.m. from May through Sept.

Saturday Market at St. Philips Plaza, St. Philip's Plaza, 4300 N. Campbell Ave., Tucson, AZ 85718; (520) 603-8116. Sat from 9 a.m. to 1 p.m. year-round.

Ventana Farmers' Market, Ventana Plaza, 5455 N. Kolb Rd., Tucson, AZ 85750. Tues 1 to 5 p.m. from Nov through Apr, 3 to 7 p.m. from May through Oct, Sat 9 a.m. to 1 p.m. year-round.

Voyager RV Resort Farmers' Market, 8701 S. Kolb Rd., Tucson, AZ 85756; (520) 603-8116. Wed 9 a.m. to 1 p.m. from Oct through May, hours and days of operation vary June through Sept, call first.

Vendor Spotlights

There are many, many wonderful and hardworking farmers, producers, growers, and cooks to be found at all our Farmers' Markets and I applaud and admire them all. For those of you interested in who the people are behind the booths and stands, these are some of the Tucson-based vendors who grow, make, and sell local food products.

Meet the Grower: Desert Treasures Groves

Chris Duggan lives amid and sells the marvelous fruit from the only citrus grove left in Tucson. Hidden away off the busy intersection of Ina and Orange Grove Roads, the citrus blossoms smell heavenly in the spring and produce over 40 varieties of juicy, flavorful fruit. Buy them at St. Philip's and Oro Valley farmers' markets.

Meet the Farmer: Menlo Farms

Paul Buseck and Dana Helfer grow and harvest their organic veggies from several garden plots of land they've lovingly created in their urban Menlo Park neighborhood, Barrio Kroeger Lane and Barrio El Rio on the southwest side of town. Passionate about sustainable agriculture, Paul has a Masters in International Agriculture Development from UC Davis and he uses his vast knowledge about dry-land farming to coax some mighty tasty vegetables from the local soil. The labor of his love is available at the Santa Cruz farmers' market. menlofarmstucson@gmail.com.

Meet the Baker: Big Skye Bakers

Tucsonan Bodie Robins uses his baking and architectural design skills to create pies big and small, some featuring crusts made with the indigenous and distinctively flavored mesquite flour. Fruit-filled and sweetened with agave syrup, his pies can also be made sugar- and gluten-free on request. Pies are sold at St. Philip's farmers' market. (520) 303-3050.

Meet the Jam Maker: Margy's Jam

Working right here in Tucson, Margy Dehlin and husband Gary cook up multiple varieties of homemade jam and jellies in unusual combinations and flavors (the blackberry habañero is addictive). You'll find her eponymous products at the Green Valley farmers' market. (520) 407-5521; margysjam.com.

Meet the Salsa Lady: Poco Loco Salsa

You can't miss fiery owner and chief salsa maker Adela Durazo who makes homemade salsas of all kinds. The lines are long for samples of her signature blends of fruit and chiles, from mild to "stupid hot," and most tasters walk away with at least one container of her tasty refrigerated salsa. She sells at Jesse Owens, Oro Valley, and St. Philip's.

Meet the Egg Man: Tom Cholley

Tom Cholley has a motto: "Happy eggs from happy chickens." He and wife Cheryl are the mother hens for 400 chickens at his Mountain Sunshine farm in Sahuarita. What started as a hobby has turned into a full-time job and Tom sells his blue, brown, and white organic eggs at the Tucson Farmers' Market East at Jesse Owens Park and the Sunday St. Philips' Market. (520) 648-7360.

Meet the Soup Maker: Jack and the Beanstalk

Long time Tucsonans Jack and Valerie Smith have been ladling out soup samples and selling their gourmet soup mixes in the distinctive red bags since the late 1980s. Many blends use the indigenous tepary bean along with special spices and herbs. Their stockpots are always full and ready to be sampled and the soups can be purchased at Jesse Owens, Oro Valley, Maynards, and St. Philip's farmers' markets. (520) 325-1341; jackandthebeanstalksoup.com.

Meet the Native Food Harvester: Skeleton Creek/Aravaipa Heirlooms

Keeping indigenous foods alive and well, Jeau and Charlie Allen are committed to showcasing the bounty of the Sonoran Desert. They use a variety of native foods to make everything from prickly-pear frozen ice pops to syrups, jams, and jellies. They also sell locally harvested mesquite meal and desert-tolerant regional and endangered food plants. You'll find them at St. Philip's Sunday market, Santa Cruz and Oro Valley markets. (520) 477-7637; pricklypops.com.

Community Supported Agriculture (CSA)

If you like to cook, becoming a member of a CSA is a great way to get super-fresh, locally grown produce and support local farmers and growers. Pickup locations are at several places around town and at some farmers' markets.

Aquaponics

There are a limited number of shares available in this unique small-scale CSA, which offers products grown strictly via aquaponics using non-GMO and native seeds. They offer produce and fish shares that can be had by contacting owner Stéphan Herbert-Fort directly at (765) 276-6427 or localrootsaquaponics@gmail.com. Details about the fascinating aquaponics method is at their website, localrootsaquaponics.com.

Menlo Farms

A series of urban plots yields bountiful produce for members of this CSA; pickup is on the southwest side of town at the farmers' market at Santa Cruz. Farmers' market at Mercado San Agustin; Mercado San Agustin is a venue at 100 S. Avenida del Convento that hosts the Santa Cruz Farmer's Market. menlofarmstucson@gmail.com.

River Road Gardens

Produce grown by this tiny, family-run operation is available from farmer Jon McNamara at his lovely garden, centrally located at the Tucson Waldorf School (3605 E. River Rd.) or at Maynards Farmers Market. (520) 780-9125; riverroadgardens.com.

Sleeping Frog Farm

One of the largest CSAs, Sleeping Frog offers fresh produce grown at their 75-acre farm in Cascabel, just north of Tucson. Multiple options and pickup locations are available for members, check sleepingfrogfarms.com/csa, or call (520) 212-3764 for details.

Tucson CSA

At one of the original CSAs in town, members can pick up veggies, herbs, and all kinds of produce at the inner courtyard of the historic Y in the University area. tucsoncsa.org; (520) 203-1010.

Pick Your Own

There's nothing fresher than picking your own fruit and veggies right out of the ground or off the tree. Here's where to go and get them!

In town:

Howard's Orchard

A secret known only to locals (but not for long), this delightful orchard is smack in the middle of a residential area in Catalina at 4101 E. Pinal St. Full of graceful old apple and peach trees, with a small plot of cucumbers and tomatoes, it's one of the nicest small scale orchards around (if not the only one in town). Owner Howard James lets you pick as long as he has fruit on the trees

and vegetables on the vines. Call for the schedule as it changes seasonally. (520) 825-9413.

Tucson Village Farm

Owned by the University of Arizona and used primarily for educational purposes, this kid-friendly garden on busy Campbell Avenue (4210 N. Campbell Ave.; 520-626-5161; tucsonvillagefarm.org) is open to the public for picking from 3 to 5 p.m. on Tues year-round.

Out of Town

Agua Linda Farms, Amado, Arizona. You can harvest all sorts of seasonal vegetables throughout the year at this small-scale, family-owned farm complete with a petting zoo. (520) 891-5532; agualindafarm.net.

Apple Annie's, Willcox, Arizona. At one of the largest you-pick-it spots, you can pick pumpkins, apples, peaches, and tons of veggies here seasonally and enjoy hayrides and special events. (520) 384-2084; appleannies.com.

Food Trucks

A fad, or here to stay? Who knows and who cares, because some great food comes out of these restaurants on wheels! These local trucks can be found all over town and at special events, monthly roundups, and festivals. Several of them also offer catering services and will do private parties. The best way to find them is to check their Facebook pages or Twitter feeds.

D's Island Grill JA, (520) 861-2271. You can't miss this bright green truck with the big yellow X where Duane Hall, originally from Morant Bay, Jamaica, makes his own home-style Jamaican food just as he makes for his family and friends. You will become a friend too when you taste his curry goat and oxtail stews and jerk chicken, all served up with rice and peas, the veggie of the day, and a hot, deep-fried Festival (a slightly sweet cornmeal hushpuppy). *The* thing to get here is Duane's homemade beef patties. He makes his own dough from scratch and cooks his beef with a special blend of secret spices. They take 20 minutes because each one is made to order. If you call in advance he will have them hot and ready for you—no waiting! If you do need to wait, enjoy the reggae tunes and chat with the cheerful Duane who hangs out Mon through Sat at the corner of Grant and 6th and at the occasional food-truck roundup.

Foodie Fleet, (520) 329-3663; facebook.com/pages/Foodie-Fleet/165531693503161. The four guys stuffed into this truck (owners Matt McDonnell, Mike O'Connell, Jeremiah Mosij, and Rick Thompson) press out some mighty good sandwiches and fry up some delish, crispy sweet potato fries too (dunk them into the sriracha mayo)!

You'll find all kinds of pressed sandwiches (the melted cheese with two kinds of cheddar and rainbow peppercorns is yummy and the goat cheese, arugula, and whiskey-pear jam is a top seller), and crispy waffles with unusual toppings.

FOOD TRUCK ROUNDUP

If you don't want to chase all over town to find a truck, you'll find most of them at the monthly Food Truck Roundup held at various venues around town. Get ready for long lines and lots of people because it seems like everyone else wants to try them all in one place too! For details on locations, dates, and times, go to tucsonfoodtrucks.com and twitter.com/TucFoodTrucks.

German Food Station, (520-270-6531); germanfoodstation.com. It's red, it's boxy, and it's only here from October through May. Owners Max and Andrea Offerman hail from Stuttgart and bring a taste of Germany to the Tucson food-truck scene. Sausages and meat loaf are specially made by a German butcher and prepared fresh on the truck and nestled into soft buns. You can get German mustard or spicy horseradish to go on top or a side order of sauerkraut. Leave room for Andrea's favorite, the unique "topkiss," a chocolate-covered marshmallow treat imported from Germany and served on a bun—skip the bun and just bite right into the rich, marshmallowy chocolate.

Guero Loco's Bubba-Que, (520) 425-6642; facebook.com/BUBBATRUCK. Owner and barbecue master Rich Park is passionate about barbecue; all his meats are smoked right on the truck for 15 to 20 hours and some unusual meaty combos come out of this smokehouse on wheels. While there are quite a few choices here, the Hawaiian is the way to go. It features a hefty portion of smoked pulled pork doused with Rich's signature smoky-sweet-spicy-tart sauce, piled high on grilled corn tortillas and topped with a jalapeño and pineapple slaw. Another favorite is the Slider, pulled pork on a grilled French roll layered with a citrusy homemade coleslaw with crunchy apples in the mix.

Isabella's Ice Cream, (520) 440-2650, isabellasicecream .com. In one of the quaintest trucks in the fleet, Dominic and Kristel Johnson scoop some mighty good ice cream out of this solar-powered, wood-paneled Model-T. Kristel creates some amazing flavors, including spicy Old Pueblo chocolate with cinnamon and a hint of cayenne pepper, and the vegan Limoncello sorbet flavored with basil, berries, or lavender. The ice cream is dense, eggy, and super-creamy, and the cups, spoons, and napkins are all biodegradable. They will happily give you samples of all the flavors, although it sure makes it harder to choose.

Jamie's Bitchin' Kitchen, (520) 869-3191; facebook.com/pages/ Jamies-Bitchen-Kitchen, twitter.com/bitchinkitchen. **Jamie Castro** is the chef here. She's taken her love of Cuban and Puerto Rican food from her 25 years of living in Miami and poured it all into her specialty sandwiches and tacos. Try the Cuban, a tasty melt of *mojo criollo*–marinated, braised pork, smoked ham, swiss cheese, homemade mustard, and pickles. Tacos come in all sorts of combinations with meats grilled to order and with a side of Cuban black beans and

What's Cyclopopsicle?

It's not a food truck, but a bicycle built for popsicles! Cyclopopsicle is the brainchild of Gus Coliadis, who married his love for artisan popsicles with his commitment to the environment. He pedals his lovely vintage bicycle with its built-in cooler full of handmade ice pops all around town, dispensing icy-cold, fruit-based delights to one and all. Chocolate-dipped mango with a chipotle pepper kick and hibiscus ginger are tops. Check his Facebook (facebook.com/pages/Cyclopsicle/141029585997262) or web page (cyclopsicle.com) or Twitter (twitter.com/Cyclopsicle) to find him, or give him at a call at (520) 477-9551.

yellow rice. Her black beans are addictive, creamy, and spicy—she makes these from scratch with a blend of secret spices.

Jones Street Bistro, (520) 979-1916; jonesstreetbistro.com. The top pick here is the Bourdain (yes named after that famous Travel Channel chef): a soft bun layered with melt-in-your mouth pork belly, deep-fried, creamy-centered pieces of *foie gras* (!), fennel slaw, and arugula. You can add an order of duck-fat-fried truffled french fries if you dare. Owner Gary Jones and son Jonathan (who trained at the Scottsdale Culinary Institute and worked with top chefs Jean-Georges Vongerichten and Michael Mina) created this calorific terrific combination. All the food on the truck is hand-crafted, from the meats to the sauces, and the quality is top-notch.

Freshly made Italian sodas, egg creams, phosphates, and naturally flavored sodas (try the lemongrass) are dispensed here too.

Pin-Up Pastries, (520) 954-6124; pinuppastries.com. Whoopie pies anyone? This adorable pink polka-dotted trailer serves up a variety of whoopie flavors, from salted caramel to mocha almond, along with cupcakes and cake pops of all kinds. Bubbly baker/owner Tracey Santa Cruz makes everything from scratch using recipes inspired by her grandma from Tennessee. The salted caramel whoopie pies sell out quickly. Cake pops are all hand-formed, hand-dipped, and hand-decorated, and the red velvet is especially good.

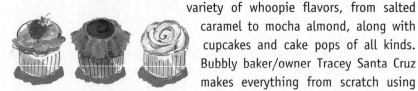

Planet of the Crepes, (520) 271-6083. Chef-Owner Jessica Kraus is a graduate of the Culinary Institute of America and her technique and innovative crepe fillings definitely set her apart from the food-truck crowd. It's fun to watch her ladling her homemade batter onto the piping-hot steel disks that cook the crepes. She manages to make a crepe with that's both crispy and tender to fold around a variety of delicious fillings. The crepes are huge and the fillings generous. A kid favorite is the chocolate, marshmallow, Nutella crepe, a sinful, calorie-filled delight. Savory crepes include the delicious duck confit with goat cheese, arugula, and tomatoes, but Jessica is always experimenting with new flavor combinations so you never know what you might find on the menu.

Robdogs. Not one of the prettiest trucks, this is more like a hot dog stand, but they do grill up some tasty dogs, including the "famous" Sonoran Dog, loaded with bacon, beans, and grilled onions (my go-to hot dog). Probably one of the least expensive choices, two dogs with all sorts of toppings can be had for just a few bucks.

Seis Curbside Kitchen & Catering, (520) 260-6581; seiscurb side.com. Jake Muñoz puts his culinary skills and cultural background (his mom's family is from Mexico and Dad is from Spain) to work here creating some super-gourmet dishes from the six (the *seis* in the name) culinary regions in Mexico. Take some time to talk to Jake about his unusual menu items—he is a fount of information about the different culinary styles and ingredients found from the Baja to the Yucatan. His chalkboard menu changes daily but (happily) always offers the Yucatan specialty *cochinita pibil,* slow-roasted pork marinated in achiote and sour oranges and wrapped in banana leaves. The *el pastor* (shepherd-style) tacos feature pork marinated in four different kinds of red chiles, grilled and served on corn tortillas with a dice of fresh pineapple—a magical combination of sweet and hot. Look for the sleek, black truck and watch the board for other unusual specials.

Street Delights, (520) 975-3677; street delights.com. Brownies, crème brûlée, pies . . . this truck is a dessert destination. The best of the lot is the peanut

Unique Roadside Stand

Roadside stands are sprinkled around various parts of town, most selling hot dogs and Mexican street food, but one that you won't find anywhere else is the Coctel de Elote or Elotes El Frida, depending on what side of the truck you're looking at! The tiny trailer attached to a pickup is parked on the west side of Irvington Road and 12th Avenue. They dish out a corn stew (*cocktel elotes*) that is simple and delicious—it's just corn kernels in a light broth with a squeeze of lime, melted cheese, and a blob of *crema*. Also on order are whole ears of roasted corn Oaxacan-style, slathered with mayonnaise and cheese. They don't speak much English here but the language of food is universal—*delicioso!*

butter brownie. Made to look like a cupcake, a crunchy brownie crust is layered with chocolate ganache and creamy peanut butter, omg!

Trucking Good Cupcakes, (520) 329-4411; 2cupcakes.com. Run by Lance Jones who bakes and his wife Elaine who frosts, this is the place for cupcakes. Red velvet, chocolate, lemon, cherry almond, and seasonal specialty flavors all find their way out of the window into your waiting hands. The to-go packaging is tops here too, with a special plastic insert to keep your cupcake centered on the way to your car—in case the cupcake lasts that long.

Vero Amore Neopolitan Pizza, (520) 954-8018; veroamorepizza
.com. Live fire, in a food truck? Yes, and it's not fake, that's a real
wood fire in the side of Vero Amore's truck, a retrofitted fire engine
to be exact. Hand-tossed dough topped with house-made tomato
sauce and fresh mozzarella along with lots of other combinations,
including vegan and gluten-free, is baked until it's sizzling hot.
The Neapolitan-style pizzas have a thin, crispy dough and are light
and fresh.

Native Foods

Many people who move to Tucson (like me!), and some who have even lived here for ages, don't realize that the arid-looking and somewhat intimidating desert landscape is home to a wide variety of edibles. While at first look the desert does not seem to have "seasons," Mother Nature still works her magic here, providing daily sunshine and bringing the amazing monsoon rains in the late summer to water the indigenous plants that supply a bounty of foods throughout the year.

The Native American people who call this region home are the Tohono O'odham (People of the Desert). They have been harvesting wild desert foods, planting and growing beans, squash, and corn, gathering wild foods and hunting game here for generations. The rich foodways of the Tohono O'odham showcase their strong link to the land, their appreciation of what nature has provided, and their amazing resilience and ingenuity. The Tohono O'odham Nation is third largest Native American sovereign nation in the United States, consisting of over 4,000 square miles) in Pima County to the south and west of the city of Tucson. The nation can be found

The **Arizona-Sonoran Desert Museum** (520-883-2702, desertmuseum.org) and **Colossal Cave Mountain Park** (520-647-7121, colossalcave.com) offer seasonal saguaro-harvesting events. Reservations are required.

in two sections, a small area surrounding the San Xavier Mission and a larger land mass about 60 miles west anchored by the capital city of Sells.

Native peoples have been sustained by the bounty of this desert, and one can even argue that the Tohono O'odham (like many other native peoples) are the original locavores, eating foods grown and harvested seasonally and locally.

The real "slow foods," these indigenous plants and animals have been boiled, sun and air dried, roasted, grilled, and stewed to create a truly place-based diet.

Here, I am happy to share with you some of the information that I have been privileged to learn from O'odham elders and community members about these amazing foods. This is just the tip of the "iceberg," so I've also included some additional resources so you can learn more at your leisure. *Si sap e-gegus* (eat well).

Edible Plants

Indigenous plants, those that grow and flourish naturally in the Sonoran Desert, fall into two categories—wild and cultivated.

Wild Foods

The O'odham have seasonally gathered many fruits and plants from the desert including:

Chiletepin peppers/*Ko'okol*—These tiny, super-hot berries turn from green to red through the summer months and dry right on the plant. Fiery reddish-orange, they are picked (carefully) and used as seasoning.

Cholla cactus buds/*Ciolim*—Hand-harvested from the spiny buck and staghorn cholla cactus in the spring, these tiny buds are cleaned of their spines with branches of greasewood and picked with tongs. Traditionally they are roasted or boiled and sun-dried for future use. The cooked buds have a citrus-like flavor and sticky texture.

Mesquite pods/*Wihog*—Yellow, fuzzy flowers turn to pods in both spring and fall. Once the pods dry, they are harvested and ground into flour, traditionally by hand in holes in the bedrock. The flour is gluten-free and has a sweet, musky flavor.

Prickly-pear fruit/*I:ibhai*—This variety of fruit ripens throughout the summer and is harvested with tongs after being brushed with branches made from the greasewood tree (the fine spines stick to the sticky leaves). The fruit is peeled and eaten fresh or cooked into a thin syrup.

Prickly-pear pads/*Nawĭ na:k*—While the O'odham don't often eat the pads, they are used widely in Mexican cooking and are harvested early in the spring, when they are small and have fewer thorns. The cooked pads have a slightly soft, sticky texture.

Saguaro cactus fruit/*Bahidaj*—After the waxy white saguaro flower blooms in early summer, a pod appears and turns from green to reddish pink, forming a delicious, red fruit inside. The fruit is harvested with long sticks made of dried saguaro ribs and cooked down into thick, smoky syrup. The fresh fruit is remarkably like a fresh fig.

Wild greens/*I'wagĭ*—the dry desert yields a variety of greens; early winter rains bring poverty weed, while summer months bring amaranth, purslane, and salt spinach.

Cultivated Foods

Cultivated foods include the "three sisters"—corn, beans, and squash. Archaeological digs in the region have unearthed sites from hundreds of years ago that have yielded tepary beans and corn kernels in ancient cooking areas.

Reading about the Foods of the Sonoran Desert

The foods of the Sonoran Desert have been the subject of several books by local authors. Here's where to discover more about the foods themselves and how to cook them.

American Indian Cooking—Recipes from the Southwest by Caroline Niethammer (University of Nebraska Press, 1974). In one of the first books to explore traditional native foodways, author Caroline Niethammer explores and explains the foods of several tribes of the Southwest, with hand-drawn illustrations, excellent explanations of the native plants, and traditional cooking methods, along with recipes.

Cooking the Wild Southwest: Delicious Recipes for Desert Plants by Caroline Niethammer (University of Arizona Press, 2011). Featuring 150 recipes, this book includes harvesting techniques and the general characteristics of over 20 desert plants, a result of Caroline's ongoing research and fascination with the foods of the Sonoran Desert. The recipes are contemporary and delicious.

Eat Mesquite! Published by the local nonprofit Desert Harvesters (an organization that promotes the use of mesquite), this spiral-bound cookbook is a wealth of information about mesquite. The 50 recipes have all been thoroughly tested (the flourless brownies are amazing!) and showcase the versatility of this indigenous ingredient. It is available for purchase on their website, desertharvesters.org, and at select specialty stores, markets, and farmers' markets in town.

From Furrow to Fire. Produced by the nonprofit seed bank, Native Seed/SEARCH, this slim paperback volume contains recipes developed and tested by members and the local community. Inspired by the seeds and plants sold in their retail store, the recipes include many dishes using indigenous ingredients. The chia fruit salad is a winner! Available at the store (3061 N. Campbell Ave., Tucson, AZ, 520-622-5561) and on their website, nativeseeds.org.

From I'itoi's Garden: Tohono O'odham Food Traditions by Tohono O'odham Community Action, Mary Paganelli (yes, that's me!) and Frances Manuel. This full-color book explores the many foods of the Sonoran Desert and the foodways of the Tohono O'odham with detailed information about planting, harvesting, and cooking interwoven with legends, songs, and personal reflections from community elders. Traditional and contemporary recipes are included in each chapter. The book is available for preview and purchase at blurb.com/bookstore/detail/1580427 and at the Desert Rain Gallery (Tohono Plaza, Main Street, Sells, AZ, 520-383-4966).

The Prickly Pear Cookbook by Carolyn Niethammer (Rio Nuevo Press, 2004). The prolific Carolyn Niethammer demystifies the prickly-pear cactus with 60 recipes culled from local and area chefs along with detailed nutrition information, instructions, and hints about how to pick, process, and cook the pads and fruit from this thorny cactus. Available at local bookstores and on amazon.com.

O'odham squash/Ha:l—A variety of *Cucurbita mixta,* this hardy squash yields edible flowers, baby squash, and a thick-skinned mature squash. The mature squash is often boiled or baked and can be skinned and dried for storage. Flavor is much like a Hubbard squash.

60-day corn/Huñ—A unique variety of white-flour corn, this plant goes from seed to ear in 60 days. Generally planted and harvested in the summer, the kernels are roasted, dried, and ground for use in soups and stews.

Tepary beans/Bawĭ—Drought resistant and delicious, the beans are planted in the spring, nurtured by the hot summer sun, watered by monsoon rains, and harvested in the fall. Thought to have originated as a wild plant, there are two varieties still grown, a white and a brown/red bean, although multiple varieties have been documented in the past. The white beans have a slightly sweet, soft texture; the brown are meaty and rich.

Where to Find These Foods

If you can't plant or gather your own from the land (note: saguaro cactus are protected in Arizona, so you can only harvest from cactus on your own land) several local stores and organizations sell indigenous foods. Here are some sources.

Arizona Cactus Ranch, (520) 625-4419; arizonacactusranch.com. Owner Natalie McGee processes her vast harvest of prickly-pear fruit into a wonderful, sugar-free, magenta juice.

Food City, foodcity.com. Seasonal produce at select locations includes prickly-pear fruit and pads, purslane, roasted agave leaves, and O'odham mature squash. Chiletepin peppers are available packaged in the spice aisles.

Native Seed/SEARCH, (520) 622-5561; nativeseeds.org. This local nonprofit seed bank has a retail store that sells seeds as well as packaged foods, books, and ingredients. You can find tepary beans, cholla buds, and mesquite flour (be sure it's local).

San Xavier Cooperative, (520) 295-3774; sanxavier coop.org. Part of the Tohono O'odham Nation, this cooperative farm plants a limited number of traditional foods and sells them from its tiny office. They offer local mesquite flour, O'odham squash, honey, tepary beans, and dried corn. Always call ahead, they have limited quantities.

Tohono O'odham Community Action, (520) 383-4966; tocaon line.org. This independent nonprofit on the Tohono O'odham Nation in Sells is dedicated to the preservation of culture and health. All proceeds from sales go toward educational programming designed to support future traditional farmers, basket weavers, and youth. Tepary beans, cholla buds, saguaro syrup, and saguaro seeds are available here.

Foodie Festivals & Events

There are so many interesting and tasty food festivals and events that take place around town throughout the year. The majority of them happen during our peak season, February through April, when the weather is spectacular and we have lots of hungry snowbirds (winter visitors) here from all over the country that swell the ranks of our full-time foodies.

February

Taste of China Festival, Chinese Cultural Center, 1288 W. River Rd., Tucson, AZ 85704; (520) 292-6900; tucsonchinese.com. Find the date of the Chinese New Year and put a big red mark on your calendar—this festival, which takes place annually during the Chinese New Year, is not to be missed! Served at the lovely

Second Saturdays Downtown

Held every second Saturday (thus the name!), this monthly event is a great way to check out the downtown scene. Every restaurant, club, coffee shop, store, and gallery is open and throngs of people walk the streets chatting and chewing. The main street, Congress Avenue, is closed to traffic and it makes for a lovely evening out. You'll find food trucks and a variety of basic food vendors lining the roads along with crafts, antique cars, musicians, and performers. Parking is at a premium, so plan accordingly! Details are at 2ndsaturdaysdowtown.com.

Chinese Cultural Center, the food available here is made right in the kitchens by locals, not by restaurants. Get here *early!* The space is limited and the lines are *long*. There is an entry fee and individual food tickets are sold only at the entrance to the center. Buy a whole bunch because it's almost impossible to navigate the crowd to get back to the ticket area and no cash is accepted for food or drinks. A series of tented booths organized by regions is set up around the grounds and each offers a different combination of unique dishes, with a separate tent for desserts. This is a very popular event and at times the food has actually run out; food tickets are not refundable so make sure you have enough time to stand in line. Live entertainment will keep you from getting bored as you wait—martial arts demonstrations, singing, and dancing take place throughout the day.

March

CRUSH Wine, Food, Art Festival, Tucson Museum of Art, 140 N. Main St., Tucson, AZ 85701 and various venues; (520) 624-2333; tucsonmuseumofart.org/crush. A huge fund-raiser for the Tucson Museum of Art, this event gives you access to a host of wine and food tastings and a gala dinner. The event starts with a series of art seminars pairing food, wine, and museum and culminates with the Crush Party and the Crush Gala. The Party takes place on the lovely museum grounds and features hors d'oeuvres from over 25 local restaurants, tastings of national, regional, and local wine and beer, and a silent auction that lets you bid on dinners, hotel stays, and rare wines. The Gala is held at an upscale dining venue with dancing, a sit-down multicourse gourmet dinner, and a live auction. Tickets are available per event.

Tucson Festival of Books, University of Arizona Main Mall, Tucson, AZ 85721; tucsonfestivalofbooks.org. Although this festival focuses on books, books, books, there's lots here for food lovers too! Local and regional cookbook authors demonstrate their signature recipes at the Culinary Tent, talk about their inspirations in seminars, and sell and sign their books. Area restaurants have booths with food for sale and there is no entry fee! Get ready for big crowds (the festival draws upwards of 100,000 people) and get to the cooking demos early—they fill up fast. The festival takes place on the Main Mall of the University of Arizona. Maps, event

OUT OF TOWN WINE FESTIVALS

Southeast Arizona is fast becoming its own little wine country with numerous area wineries. Several host small-scale festivals in April featuring their unique vintages, tastings, blessing ceremonies, and grape-stomping. While food is not the top draw here, if you're in the mood for a lovely drive out of town, check these out:

Blessing of the Vine (April), Harvest Festival (July), Sonoita Vineyards, 290 Elgin-Canelo Rd., Elgin, AZ 85611; (520) 455-5893; sonoitavineyards.com. The Blessing of the Vine event in April includes wine and food pairings and horse-drawn wagon rides while the Harvest Fest gives you a chance to stomp grapes a la Lucille Ball (my favorite part). Food is available at an extra cost from local restaurants.

Southeast Arizona Wine Growers Festival, Kief Joshua Vineyard, 370 Elgin Rd., Elgin, AZ 85611; (520) 455-5582. Held at the lovely Kief Joshua Vineyards, winemakers from all four wine regions of Arizona offer samples of their wines here. For an entry fee you get eight tastings along with live music. Food is provided (at an extra cost) by a local steakhouse and a local chef who specializes in sandwiches and makes a mean omelet.

times, parking details, and author listings are all available on the website. If you want to rub shoulders with the culinary writers featured on the culinary stage, you have two chances. The local Slow Foods convivium hosts a reception where you can taste local wines, beers, specialty cocktails, and hors d'oeuvres, and there's a sit-down dinner with wine pairings at a local restaurant (tickets and information at slowfoodtucson.org).

April

Flavors of the Desert Fund-raising Dinner, Native Seed/SEARCH; (520) 622-0830; nativeseeds.org. This multicourse buffet dinner is a fund-raiser for the seed bank Native SeedSEARCH (see the Native Foods Chapter for more details about the organization). It takes place at different venues annually, from botanical gardens to casino ballrooms, with different guest chefs who develop a special menu using local and indigenous ingredients in creative and delicious ways. Highly popular, tickets sell out fast and they are worth it. Chefs and Native Seed/SEARCH staff really pull out all the stops to create a delicious, truly place-based dinner, spending months designing the menu.

Taste of Chocolate, tucsontasteofchocolate.org. What could be better than an event where *everything* is chocolate? Chocoholics rejoice and head to this tasty event sponsored by the Rincon Rotary Club. An admission fee buys you access to chocolate treats made by top restaurant chefs, caterers, pastry chefs, bakers, and artisan chocolatiers. Held at the Doubletree Hotel in midtown, this event features table after table of mouthwatering tastings, from beautiful artisan chocolate confections to breads, cakes, and even some savory dishes incorporating mole and pasta! Not just a tasting, this is also a competition. Culinary participants are competing for top prizes in a variety of categories and you, along with top local food writers, get to be the judge—so be sure to fill out your ballots. The proceeds benefit the Rincon Foundation's scholarship program and the Third Grade Dictionary Project that aims to place a dictionary (a real paper one) in the hands of every third grader.

Tucson Taco Festival, Rillito Park, 4502 N. First Ave., Tucson, AZ 85718; (480) 466-0579; tucsontacofestival.com. If you love tacos, this is the event for you. Over 25 taco teams, both professional and amateur, battle it out for a cash prize and trophies. The winning team takes home a cool $5,000 and the title of Grand Champion. The event takes place at the east side of the infield at Rillito Park, a large park and horse-racing track. There's an admission fee and a fee for food on site from booths offering hundreds

of varieties of tacos along with salsas and guacamole. You'll need tickets for most of the food; only some booths take cash.

Other highlights include *lucha libre* wrestling (think Jack Black in the hysterical movie *Nacho Libre*), hot chile eating contests, live bands, and a boutique tequila-tasting tent (entry for this is a separate fee and includes tastings and a margarita competition featuring local bartenders). I can't tell you what kind of tacos to expect, it all depends on what the contestants make using chicken, beef, pork, and fish, so anything goes. If you happen to be there

OUT OF TOWN

Handmade tortilla-making demonstrations take place at Tumacacori National Historic Park located about 50 miles south of town (1895 E. Frontage Rd., Tumacacori, AZ 85640; 520-398-2341; nps.gov/tuma/index.htm). On select weekdays and weekends seasonally, local expert Hilda Alegria makes the dough, pats it, stretches it, and cooks it deftly at an outdoor *ramada* over a wood fire. Kids love to watch and to taste these hot off the griddle (samples are free, although a donation is welcome). While I wouldn't drive there just for the demo, if you find yourself in the area or live in the area, it's worth a stop to see the remains of one of the region's oldest missions and other cultural demonstrations including traditional basket weaving. There is an admissions fee to enter the park grounds where the demo takes place.

midday, volunteer for the taco-eating challenge—the MC will call for participants from the crowd.

June

Garlic and Onion Festival, Agua Linda Farm, 2453 E. Frontage Rd., Amado, AZ 85645; (520) 891-5532; agualindafarm.net. This family-owned farm is just delightful. Farmer Stewart Loew and his wife and kids work the land and are truly committed to sustainable agriculture. Set in a shaded grove on the property, this small-scale, family-friendly festival celebrates garlic and onions in all their glory. A modest admission fee gets you hayrides, access to the petting zoo, and live music from local bands. Food choices include the stars of the festival—garlic and onions! You'll find sandwiches, juicy farm burgers, deep-fried onion rings, and a special plate lunch (for a separate charge). If you're inspired by the food, you can take home armloads of onions and garlic grown right on the farm.

September

Tucson Greek Festival, St. Demetrios Greek Orthodox Church, 1145 E. Ft Lowell Rd., Tucson, AZ 85719; (520) 888-0505; tucson greekfest.com. Get ready for lots and lots of food! Hosted by the St. Demetrios Greek Orthodox Church, this extremely popular and

Out of Town

Apple Annie's Orchard in Willcox (2081 W. Hardy Rd., Willcox, AZ 85643; 520-384-2084; appleannies.com) hosts a variety of seasonal fruit-themed events throughout the year. Apples, peaches, pumpkins—Annie's puts on family-friendly festivals for them all, featuring pancake breakfasts, hayrides, burger lunches, and homemade ice cream. The kids (and you!) will love it. About 60 miles southeast of town, it's worth the drive.

crowded festival offers 4 days filled with food and fun. For a small entry fee you'll get access to cooking demonstrations, lectures, exhibitions, and classes but best of all, you will be able to buy and eat lots of food. Inside are tables covered with Greek desserts, all made by church members. Look for *finikia* (honey-dipped cookies), *kourabiedes* (powdered sugar cookies), and ouzo cake by the piece. These are not things you will find in restaurants but are homemade and delicious. You can pick and choose your favorites or buy an assortment already packaged. For savory items, head outside for spanakopita, Athenian roast chicken, pastitsio, and roast lamb, also homemade. These dishes and more are offered cafeteria-style, with photos and descriptions to help you choose what to put on your tray. Do not miss the *loukoumades,* deep-fried, warm, honey-drizzled fritters that are made at a separate outdoor stand. There's more—Greek beer, Greek wine, Greek coffee, Greek music, pan-Athenian dancers, games, rides, and lots and lots of people. Get there early, the best time to go is when the doors open on the very first day of the festival.

ARIZONA RESTAURANT WEEK

Many of Tucson's top restaurants participate in the statewide Arizona Restaurant Week event, offering a prix-fixe special menu showcasing signature dishes. It takes place for one week in mid-September and is a great way to try out new places or visit old favorites. Check arizonarestaurantweek.com for a full listing and details.

October

Tucson Culinary Festival Reserve and Grand Tasting at Casino del Sol Resort, 5655 W. Valencia Rd., Tucson, AZ 85757; (520) 343-9985; tucsonoriginals.com. Held in the giant ballroom at the Casino del Sol Resort, this upscale, ticketed event offers an opportunity for gourmet food and wine lovers to sip and sup on fine wine (rare and boutique wines take center stage) and fine foods prepared by area top chefs from over 40 restaurants. This is not your grandma's casino with penny slots—the luxury hotel rises up from a circular drive and is home to top-rated accommodations. Wear your fancy duds because you will want to see and be seen at this popular event.

Tucson Meet Yourself Festival, various venues in downtown Tucson; (520) 370-0588; tucsonmeetyourself.org. Despite its some-what odd name, this is *the* biggest food event in town. The 3-day festival takes place in six areas of the downtown, from the intimate Presidio courtyard to the open Presidio Park, and there is no entry fee. But take your wallet because absolutely every kind of food is here and you'll want to try it all. Booth after booth of foods from every imaginable cuisine and culture (over 60 countries and cultures are represented) are available from restaurants, community and non-profit organizations, clubs, churches, grandmas, you name it! The list of participants is far too long to list, so check the website and the special sections of the newspaper in advance for a detailed event listing and map. Go early, plan to stay all day, and good luck with parking—it's not easy to find spaces on the street, so leave plenty of time and think of parking in the lots sprinkled around downtown. Along with the food booths, you'll find iron chef contests and food demos at the Kitchen Stadium, music, dancing, and tons of vendors hawking everything from knickknacks to artisan crafts.

World Margarita Championship, venues change annually, (520) 343-9985; tucsonoriginals .com. You'll need a ticket to this competition where mixologists from Tucson Originals restaurants compete aggressively to create a cocktail that deserves the title of "World's Greatest Margarita." Guests will have the chance to taste these contenders to the margarita throne paired with a variety of savory foods from the same restaurants. See if you can choose the winner—your vote will be tallied along with the judging panel's to determine the winner.

November

Pecan Festival, The Green Valley Pecan Company, 1652 E. Sahuarita Rd., Sahuarita, AZ 85629; greenvalleypecan.com. Held in the parking lot of the massive Green Valley Pecan Company, this small-scale festival offers a fascinating chance to see pecan harvesting. Family owned and operated since 1937, the Green Valley Pecan Company is home to the world's largest irrigated pecan orchard with over 7,000 acres and 104,000 trees. While you can't get into the plant to see how the nuts are processed (believe me

More Tucson Events!

Although you might not find gourmet fare at these venues, they are some of Tucson's biggest events and should not be missed!

Fourth Avenue Street Fair—Fall and Spring: A top draw for visitors and residents alike, these enormous street fairs take over Fourth Avenue with tented booths selling everything from crafts to food. You will find the usual vendors here, sausage and peppers, hamburgers and hot dogs, but there are specialty purveyors and some gourmet and local products available too. And you can always take a break and visit one of Fourth Avenue's terrific restaurants or coffee shops. It's super-crowded and street parking is almost impossible to find so get there early. More info is at fourthavenue.org.

La Fiesta de los Vaqueros: Ah, the rodeo! Yee-ha! Put on your boots and your cowboy hat and head to one of Tucson's most popular events. Bull riding, broncos, kids hanging onto sheep, and a whole bunch of food vendors offering everything from tri-tip beef sandwiches, barbecue, pulled pork, the ubiquitous kettle corn (sweetened popcorn), and loads of ooey-gooey desserts keep people coming here year after year since it started in 1925! Go to tucsonrodeo for tickets and details.

Pima County Fair: Funnel cakes, curly fries, candy apples, deep-fried everything . . . the fair is definitely not a gourmet destination but it is lots of fun and you will find tons of things to eat here, even if they're not all good for you! Check out the rides, the animals, the sideshows, the games, and have some fun! Check pimacountyfair.com for dates and details.

I tried!), you can tour the orchard during the festival and see the mechanical harvesting process. While the majority of the products are sold by mail order, a tiny retail store on site has bins and bags of delicious pecans for sale in every possible form—roasted, chocolate covered, brittled, spiced, and more. They very generously offer samples of just about everything at the store and during the festival (I loved the chocolate camelback, toffees, and the mesquite spiced). Stick with the nuts and pass on the selection of refrigerated pecan pies that are made by an outside vendor. Food choices at the festival are limited to barbecue and Mexican food.

December

Tucson Tamal and Heritage Festival, Casino del Sol, 5655 W. Valencia Rd., Tucson, AZ 85757; (520) 838-6793; casinodelsol.com/events/tamal-festival. Christmas in Tucson means tamales. Those delectable steamed corn husks wrapped around all sorts of fillings can be addictive, and this is the place to learn all about the significance of tamales in Hispanic culture. This free annual event takes place at the outdoor AVA amphitheater at Casino del Sol and features a tamale contest and live entertainment, including dancing and *folklorico* music. It's a great way to get into the holiday spirit. You can buy all sorts of tasty tamales from the over 100 tamale vendors on site.

Recipes

I love recipes, it's always interesting to see what ingredients and methods talented chefs and cooks use to create the foods we love on their menus. And it's even more interesting (and sometimes challenging) to recreate them at home. Here, top chefs from some of Tucson's award-winning restaurants and spas have generously contributed signature recipes, showcasing unique style and creativity. Enjoy!

Clear, Ageless Skin Smoothie

Miraval has become synonymous with health and fitness, not to mention Oprah, who loves to visit this Tucson-based top spa and health resort. A team of top chefs make the magic happen here, creating beautiful, healthy, and seasonal beverages, entrees, desserts, and cocktails that keep celebrities and health-minded guests coming back year after year to dine at their Cactus Flower Restaurant and sip smoothies at the Palm Court smoothie bar. Here they share the recipe from their book Mindful Eating *(Hay House, 2012) for a signature smoothie that distills the essence of nutrient-rich fruits and vegetables. A juicer brings out the very best texture and flavor in this bright green smoothie. Calories: 170; total fat: 0 g; carbohydrate: 44 g; dietary fiber: 7 g; protein: 2 g.*

2 cups cucumber, with skin on
1 cup Granny Smith apple,
   stemmed and seeded
1 cup celery hearts

1 heart of romaine lettuce,
   about 6 ounces
⅓ cup fresh pineapple

Combine all of the ingredients in the bowl of a heavy juicer or blender and process on high speed until smooth and frothy.

Pour into a tall glass and serve immediately.

Courtesy of Miraval Resorts, reprinted by permission from
Mindful Eating (Hay House Inc, 2012). (p. 89)

Fresh Organic Apple-Cumin Vinaigrette

This is the signature dressing at The Tasteful Kitchen, known for its healthy, nutritious, and delicious cuisine. Chef and co-owner Sigret Thompson has always had a keen interest in cooking as well as health, nutrition, fitness, art, and design. She spent several years in major cosmopolitan cities such as New York, London, and Sydney, where she had the opportunity to develop those interests further. Now her life experiences and knowledge are brought together and are expressed at The Tasteful Kitchen, where she creates unique vegetarian, vegan, and raw dishes that are both delicious and artfully presented.

This dressing is so versatile it goes well with almost every type of salad. It is light and refreshing, slightly sweet, and a little tangy. If cumin is not for you, Sigret suggests leaving it out and using fresh ginger instead.

Yield: 1⅔ cups

- 1 crisp organic apple, any variety will do
- 2 tablespoons apple cider vinegar
- 1 lemon, juiced
- ¼ cup water
- 1 teaspoon cumin
- 1 tablespoon agave nectar
- 1 pinch of salt
- ½ cup olive oil

Peel, core, and rough chop the apple.

Place the chopped apple and all remaining ingredients into the blender and blend until a smooth consistency is achieved.

Pour dressing into a jar or squeeze bottle and store in the fridge for up to 2 weeks. The vinegar and lemon juice act as natural preservatives. Shake well before using. It makes about 1⅔ cups.}

Try the dressing on organic spring mix with chopped celery, jicama, walnuts, and oranges.

Courtesy of Sigret Thompson, Chef and Co-Owner of
The Tasteful Kitchen—Unique Vegetarian Cuisine (p. 169)

Ceviche with Minted Ginger Syrup & Candied Jalapeños

Chef Janos Wilder is one of Tucson's star chefs. Named the Top Chef of the Southwest in 2000 by the James Beard Foundation, he continues to innovate and is truly a culinary genius. Born in Redwood City, California, he began his culinary career as a teenager at a local pizza parlor, followed by many years as a chef at restaurants in California, Colorado, and Tennessee. In 1982 he traveled to France where he studied French cooking and honed his classical techniques at several Michelin-starred restaurants in Bordeaux. Now chef-owner of Downtown Kitchen+Cocktails and chef consultant to the innovative Kai Restaurant in Chandler, Arizona, Janos is also the author of several award-winning cookbooks. Downtown Kitchen+Cocktails showcases his unusual combinations of Asian, Mexican, and regional ingredients. This popular appetizer is a perfect balance of sweet, heat, salty, and sour.

Yield: 4 portions

Ceviche

12 ounces sushi-grade ahi, cut into medium dice

sea salt

½ cup fresh tangerine juice

2 tablespoons sesame oil

2 tablespoons fermented fish sauce

¼ cup minted ginger syrup (see recipe below)

¼ cup dried pineapple, small dice

16 pink grapefruit supremes

16 candied jalapeños (see recipe below)

16 whole roasted almonds

Place the ahi in a medium stainless, glass, or other noncorrosive bowl.

Salt the fish and toss lightly.

Whisk the tangerine juice, sesame oil, fish sauce, and minted ginger syrup together and pour over the ahi.

Lightly toss with the pineapple, grapefruit supremes, candied jalapeños, and whole roasted almonds.

Minted Ginger Syrup

1 cup fresh mint leaves, packed
¼ cup spinach leaves, packed
¼ cup freshly grated ginger

1 cup simple syrup (recipe follows)

To blanch the mint and spinach leaves

1 quart water

1 tablespoon salt

Separately blanch the mint and spinach quickly in boiling, salted water and shock in ice water.

Squeeze out all excess water.

Thoroughly puree the blanched mint, spinach, and ginger. Add puree to simple syrup and strain through fine-mesh strainer or cheesecloth. Discard leaves, reserving the green minted ginger syrup and refrigerate.

Candied Jalapeños

3 jalapeños, sliced into ¹⁄₁₆-inch rounds and seeded
1 cup simple syrup (recipe follows)

1 whole jalapeño, cut in half lengthwise and seeded

Simmer the jalapeño slices in the simple syrup until they soften a bit, remove the slices, and set aside.

Remove the syrup from heat and puree with the two halves of the jalapeño.

Strain, reserving the liquid.

Put the slices back into the syrup and refrigerate.

Heavy Simple Syrup

2 cups water   **2 cups granulated sugar**

Place water and sugar in a saucepan.

Bring water and sugar to a simmer and cook until the sugar is completely dissolved.

Yield: 2 cups

Courtesy of Janos Wilder, Chef-Owner Downtown Kitchen + Cocktails (p. 144)

Traditional Green-Corn Tamales

Tucson Tamale Company produces over 20 different varieties of tamales and owner Todd Martin is a real tamale aficionado, traveling the world to research new techniques and combinations. He loves to experiment with different and unusual flavors and he also makes vegan and vegetarian varieties, all available at his small retail store, cafe and at local markets and farmers' markets. Todd did not come to tamales naturally; a former manager at Intuit, he exchanged his pinstripes for an apron in 2008 after being inspired by making tamales with his wife's family. Traditionally, people gather at holiday time to make tamales en masse for family and friends. This recipe will definitely feed a crowd or a very big family—it makes 5 dozen! Tamale-wrapping is a real art form, so if you've never done it, Todd suggests watching some YouTube videos to get the hang of it!

Yield: 5 dozen tamales

- 20 ears fresh white corn, removed from husk
- 1 pound maseca (instant corn masa flour, available in most Hispanic markets and grocery stores and online)
- 2 tablespoons salt
- 2 tablespoons baking powder
- 2–3 cups water
- 1 pound dry corn husks
- 3 pounds fresh roasted green chiles
- 1½ pounds grated cheddar cheese

Put all the fresh white corn in a processor and grind until it is soupy. Put in mixing bowl with maseca, salt, baking powder and 2 cups water. Beat on medium speed for 10 minutes. Add more water if masa is too thick. Put masa in fridge for one hour.

Soak the corn husks in warm water. They should soak for at least one hour. Leave them in the water until you are ready to use them.

Peel and clean the green chiles, getting rid of as much of the seeds and skin as you can. Dice the chiles and put them in a stainless mixing bowl. Add the grated cheddar and combine with the chiles.

Take a soaked corn husk and lay it rib side down (you will be putting the masa on the smooth side of the husk. Scoop 2 ounces (¼ cup) of masa on the husk. Then press 1½ ounces (¼ cup) of the cheese-chili mix into the center of the masa. Grab the husk on either side and bring the sides together, rolling the masa into a cigar shape. Finish wrapping the tamale by wrapping the remaining side of the husk around itself. There will be a tail that you fold up toward the top of the tamale. Place the tamales in a steamer basket.

When all the tamales are wrapped and in the steamer basket, have your water boiling, ready to steam them. Place the steamer basket in the pot. Cover and cook for 45 minutes. Remove the steamer basket from the pot and let the tamales cool for 15 minutes. They are now ready to eat. Wrap up all that you don't eat and they can be frozen for later.

Courtesy of Todd Martin, Owner, Tucson Tamale Company (p. 54)

Tepary Bean Soup

Corporate Chef Scott Uehlein oversees the vast culinary operations at Canyon Ranch Health Resorts. A brilliant chef and graduate of the Culinary Institute of America, he travels the globe developing new, innovative recipes for the Ranch's resorts, affiliated cruise ships, and health spas. Always on the cutting edge of cuisine, Canyon Ranch is known for its healthy, delicious, and nutritious food, and Chef Uehlein is their master chef. His many creative recipes can be found in the cookbook Canyon Ranch Nourish: Indulgently Healthy Cuisine (*Viking Studio, 2009*). *Scott is committed to using sustainable, local, and indigenous ingredients whenever possible, taking great efforts to source only the very best products. Here he uses the indigenous tepary bean to create a light, smoky, delicious soup low in carbs and high in protein.*

1 cup brown tepary beans, soaked overnight and rinsed*

⅓ cup diced yellow onion

¼ cup peeled and diced carrots

¼ cup diced celery

1 teaspoon minced fresh garlic

1 tablespoon olive oil

1½ quarts chicken stock

Dash liquid smoke

¼ teaspoon dry basil

Pinch dry oregano

Pinch dry thyme

¾ teaspoon salt

Pinch black pepper

½ teaspoon Worcestershire sauce

1½ teaspoons chopped fresh parsley

½ teaspoon lemon juice

* Sources for these native beans can be found in the Native Foods Chapter.

In a large saucepot add soaked beans and cover with fresh water and bring to a boil. Reduce heat to low and simmer for 3 hours. Drain.

In a separate large saucepot, sauté onions, carrots, celery and garlic in olive oil until onions begin to turn translucent.

Add beans and stir. Add stock, liquid smoke, basil, oregano, and thyme. Bring to a boil, reduce heat to low and simmer for 1 hour, or until beans are soft.

Beans should begin to fall apart and thicken broth.

Once soup begins to thicken, add remaining ingredients. Simmer briefly.

Makes 5 (¾-cup) servings, each containing approximately:
160 calories
24 grams carbohydrate
3 grams fat
0 milligrams cholesterol
8 grams protein
311 milligrams sodium
6 grams fiber

Courtesy of Scott Uehlein, Corporate Chef, Canyon Ranch Resorts (p. 67)

Black Rice Horchata

Chef Ryan Clark wears many toques—chef, pastry chef, and mixologist. Winner of Tucson's Iron Chef and Copper Chef competitions and an all-around nice guy, he creates masterful cuisine and drinks at The Lodge on the Desert. This amazingly creamy, rich cocktail is inspired by the local nonalcoholic drink horchata. A refreshing mix of rice, water, almonds, cinnamon, sugar, and vanilla, it can be found in bottles, coolers, premixed in bags, and ladled out of glass jugs at Hispanic markets around town. Here Chef Ryan has kicked it up a notch with a healthy dose of cinnamon-infused bourbon. Before filling the glasses, he dips the rims in sparkly cinnamon sugar.

Yield: 1 quart

- 1 cup black rice (also referred to as "forbidden rice," available in Asian and specialty markets and online)
- 1 cup almonds
- 1 cup basmati rice
- 1 (2-inch) piece cinnamon stick
- ¾ cup sugar
- ¼ teaspoon vanilla extract
- 9 cups water

Mix all ingredients together with 4 cups of the water and let rest overnight in the refrigerator.

The next day, puree the ingredients in a blender with the remaining 5 cups of water and strain through cheesecloth.

Keep cold.

To make a cocktail, add 1 part cinnamon-infused bourbon to 5 parts Black Rice Horchata.

To make cinnamon infused bourbon, place 1–2 sticks of cinnamon into your favorite bourbon and let it infuse into the alcohol over several days.

Cheers!

Courtesy of Chef Ryan Clark, Lodge on the Desert (p. 37)

Appendix: Eateries by Cuisine

American

Abbey Eat + Drink, The, 63
Blue Willow, 18
Bobo's, 19
Cafe 54, 138
Cafe a la C'art, 137
Claire's Cafe, 83
CORE Kitchen + Wine Bar, 85
Cup Cafe, 150
Cushing Street Bar and Grill, 151
Dakota Cafe & Catering, 22
Delectable's, 161
El Corral, 68
Feast, 25
Frank's/Francisco's, 27
Gus Balon's, 31
Happy Rooster Cafe, 115
Hub Restaurant and Creamery, 149
Jonathan's Cork, 116
La Cocina, 153
Le Buzz Caffe, 117
Mays Counter Chicken and Waffles, 40
100 Estrella Restaurant and Lounge, 103
Pastiche Modern Eatery, 44
Pat's Drive In, 104
Son's Bakery Cafe, 51
Todd's Restaurant, 108
Union Public House, 55
Wilko, 172

Asian

Kampai, 87

Barbecue

Bone In Steak and Smokehouse, The, 111

BrushFire BBQ Company #1, 20
Original Mr K's BBQ, 127

Beer
Frog and Firkin, 162
Nimbus Brewing Company, 126
1702, 168

Bosnian
Alisah's Restaurant, 78

Breakfast
Millie's Pancake Haus, 42

Brewpub
Gentle Ben's Brewing
    Company, 163

Burgers
Lindy's on Fourth, 166

Cajun
Parish, The, 90

Cheesesteak
Frankie's, 27

Chinese
China Pasta House, 160
China Phoenix, 80
Dragon's View Chinese
    Restaurant, 100
Golden Phoenix Restaurant, 125
Impress Hot Pot, 33

Continental
Anthony's in the Catalina, 66
Arizona Inn, 61
Dish, The, 23
Grill at Hacienda del Sol Guest
    Ranch Resort, The, 76
Monterey Court Cafe, 101

Deli
Shlomo & Vito's New York
    Delicatessen, 71

Eclectic
Eclectic Cafe, 113

Ethiopian
Cafe Desta, 139

Farm to Table
Pasco Kitchen and Lounge, 167

French
Agustin Brasserie, 97
Ghini's French Caffe, 28
Joel's Bistro, 164
Le Rendez-vous, 35
Maynards, 154

Fusion
Downtown Kitchen + Cocktails,
    144, 274

Global/SW
Acacia Real Food & Cocktails, 64

Greek
Athens on 4th Avenue, 157
Greek Taverna, 30

Indian
New Delhi Palace, 118
Saffron Indian Bistro, 91
Sher-e-Punjab, 49

International
AI Bistro, 17

Italian
Cafe Milano, 141
Caffè Torino, 80
Caruso's, 173
Dry River Company, 114
Tavolino, 72
Vivace Restaurant, 57

Jamaican
CeeDee Jamaican Restaurant, 21

Japanese
Ginza Sushi, 70
Yoshimatsu Healthy Japanese
    Food, 58

Korean
Takamatsu, 52

Latin
Miguel's, 87

Malaysian
Neo of Melaka, 43

Mediterranean
Primo, 104

Mexican
Blanco Tacos + Tequila, 66
Boca, 159
Cafe Poca Cosa, 142
El Guero Canelo #1, 130
El Indio, 131
El Mezon del Cobre, 24
El Molcajete, 25
El Torero, 124
La Indita, 165
Las Brasas Mesquite Grill, 126
Lerua's, 36
Los Portales, 132
Mi Nidito, 134
Taqueria Pico de Gallo, 135
Teresa's Mosaic Cafe, 107
Tooley's Cafe, 171
Tucson Tamale Company, 54, 277
Zivaz Mexican Bistro, 60

Middle Eastern
Shish Kebab House, 50
Zayna Mediterranean, 59

New American
Wildflower, 92

New Mexican
Poco and Mom's, 119

Pizza
Brooklyn Pizza Company, 159, 217
Empire Pizza & Pub, 148
Scordato Pizzeria, 48
Tino's Pizza, 54

Polish
Polish Cottage, 47

Pub
Canyon's Crown Restaurant and
   Pub, 112
Noble Hops Gastropub, 88

Seafood
Kingfisher, 34

Southwestern
B-Line, 158
Desert Rain Cafe, 98
Flying V Bar & Grill, 69

Gold at Westward Look Resort, 74
Lodge on the Desert, 37, 281
Ocotillo Cafe at the Arizona
    Sonora Desert Museum
    Restaurant, 109
Tanque Verde Ranch, 121
Tohono Chul Tearoom, 205

Spanish
Casa Vicente, 143

Steak
HiFalutin', 86
Little Abner's Steakhouse, 101
McMahon's Prime Steakhouse, 40

Pinnacle Peak Steakhouse, 45
PY Steakhouse, 105
Silver Saddle Steak House,
    The, 128

Vegetarian
Govinda's, 29
Lovin' Spoonfuls, 39
Tasteful Kitchen, The, 169, 272

Vietnamese
Com Tham Thuan Kieu, 84
Ha Long Bay, 32
Pho # 1, 46

Index

A

Abbey Eat + Drink, The, 63
Acacia Real Food & Cocktails, 64
Agua Linda Farms, 238
Agustin Brasserie, 97
AI Bistro, 17
Alejandro's Tortilla Factory, 177
Alisah's Restaurant, 78
Allegro—il gelato naturale, 215
Anita's Street Market, 177
Anthony's in the Catalinas, 66
Apple Annie's, 238
Apple Annie's Orchard, 263
Aquaponics, 236
Arizona Cactus Ranch, 255
Arizona Inn, 61
Arizona Restaurant Week, 264
Arizona-Sonoran Desert
    Museum, 249
Athens on 4th Avenue, 157

B

Babylon Market, 178
Bashas', 178

Bear Canyon Open Air Market, 231
Bentley's House of Coffee and
    Tea, 206
Beyond Bread, 81, 193
Big Skye Bakers, 233
Blanco Tacos + Tequila, 66
B-Line, 158
Blue Banana Frozen Yogurt, 216
Blue Willow, 18
Bobo's, 19
Boca, 159
Bone In Steak and Smokehouse,
    The, 111
Brooklyn Pizza Company,
    159, 217
BrushFire BBQ Company #1, 20

C

Cafe 54, 138
Cafe a la C'art, 137
Cafe Desta, 139
Cafe Marcel, 218
Cafe Milano, 141
Cafe Poca Cosa, 142

Caffè Torino, 80

Canyon Ranch Health Resorts, 67, 279

Canyon's Crown Restaurant and Pub, 112

Caravan Mid Eastern Foods, 179

Carnicerias, 191

Cartel Coffee Lab, 207

Caruso's, 173

Casa Vicente, 143

CeeDee Jamaican Restaurant, 21

Chantilly Tea Room, 202

Cheri's Desert Harvest, 198

China Pasta House, 160

China Phoenix, 80

Chocolate Iguana, 208

Claire's Cafe, 83

Coctel de Elote, 246

Colossal Cave Mountain Park, 249

Com Tham Thuan Kieu, 84

CORE Kitchen + Wine Bar, 85

Crave Coffee Bar, 208

CRUSH Wine, Food, Art Festival, 258

Cultivated foods, 251

Cup Cafe, 150

Cushing Street Bar and Grill, 151

Cyclopopsicle, 243

D

Dakota Cafe & Catering, 22

Delectable's, 161

Desert Rain Cafe, 98

Desert Treasures Groves, 233

Dickman's, 191

Dish, The, 23

Downtown Kitchen + Cocktails, 144, 274

Dragon's View Chinese Restaurant, 100

Dry River Company, 114

D's Island Grill JA, 240

E

Eclectic Cafe, 113

El Charro Cafe, 146

El Corral, 68

El Guero Canelo #1, 130

El Herradero Carniceria y Panaderia, 180

El Indio, 131

El Mezon del Cobre, 24

El Minuto Cafe, 148

El Molcajete, 25

El Torero, 124

Empire Pizza & Pub, 148

Epic Cafe, 209

European Market, 181

F

Farmers' Market at the Shoppes at
    La Posada, 231
Feast, 25
Flavors of the Desert Fund-raising
    Dinner, 260
Flying V Bar & Grill, 69
Food City, 255
Food Conspiracy Co-op, 181
Foodie Fleet, 240
Food Truck Roundup, 241
Fourth Avenue Street Fair, 267
Frankie's, 27
Frank's/Francisco's, 27
Friday Farmers' Market, 231
Frog and Firkin, 162
Frog's Organic Bakery, 194
Frost, A Gelato Shoppe, 219
Frosty Jake's Frozen Custard, 219

G

Garlic, Onion and Music
    Festival, 262
Gentle Ben's Brewing Company, 163
German Food Station, 241
Ghini's French Caffe, 28

Ginza Sushi, 70
G&L Import, 182
Gold at Westward Look
    Resort, 74
Golden Phoenix Restaurant, 125
Gourmet Girls Gluten Free
    Bakery, 195
Govinda's, 29
Greek Taverna, 30
Green Valley Farmers'
    Market, 225
Grill at Hacienda del Sol Guest
    Ranch Resort, The, 76
Guero Loco's Bubba-Que, 241
Gus Balon's, 31

H

Ha Long Bay, 32
Happy Rooster Cafe, 115
HiFalutin', 86
Holy Trinity Monastery, 201
Howard's Orchard, 237
Hub Restaurant and Creamery, 149
Hub Restaurant and Ice
    Creamery, 220

I

Impress Hot Pot, 33

India Dukaan Fine Food
   Market, 183
India Food & Gifts, 183
Isabella's Ice Cream, 242

J
Jack and the Beanstalk, 235
Jamie's Bitchin' Kitchen, 242
Joel's Bistro, 164
Jonathan's Cork, 116
Jones Street Bistro, 243
Joy Asian Market, 184

K
Kampai, 87
Kimpo Oriental Market, 184
Kingfisher, 34

L
La Baguette Bakery, 195
La Baguette Parisienne, 196
La Cocina, 153
La Estrella, 196
La Fiesta de los Vaqueros, 267
La Indita, 165
La Mesa Tortillas, 197
Las Brasas Mesquite Grill, 126
Le Buzz, 210

Le Buzz Caffe, 117
Le Rendez-vous, 35
Lee Lee Market, 185
Lerua's, 36
Lindy's on Fourth, 166
Little Abner's Steakhouse, 101
Lodge on the Desert, 37, 281
Loews Ventana Canyon, 205
Los Portales, 132
Lovin' Spoonfuls, 39

M
Margy's Jam, 234
Mariscos Chihuahua, 129
Maynards, 154
Maynard's Market, 186
Mays Counter Chicken and
   Waffles, 40
McMahon's Prime Steakhouse, 40
Menlo Farms, 233, 236
Mexican treats, 221
Miguel's, 87
Millie's Pancake Haus, 42
Mi Nidito, 134
Miraval Arizona Resort & Spa, 89
Miraval Resorts, 89, 271
Mona's Danish Bakery, 199
Monterey Court Cafe, 101

N

Nadine's Bakery, 199
Nan Tian BBQ, 193
Native Seed/SEARCH, 255
Neo of Melaka, 43
New Delhi Palace, 118
Nimbus Brewing Company, 126
Noble Hops Gastropub, 88
Nur Market International
  Foods, 186

O

Oasis Fruit Cones, 220
Ocotillo Cafe at the Arizona Sonora
  Desert Museum Restaurant, 109
100 Estrella Restaurant and
  Lounge, 103
Original Mr. K's BBQ, 127
Oro Valley Farmers' Market, 226

P

Parish, The, 90
Pasco Kitchen and Lounge, 167
Pastiche Modern Eatery, 44
Pat's Drive In, 104
Pecan Festival, 266
Pho # 1, 46
Pima County Fair, 267

Pinnacle Peak Steakhouse, 45
Pin-Up Pastries, 244
Planet of the Crepes, 244
Plaza Palomino Farmers'
  Market, 232
Poco and Mom's, 119
Poco Loco Salsa, 234
Polish Cottage, 47
Primo, 104
PY Steakhouse, 105

R

Raging Sage, 210
Reserve and Grand Tasting at
  Casino del Sol Resort, 265
Revolutionary Grounds, 211
Rincon Market, 187
Rincon Valley Farmers' and
  Artisans' Market, 227
Risky Business, 120
River Road Gardens, 236
Roasted Tea & Coffee Shop, 212
Robdogs, 245
Roma Imports, 188

S

Sabine's Cafe Passe, 213
Saffron Indian Bistro, 91

Santa Cruz Chili & Spice
    Company, 190
Santa Cruz River Farmers'
    Market, 228
San Xavier Cooperative, 255
Sauce, 92
Sausage Deli, 47
Savaya Coffee Market, 213
Scented Leaf Tea House &
    Lounge, 203
Scordato Pizzeria, 48
Seis Curbside Kitchen &
    Catering, 245
Seven Cups Tea House, 204
1702, 168
17th Street Market, 188
77 N. Artworks and
    Marketplace, 231
Sher-e-Punjab, 49
Shish Kebab House, 50
Shlomo & Vito's New York
    Delicatessen, 71
Silver Saddle Steak House,
    The, 128
Skeleton Creek/Aravaipa
    Heirlooms, 235
Sleeping Frog Farm, 236
Small Planet Bakery, 196

Something Sweet Dessert
    Lounge, 222
Sonoran Delights, 223
Sonoran Desert foods, 252
Son's Bakery Cafe, 51
Sparkroot, 214
Street Delights, 245
Sun Oriental Market, 189

T

Takamatsu, 52
Tanque Verde Ranch, 121
Taqueria Pico de Gallo, 135
Tasteful Kitchen, The,
    169, 272
Taste of China Festival, 256
Taste of Chocolate, 260
Tavolino, 72
Teresa's Mosaic Cafe, 107
Time Market, 190
Tino's Pizza, 54
Todd's Restaurant, 108
Tohono Chul Tearoom, 205
Tohono Chul Tearoom in Tohono
    Chul Park, 94
Tohono O'odham Community
    Action, 255
Tooley's Cafe, 171

Trucking Good Cupcakes, 246
Tucson CSA, 237
Tucson Farmers' Market at
    Maynards, 229
Tucson Farmers' Market at St.
    Philip's Plaza, 230
Tucson Farmer's Market East, 229
Tucson Festival of Books, 258
Tucson Greek Festival, 263
Tucson Meet Yourself
    Festival, 265
Tucson Taco Festival, 261
Tucson Tamal and Heritage
    Festival, 268
Tucson Tamale Company,
    54, 277
Tucson Village Farm, 238
Tumacacori National Historic
    Park, 262

U

Union Public House, 55
University of Arizona Meat
    Sciences Laboratory, 192

V

Ventana Farmers' Market, 232
Vero Amore Neopolitan Pizza, 247
Village Bake House, 200
Viro's Real Italian Bakery, 200
Vivace Restaurant, 57
Voyager RV Resort Farmers'
    Market, 232

W

Wildflower, 92
Wild foods, 250
Wilko, 172
Wine Festivals, 259
World Margarita Championship, 266

Y

Yoshimatsu Healthy Japanese
    Food, 58

Z

Zayna Mediterranean, 59
Zin Burger, 73
Zivaz Mexican Bistro, 60